THE NORTH SEA

N

The Calendar Year

Grimsby

Lincolnshire Wolds

Louth

River Witham

Gunby Hall

Boston

Walsingham Abbey

Sandringham

Blickling Hall

The Fens

King's Lynn

River Welland

Burghley House

Peterborough

River Nene

Part of Norfolk

Great Ouse

The Calendar Year

The Calendar Year

A CELEBRATION OF EVENTS IN THE YORKSHIRE TELEVISION REGION

General Editor: Maurice Colbeck

With photography by Derry Brabbs

THE CALENDAR YEAR

First published 1983

Published by EP Publishing Limited and Yorkshire Television Enterprises Limited

Diary of Events Copyright © 1983 Maurice Colbeck
Things to do and places to go Copyright © 1983 EP Publishing Limited
Introduction (including photography) Copyright © 1983 Yorkshire Television Limited
Photography (unless otherwise acknowledged) Copyright © 1983 Derry Brabbs
Calendar Copyright © Yorkshire Television Limited

ISBN 0 7158 0854 0

British Library Cataloguing in Publication Data

Colbeck, Maurice
    The Calendar year.
    1. Festivals – England – Yorkshire
    2. Recreation – England – Yorkshire
    3. Yorkshire – Recreational activities
    I. Title
    790'. 09428'1   GV181.2

First edition 1983

Text set in 10/10 pt Novarese by The Word Factory, Rossendale, Lancashire, England

Colour Reproduction by La Cromolito, Milan, Italy

Printed and bound in Italy by Sagdos, Brugherio, Milan

Acknowledgements

Compiling *The Calendar Year* would have been impossible without the aid of a veritable army of helpers to whom I cannot adequately express my gratitude. The danger inherent in lists is that someone — usually one of the most deserving — is left out. It is a risk I must take, begging forgiveness in advance for any omissions.

After our distinguished guest contributors, the Duchess of Devonshire, Lord Harewood and Richard Whiteley, and the designer, John Ridyard, I must mention the EP Publishing editorial and production team — especially Frances Royle, whose enthusiasm, determination and optimism have been a constant tonic and incentive; also Jane Cockerton and Catherine Hepworth, upon whose shoulders a vast amount of the enquiry and compilation work has fallen. Only those who have attempted such a task as theirs can appreciate the frustrations and irritations involved, and the success which has crowned their labours.

My thanks should also go to Derry Brabbs, whose contribution to this book has been more than the photographs, beautiful though they are. His helpful suggestions have been gratefully received — and usually implemented.

I am indebted also to the following for information and the checking of manuscripts: Colin T. Adamson, Sid Alderson, Cyril Bainbridge, G. Norman Benson, Arnold J. Burton, Devina Cannon, P.N. Calvert, Stephen Caunce, C.D. Chippindale, Donald A.H. Cox, Sheila M. Cooke, Roger Crees, Clarence Daniel, J.H.B. Douglas, Harry East, E.A. Fairbrother, L.J. Feiweles, Christopher Gilbert, G. Glendinning, Sue Green, Graham Greenfield, Edward Hart, D.A.R. Hinchcliffe, C.C. Hitch, Len Horton, John T. Houghton, Moira Hunter, Antony Jarvis, Keith A. Jenkinson, F.C. Jolly, Edmund Lamb, R. Lantaff, John Layton, Peter Long, Gregor MacGregor, Jean MacQuarrie, Clive W. Malpass, A.S. Marshall, J.A. Milne, Mrs B.E. Moore, John Netherwood, June Oldham, David Parker, J.C. Penniston, John Rawnsley, Wendy Riley, Alison Ross, R.H. Ruston, Rachel Semlyen, R.T.G. Sharp, Douglas Smith, Charles Stratton, Garry Stringfellow, Barry Thorpe, Ian Topham, H. Tweed, D.J. Waterman, Jack Watmough, Christine Whitehead, Catherine M. Wilson and Clive Wilson.

Constance Drake kindly allowed me to quote from the *The Pace Egg*, of which her father, H.W. Harwood, and F.H. Marsden were joint authors; and this reminds me also of the help received from the library staff of the *Halifax Courier*. Nor must I forget the Tourist Boards whose staffs supplied much valued material.

Books consulted include *Brass Triumphant* by Cyril Bainbridge (Frederick Muller, 1980); *Headingley Test Cricket 1899-1975* by Ken Dalby (Olicana Books, 1976); *Laughter at the Wicket* and *Cricket is for Fun* by Harry East (Whitethorn Press, 1980 and 1981); *Origins of Festivals and Feasts* by Jean Harrowven (Kaye and Ward 1980); *The Hill Shepherd* by Edward Hart (David and Charles, 1977); *Customs and Traditions of England* by Garry Hogg (David and Charles, 1971); *English Traditional Customs* by Christina Hole (B.T. Batsford, 1975); *Rites and Riots* by Bob Pegg (Blandford Press, 1981); *A Calendar of Country Customs* by Ralph Whitlock (B.T. Batsford, 1978) and *Events in Britain* by Bernard Schofield (Blandford Press, 1981).

Maurice Colbeck
June 1983

Contents

Something to Celebrate

Events change, so check first

Even the best established customs and traditions are liable to change their times and venues, or even to cease without warning. Therefore, whilst every effort has been made to ensure the accuracy of the information given, to avoid disappointment, readers are advised to check dates and places before setting out to visit any events listed in these pages.

Since it is of course impossible to list every occurrence of interest in an area as large as ours, this has not been our intention; we have tried instead to offer a varied and representative selection from what seemed most colourful, spectacular or entertaining. Inevitably some readers will find that a favourite event or observance has been omitted: we can only plead the difficulty of our otherwise delightful task and offer the hope that some items omitted from this volume may perhaps find a place in future editions. We have done our best to check our facts, but since human enterprises are rarely free from error we shall be grateful — if not exactly overjoyed — to be told of ours.

What to include in a book like this? What to leave out? Should it be all folk and festivals? A diary of dahlia and dog shows? A surfeit of sport? Since we could not possibly include *all* shows or all sports or all customs, how discriminate amongst them? Which should be merely mentioned and which described at length?

It was comparatively easy to decide which events to photograph, because some obviously lent themselves to Derry Brabbs's enriching talent. Easy, too, to write entertainingly about some events; not so easy to write about others. In the end we decided that what mattered was the degree to which the events reflected the life and character of the region. But here again was a difficulty, because the Yorkshire Television region is by no means confined to Yorkshire and Humberside but includes Lincolnshire and parts of several other Midland and Eastern counties; and all these areas have their own cultures and customs.

But if they have their differences, they also have much in common. Geographically, they share the eastern side of England. They are *producing* counties, industrially and agriculturally. They cherish their character and traditions. They are all proud to be themselves, just as I am proud to be the General Editor of such a book — not only because I am a Yorkshireman but precisely because this book covers so much more than Yorkshire. Inevitably I feel that my native county with its dales and moors and coastline offers an unsurpassable variety of riches. But I recognise that the Lincolnshire man and the East Anglian find in their flat, fertile, sea-washed lands, their ancient towns and churches mysteriously brooding under vast luminous skies, a peculiar magic that has no equal. But even with all our differences we are surely drawing closer together. One spectacular symbol of this is the Humber Bridge. Another is Yorkshire Television itself, proving as it does that London has no monopoly of creative talent.

And there, perhaps, we have the purpose of this book in a nutshell: it is a celebration of regional life. For surely, an area which can produce events as disparate as the oldest horse race in England, the Kiplingcotes Derby, run once a year on Humberside; the World Coal Carrying Championships of Gawthorpe; the heroic, ice-breaking New Year swim at Todmorden and the elaborate and beautiful well dressings of Derbyshire has something to celebrate. To honour this region as it truly deserves would require an entire library; but here, between the covers of a single book, is our tribute.

Maurice Colbeck
June 1983

Introduction

by Richard Whiteley

We call it Calendarland. It's not perfect, but there isn't really a perfect word to cover the geographical area served by the *Calendar* television programme. It's not Yorkshire, because it extends far beyond the traditional county boundaries. It's not 'The North' or even 'The North East', because Norfolk is hardly in either of those categories. 'East of the Pennines'? Well – geographically correct, but hardly a warming or welcoming phrase.

So – on balance – Calendarland says it all.

It would be arrogant to claim that a mere television programme can somehow join nearly six million people into one giant happy family. A hundred and fifty miles separate our northernmost viewer from our southernmost. In a part of the world where everr people in neighbouring villages are thought to be totally different from each other, no one can pretend that the landlady from Scarborough, the docker from Hull, the social worker from Huddersfield, the hill farmer from Edale, the miner from Bolsover, the engineering worker from Lincoln and the bulb grower from Spalding all have a common outlook and attitude. And yet, especially in changing and uncertain times, people do like to belong to something; for example, every Yorkshireman is a spiritual member of the Yorkshire County Cricket Club – even if there are only twelve thousand paid up members!

And so I think it is with *Calendar*. Every night we try to bring a diverse population together for a short time – to laugh at the same things, to share a social concern and to enjoy a glimpse of other people's countryside and meet other people's local characters. Again, it would be arrogant to assume that Yorkshire Television's *Calendar* is, or was, the sole parent of this family of the airwaves. The North had had its own television service for twelve years, but in 1967 the then ITA decided that the Northern franchise area should be split down the middle – and that the Yorkshire area, as they termed it, should have its own programme contractor.

So in July 1968 the company came on the air – only thirteen months after it was awarded the franchise. (Details of the birth pangs later!) And from the very beginning one of the highest priorities was to establish a programme for and about this special region.

Many ideas abounded in the pre-transmission days. At one point it was going to be three times a week – not daily – and for weeks its working title was *The Thrice Weekly News and Views Programme*. I don't think that title would have caught on. But Donald Baverstock, the Programme Controller, who thought of one very good daily programme title – *Tonight*, for the BBC, came up with another – *Calendar*. It was crisp, economical, relevant and strong. And it's turned out to be popular.

DAY ONE

We've laughed about it since . . . but we didn't at the time. It was just after eleven o'clock on Monday 29 July, 1968. July had been a hot and sunny month . . . right up to the day before, which was glorious. Monday dawned dull and drizzly.

By eleven o'clock it was dryer, a bit brighter . . . but still overcast. A mile up the road at Headingley the Australians were playing the Third Test, and it looked as if it might peter out into a draw. But the nation's and the world's press were more concerned about the plight of the people in Czechoslovakia – just invaded by the Russians. It was not a good day.

But just after eleven o'clock, in spite of everything, there was some excitement. A Yorkshire lady – born Katharine Worsley, now Duchess of Kent – was about to open and put on the air Yorkshire Television.

A few words at the front door in the presence of assorted dignitaries . . . a press of a switch . . . and immediately the viewers would be transported to Headingley to join the crowd at the Test. The first and only time ITV had ever covered a test match live.

Yorkshire Television would be well and truly – on the air.

In fact, YTV already was on the air. The cameras were shooting the actual opening ceremony. It was impressive. The Lord Lieutenant of the County. The Lord Mayor of Leeds. A platoon of local MPs. Councillors, builders, executives and, of course, Royalty.

'There's a most distinguished crowd here for the opening,' intoned the commentator – specially imported from London to describe this august occasion. And as the cameras lingered over the guests, there was a word about each.

As opening time – and the arrival of the Royal party – drew near, it happened.

'We were expecting the Prime Minister himself here this morning,' the London voice went on, 'but I can't see him anywhere'. Which was a pity, as at that precise moment the screen was filled with the silver-haired, pipe-smoking Yorkshireman grinning benignly at the folk whence he came.

No, we didn't laugh at the time. Wise men watching on monitors round the building forecast worse to come, and in those early days, to a point, they were right.

Of course, the PM didn't mind not being noticed. Because he didn't know he hadn't been noticed. Mind you – it was generous of him to turn up at all. Only two weeks before he'd been put to tremendous inconvenience by the infant YTV. He'd agreed to film a welcome message at Downing Street at a certain time. The film crew duly arrived – but for some reason never fully explained, they sat in their van outside Number Ten not daring to knock on that famous door. Two hours later an irritated Yorkshireman, having put off several appointments, sent one of his staff to look out of the door and found the nervous crew waiting to be invited in.

Anyway – YTV was on the air. And that in itself was a tremendous achievement. Just thirteen months after being allocated the Yorkshire area franchise by the ITA, and only eleven months after building started on the studios, the place was on the air and working – just about. Because something was determined to stop us getting cleanly on the air in those early days of YTV.

11

I'm not sure what the scientific name for it is . . . suffice it to say that the two simple words 'brick dust' sent shivers down the spines of those there at the time . . . and even now I'm sure will make the hair on the back of their necks stand up and quiver.

Make no mistake . . . to build a studio complex from scratch in eleven months was remarkable. It certainly wouldn't be attempted now. The actual construction work alone was a daunting task, but combine that with the complex electronic work necessary – the miles of cabling and sensitive wiring and technical installation work . . . It makes building the Humber Bridge look like playing with Meccano.

Precautionary measures were, of course, taken. But brick dust inside sophisticated transistorised television equipment was a new phenomenon. Most people build their building . . . then put the electronic bits inside it. At YTV they had to do both at the same time. Now local people were curious about this novel and exciting building going up on Kirkstall Road. They wanted to see it – they were inquisitive. So was the dreaded brick dust. It insisted on creeping everywhere. Not just on things where you could see it and shoo it away . . . but actually inside things where it lurked out of sight, intrusive and sinister in its purpose of generating havoc and mayhem.

Much of television production involves pressing buttons. Thousands are pushed every day by battalions of nimble fingers. The evil brick dust saw to it that when a button was pushed, there was a good chance that nothing would happen. The more crucial the button – like the one that puts Coronation Street from Manchester on Yorkshire screens – the more likely that the brick dust gremlin would have its evil way. So, unknown to the brave

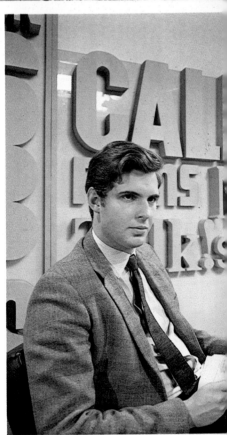

toilers, brick dust was lurking, ready to do its worst as the beautiful young Duchess was putting us on the air. The dust gremlin carefully timed its first major assault to coincide with the first edition of *Calendar*. This was to be the company's flagship – the local programme long desired by the Yorkshire public.

Calendar is always a live programme. It has to be. News must be live. But that first day – anticipating, obviously, first night difficulties, and knowing a VIP audience of TV moguls would be watching in their rooms at the Queens Hotel as they dressed for the party afterwards – it was decided to record the programme at five o'clock.

Somehow the archives have failed us – and the tape of that programme has been lost. A real pity.

The first face on was that of a young man – an old Etonian and now an MP. Clever, charming, ambitious, influential, but unskilled in the art of television presentation. He wished everybody a very good evening – and embarked on the opening menu. Imagine his dismay when halfway through, the teleprompter which he was following with glazed eyes and a terrified expression suddenly, and for no apparent reason, started going backwards. Had it gone any faster he would have been closing the programme before he'd opened it. In a wild panic he linked to the news bulletin.

Now, one of the new ideas was that the newscaster should read the news standing up. Newscasters normally sit hunched at desks, elbows on the table – back arched and shoulders round. But standing up at a lectern was like reading the lesson, back straight, head up, chin out, eyes forward, confronting the viewer with the glad tidings head on. And as a newscaster is only shown as head and shoulders, nobody would know he was standing up. The effect would be impressive – perhaps start a new trend in newscasting. The lectern was to be YTV's secret. It was the shortest-lived secret in the history of television.

As the unfortunate linkman wildly thrashed about for something to say and then linked in to the news, there was no camera ready to take the shot of our man at the lectern. 'Find me the newscaster!', screeched the director hysterically from behind his control desk. All cameras swung onto the lectern, and every one showed a full shot of a man – a distant speck in the corner of the studio, standing unbelievably – at a lectern! The secret was out.

Things were getting chaotic now. The director, lean and nervy at the best of times, was by now panic-stricken. He pushed his chair back from the control desk, took his perspiring head in his hands, and rushed up and down the control room sobbing 'It's going to be a disaster!' 'Sit down,' said the production assistant, who by this time had taken over the director's function. 'It *is* a disaster . . .

And so the minutes ticked by. A film on the man from Sheffield with the biggest head in Yorkshire was cued – but didn't appear. Another film about a missing girl in York appeared – in negative. (These were black and white days.) Another film about pollution in Wakefield appeared but only lasted twenty-three seconds then, clearly with other ideas, suddenly stopped.

Our presenter – now ghastly pale even under the layers of Sunfrolic liquid make-up, eyes reflecting a combination of fear, panic and that 'I wish I was dead – surely this is all a dream' feeling, talked unconvincingly about gremlins. Then things looked as if they might improve. A beautiful London model (born in Halifax) came on to be interviewed about stainless steel underwear.

THE CALENDAR YEAR

The interviewer, chubby, lovable, polite and just three weeks out of Oxford University, soldiered on. He looked bewildered; and it must be said, with his beautiful softly-spoken tones and flaxen hair and his obvious embarrassment in talking about underwear, he looked just a little out of his depth.

Then an interview. 'Three minutes and wind it up', said the floor manager to the interviewer. Three minutes later – 'Thank you very much – and that's all from us – good night.' Sadly there were still two minutes of the programme to go. The floor manager had meant wind the interview up – not the whole programme.

And so, eventually, the programme ended. It was a nightmare. But it was still only ten to six. The programme was on tape – we could try again and do it live! But executive decisions were taken – it was too great a risk. There was nothing we could do but go sheepishly to the pub across the road which was our watering-hole and viewing-room and see the programme go out.

A lot of people were watching that night. After all, the opening of a large TV station was a major event. They all had their own expectations. And they all reacted to that first programme in their own way. Even at this distance in time we must not intrude on private grief – or seek to resurrect the painful memories which time has eased. Suffice it to say it was quite an opening. We were on the air. Things could only get better . . . which, of course, they did. But not without more traumas on the way!

It was perhaps fortunate that five days after going on the air, there was a technicians' strike, and the whole of ITV was off the air for two weeks. It did give us a breathing space, and during that time people came and went, so when we went back on the air we had a man with a Yorkshire accent as a presenter and a man who'd produced a nightly show before as a producer.

Calendar slowly began to build a name for itself.

Let me just remind you of the original team of presenters and reporters.

Jonathan Aitken was the first face to introduce *Calendar*. A tall, urbane, ex-public schoolboy. He was a young Tory candidate – now he's a Tory MP, has interests in the City and is on the board of the breakfast TV company – TV-am.

Michael Partington, ex-local journalist – editor of the *Pudsey News* at twenty-one – then with ITN and Anglia. He was neat and immaculate. Every day he brought a black briefcase to the office, although as far as I could see he only used it to take wrapped sugar lumps home to his children! He is now a producer at Tyne Tees.

Austin Mitchell was brought in after the first week – lured from Oxford and the realms of impressive academe back to his native Yorkshire, where he could speak with a Yorkshire accent and get paid for it. A mischievous smile and hyena-like laugh. He is the only TV presenter I've known who used to go into the make-up room before transmission and ruffle *up* his hair. He was eminently suited to be an MP, which of course, he now is.

Liz Fox, everybody's favourite. Marvellous big smile, warm, musical, happy voice, and that era of the mini skirt in the late sixties certainly showed her off to full advantage. She's now living in Bristol – married with two children – and working in television as a freelance.

Simon Welfare – very intelligent – possessor of all sorts of obscure bits of knowledge. His wedding occupied a full page of photographs in the September 1968 issue of the *Tatler*. The opening

of the YTV studios merited one picture! He became a producer in the science department at YTV, and made the *Arthur C. Clarke's Mysterious World* series.

Barry Cockcroft was in on the very first week of *Calendar*. An old stablemate of Michael Parkinson at Granada, he found his true interests lay in film-making so he's been standing behind the camera for fourteen years or more – producing and directing some of the most memorable documentaries ever. He found Hannah Hauxwell; need I say more?

Paul Dunstan came in the autumn of that year. A meticulous newsreader – clear and serious. Off-camera, a joker – he attained new heights in the art of putting caption bubbles on photographs of colleagues and celebrities. He's now a documentary producer.

Other faces came and went. John Wilford and John Fairley, who were meant to be behind the scenes, as producers, but on occasions stepped in to read the news bulletins. Wilford developed a habit of putting each completed newscript on the bottom of the pile – and will long be remembered for reading the same news story twice. Of Fairley, someone observed that he appeared to know more about the news than he was prepared to tell you.

And finally in that opening team there was me. What can I say about myself that won't be libellous? And I'm still here doing the same job. A man with a great future behind him.

The on-screen team became friends of the family; news stories which previously had gone largely unreported on TV before began to be covered and shown on the screen. Annual events which had never been seen on television were filmed and brought to a wide audience. Characters began to emerge; a procession of people well-known, unknown, and soon to be well-known – like one Arthur Scargill, an eager twenty-eight-year-old branch official at Woolley Colliery – were interviewed, on location or in the studio.

The ancient game of knurr and spell, known to hundreds of people for generations, was introduced to millions. Eventually, huge crowds turned up to the World Knurr and Spell Championships at Elland – to meet newly-acquired folk heroes such as the Colne Giant.

And although *Calendar* was the programme for the region, other programmes from Yorkshire Television which were shown on the network began to show the area to the rest of the world. *Tom Grattan's War*, about a country schoolboy's adventures during the First World War, was shot in the Dales – a polished series set against the green fells, blue skies, limestone walls and crags of Upper Wharfedale. *Gazette* – about a small country weekly newspaper; *Hadleigh* – about a Yorkshire squire; *Castlehaven* – a twice-weekly series set in Whitby; and so the list went on. In the opening months of Yorkshire Television an impression had been made. Yorkshire had got on the air in record time and was building a reputation.

But then, just as things were beginning to go right . . . something happened that nobody had ever thought possible.

19 March, 1969 was a cold day . . . dull . . . a chill wind, cheerless. As it began to get dark – fairly early that night – workers and shoppers in the towns and cities bustled to get back to the warmth of their homes.

But high on the hills it was not just cold. It was bitter – and had been for days. The Pennine winds howled across hillsides locked under a carpet of frozen snow. Ice built up and sagged the telephone wires which valiantly struggled across the bleak moorland, calling at each lonely farm on their way.

Way below in the West Yorkshire valleys lights began to twinkle as dusk fell. Coal fires began to crackle in grates. Gas fires popped into life. In thousands of kitchens comforting smells began to emerge as tea was cooked. Home came the schoolchildren, ravenous and cold. It was good to come in to the warm.

Around five o'clock, YTV was screening a pop show. At the studios, the production team of that night's *Calendar* were gathering in the Green Room, getting ready for transmission. The main item was to be about lifeboatmen, and how they'd been coping with the severe winter conditions. Arthur Scargill arrived to be interviewed live. The pop show was on in the background. Nobody was really watching.

On the floor above, in master control, twenty monitor screens glowed with various pictures. Next door, in presentation control, a similar scene. The transmission controller is responsible for the minute-by-minute output of the station. He has to look at a lot of television.

He may have looked away for a moment. The pop show was just – well – another pop show. But suddenly, at three minutes to five, there was a rumbling which sounded like an earthquake two hundred miles away. It wasn't a pop record. There was no pop show. The screen was blank. So were the fifteen other monitors. So were the monitors in master control.

THE MAST

There was stunned surprise. Controllers are prepared for most eventualities – but no one could explain this.

But then no one had thought that the transmitter mast could fall down. Apparently, it can. And it did.

The dozen or so engineers in the transmitting station at Emley Moor had a lucky escape. The transmitter mast was twelve hundred and fifty feet high, a giant metal cylindrical finger pointing ever upwards, supported by giant wire guy ropes. When the mast toppled, it could have fallen on the transmitter building. It could have fallen on a terrace of cottages across the road. In fact it must have creased up as it dropped – it fell across the road and over the land beyond, coming to rest in an almost perfect zig-zag formation, each of the huge tubular sections at an angle to the next. One of the wire guy ropes, however, sliced through the roof of the tiny Methodist chapel like a giant cheese-cutter, leaving it neatly cut into two pieces. Lucky for the caretaker that he had left the chapel ten minutes earlier.

To arrive at the scene about an hour later was to be present at an awesome sight. It was foggy, it was cold, it was weird – because it was so quiet. And it was somehow horrific to see the mast sprawled out in its hideous configuration. It had dominated the skyline for thirty miles around; now it lay twisted and helpless on the ground. It was like seeing a dinosaur, monarch of its terrain, suddenly stricken, and after painful and agonising death throes finally lying still.

Of course the ITA engineers were shocked. So too were the bosses of Yorkshire Television. Ironically, at five o'clock they had all been at Leeds University dutifully attending a lecture given by the Chairman of ITA, Lord Hill. A message was brought in to Ward Thomas, the Managing Director. I imagine the colour drained from

his face. There's not much future in running a television company which doesn't have a transmitter to put its programmes out to the viewers.

At daybreak the next day you could see the extent of the collapse. There was a concrete stump where the mast had had its base, and then the mast tracing out its pattern on the ground. And you could not fail to see a group of very puzzled engineers, and a cluster of very worried TV executives.

It was a moving occasion. When the Emley mast – or indeed any transmitter mast – towered into the sky, its red navigation lights indicating its progress upwards, it was powerful. Because up through the slim finger, up the giant cables from the transmitter house, to the aerial on top of the mast went the pictures and the sound – silently and instantly. And then out from the top streamed the electronic signal, unseen, to hundreds and thousands of homes – bringing friendship, warmth and entertainment. A lifeline perhaps. At three minutes to five on the previous evening, that lifeline was cut.

The engineers worked fast. A temporary mast was erected over the weekend, and by Sunday evening much of West Yorkshire had pictures. Meanwhile a new mast was located in Sweden – shipped to Hull, and erected in amazing time by a squad of Polish riggers. And then, three years later, a brand new mast was built – like a giant lighthouse made of white concrete. It's a fine landmark now, and on a sunny day, as the white finger of concrete reaches up into the blue sky, as impressive a sight as any example of modern engineering and architecture.

And spare a thought for the villagers of Emley, nestling a mile down the road from the mast. For thirteen years they'd looked out every day, and there it was, on top of the hill – a gaunt figure, but almost comforting, because of its very presence – like a protector. Suddenly it was gone. The skyline was clear, and the village and moorland around were left on their own. They too might laugh about it now, but I'm sure they didn't then.

The *Calendar* day normally begins approximately one minute after the end of the previous day's edition.

As presenters, reporters, producers and production staff stagger wearily from studio or control room they are seeking only two things in life; one to be told how good they've just been, the other, reassurance of a more fluid nature to help ease away the pressure of the previous hour or so. But there's generally somebody hovering outside who will say 'About tomorrow – can you be outside Grimethorpe Miners' Welfare Club at eight-thirty in the morning?' Now, tension and adrenalin affect different people in different ways. Most of the production team and on-screen people are on a bit of a high in the minutes following live transmission and their resistance is low. You therefore find yourself weakly agreeing to go to Grimethorpe.

I find it inadvisable to drive a car straight after the programme because (although I hope you're not) it feels as though you're a bit drunk, and out of touch with reality. I remember one producer who would be actually revving up his car in the car park and on his way home while the end title music was still running – so quick was his retreat from the rigours of the control room. Odd – but he was Scottish.

A DAY IN THE CALENDAR

Anyway, the Grimethorpe syndrome is an example of planning ahead – the secret of putting together a daily live news programme.

Of course, by its very nature, news is something that you cannot always plan ahead for. News happens often when you're least expecting it, so you have got to be prepared to cover it when it does break. So the next day's *Calendar* begins the day before, and the news editor ought to be able to go home and sleep soundly, safe in the knowledge that he has planned activities for all his reporters and camera teams the next day. But he rarely goes a night without being telephoned by the police or fire brigades of eight counties to inform him of some excitement. (Who'd be married to a news editor?)

Eight-thirty next morning, a lone figure sits propped up at a desk by a cup of coffee and a bacon sandwich.

It's a large open-plan newsroom. Forty yards away a phone rings. The figure groans as he makes his way between desks, chairs, piles of newspapers and a large box which contains remaindered copies of Austin Mitchell's book about politics in New Zealand in the early sixties. By this time the phone has stopped ringing. So it's back to the desk, and the task of reading all the morning newpapers and drawing up a news schedule, giving a digest of the events of the day and a basis for the skeleton of that night's programme.

Gradually, the newsroom begins to fill up. Typewriters begin to clatter, and this sound together with that of animated conversation and raucous laughter fills the morning air.

Weary from a fitful and sleepless night, the news editor deploys his forces. Already his diary will inform him of pre-ordained events – a visit by a Government minister to Sheffield, the opening of a new sports centre in Bradford, a press conference to launch a report on race relations in Huddersfield, the closing down ceremony of an old wash-house in Armley and so on. At his disposal he has reporters and crews in Hull, Grimsby, Lincoln, Sheffield and two more in Leeds. So the stories are selected and the tasks assigned.

Meanwhile the producer of the day has looked at his diary to find certain items fixed. A well-known actor is coming in to talk about his newly published autobiography. An MP has been booked to be interviewed in a London studio. A troupe of Korean karate experts is coming in; they'll do a live studio demonstration.

By ten o'clock a picture of the day is emerging, and the team meet in conference. Coffee is drunk, merry quips are exchanged, rival football teams are discussed and office gossip bartered.

Eventually order prevails – the news editor reports on the projected activities of his crews, as does the Belmont news editor, who produces a separate news bulletin of interest to the viewers served by the Belmont transmitter between Grimsby and Lincoln.

Other ideas are then discussed and either approved or rejected by the producer; the likely practical and technical difficulties of the day ahead are mentioned; eventually the meeting ends and everyone goes back to the appointed task.

Generally, the morning is frustrating. The man you particularly want to take part in a studio discussion has gone to London for the day and is unavailable. The MP in the London studio says he now has a committee meeting he can't miss – so he can't do the interview. The film crew on their way to see the old lady in Cleckheaton who's got the only cat in the country that can smoke a pipe and drink a pint of beer arrive at her house to find she's out . . .

the piece of film required from the film library to make an item really come alive can't be traced . . . someone offers to get you a coffee from the canteen – you ask for black, no sugar; it comes white, with. But soon it's lunchtime. There's a five-minute lunchtime news bulletin; when this is safely out of the way, the producer and news editor get together to draw up the 'running order' for that night's programme.

The crews out on the road have kept in touch with base by radio – and reported on the success or otherwise of their missions. And during the morning, regional correspondents, called stringers, have been constantly ringing in with news stories from their own localities. Often a crew will have been diverted from its original task, to go and cover a story that has broken during the morning. The producer may find, having done a rough addition, that he won't have enough material to fill the time – the MP interview has fallen down, and the studio discussion doesn't look as though it's going to be as strong as he'd hoped.

Well, he could extend the interview with the actor – or indeed with the Korean karate kings – he could put in a ready-edited film which one of the reporters did about a man from Wetwang who models toby jugs out of the likenesses of members of the Conservative Cabinet, or he could look for another item altogether. There's a well-worn phrase, often applied by founder member Graham Ironside, for this process – 'The Lord will provide'. And normally He does. The morning post usually brings something interesting that makes an item or somebody meets somebody interesting in the pub at lunchtime.

So by half past two the running order is taking shape. Some items have fallen down, others have developed; and the running order lists the actual shape of the programme as it will appear on the screen.

At the news desk, sub-editors are writing news scripts, while in the film editing rooms the stories which have already come in from the reporters and camera crews are being edited. The perennial disadvantage of film is that once a story has been shot, the film has to be physically taken to the laboratories for processing, and then edited. Now film is being phased out and replaced by video tape. This records sound and picture straight on to a cassette videotape, which can be instantly played back – so much time is saved by cutting out the need for processing. Often, at a distant location, the cassette can be replayed and the picture received back in the newsroom, by landline or a microwave link. This process is called ENG – Electronic News Gathering.

Four o'clock is the time when the newsroom is busiest – there's certainly the most noise. Reporters are getting back from the field, and cutting their reports. Captions and slides are being ordered and made. Maps are being drawn. Films which run too long are chopped down. Late scripts are being typed, films which haven't yet arrived in the editing rooms are chased up – did the one from Chesterfield come in a taxi? The taxi's broken down on the M1 near Wakefield.

As the activity upstairs in the newsroom reaches its conclusion, much of the action switches to the studio on the ground floor. Here the director is going over the running order with the studio crew. These are the people who put the programme out – the cameramen, sound engineers, lighting men, vision mixer, production assistant, floor manager, scene and prop men.

The director has plotted out his programme from the running order which he received an hour earlier. He gives the cameramen their orders – where each will be to get the best shots of the Korean karate men. The sound people say they'll need to wheel in a microphone boom to cover that item for sound. Normally on *Calendar*, desk or stand mikes are used. The designer has done a fancy oriental background for the item; she discusses that with the lighting director.

The guests for the studio interviews are arriving now. They are met and ushered into the 'Green Room', a poky little square room next to the studio with brown walls and a brown carpet. (Brown room would be more appropriate, but doesn't sound as momentous.) Here they are offered a drink (tea or coffee believe it or not) and if they are very lucky, a chocolate biscuit. In the case of the Korean karate brigade, some sort of plan of their demonstration is worked out. Apparently, they'll be needing two volunteers recruited from the newscasters – oh and just one other thing – they'll be required to strip to the waist. Velly intelesting!

The make-up room is paradise. Perhaps not the description the girls (sorry, artists) who work there would use, but for world-weary presenters and interviewees, it's heaven on earth. Well, as near as you can get to heaven on Kirkstall Road. Where else can you go in one end looking dishevelled, greasy-haired, blotchy-skinned and generally thoroughly unattractive, and come out the other end ten minutes later with hair shining like mink, wonderfully groomed, a glowing and healthy complexion – totally blemish-free and perhaps just a hint of a suntan – after a full make-up liquid base, eyes shadowed, eyelashes mascara-ed and the whole visage gently powdered off. And you're getting paid for that treatment. It's not really surprising that hardly any television presenters wash their make-up off after the show. You get some funny looks in the queue for the cinema later that evening but generally speaking it's great for the morale.

In the control room, the production assistant is doing her sums. The presenters and newscasters have rehearsed their scripted links and news bulletins. There's a timing on everything. Then the times of the edited film and ENG stories come in. With five minutes to transmission she adds all the time up – and tells the producer the words he least wants to hear: 'You're five and a half minutes over'.

'Cut items seven and eight,' comes the order; 'also cut stories eleven and twelve from the news.' The karate men are cut down from five minutes to four and a half, and with only a minute to go adjustments are still being made. That film from Chesterfield which arrived late via the broken-down taxi is not yet edited and ready for telecine, so we've to go on the air without it and try to get it in somehow. 'One minute Studio Two', a disembodied voice announces to the control room; in fact it comes from transmission control, warning the studio they're on air live in a minute. It has happened that the control room has been so busy they've forgotten to go on the air.

So to the countdown. At seven seconds 'Roll VTR titles . . .; at zero the YTV identification; then the *Calendar* music and 'Super Calendar' caption – the title comes over the opening pictures – then 'Lose it . . . coming to Richard on three in five seconds . . . cut to three . . . cue Richard.' And so once again – you're on the air.

THE CALENDAR YEAR

From here on, there's no going back – you've started so you've got to finish. There was one exception to this. In the bad old days, in the sheer panic-stricken opening week, one programme we did got off to such a disastrous start that after three appalling minutes the director faded the screens to black, called for all the films to be rewound, and then we started again from scratch – with the 'Hello, good evening' and all.

So, once launched on the air – that's it. As a presenter you do have an inkling of any trouble ahead thanks to the earpiece (about which more later). Through it you can hear all the chat in the control room; it is not always easy to do a serious interview when in one ear they're chatting about the malfunction of the downstream key on the vision mixing desk. Of course, things do go wrong. Mainly, though, things go right – and in about thirty minutes of air time, the day's work of about one hundred and fifty people comes to fruition. Not just the people in the studio, but the telecine operators, the graphics people, the despatch riders who ferry film and news material across our vast region, the girls who work the autocue machines (no, we don't have to learn all the words), the secretaries; and, of course, the canteen staff and the tea ladies.

Meanwhile, the Korean karate men are about to do their worst. I'm doing an interview with their leader – American actually, not Korean. He has a part-time job as well – he personally trains the President's bodyguards in the art of self-defence. Anyway, he throws me around for a minute or two and then introduces his henchmen and calls for the volunteers.

Enter Geoffrey Druett, stripped to the waist and with a cucumber lashed and tied with camera tape to his chest. Henchman brandishes great sharp sword – and slices a sheet of paper in half to make the point. He stands in front of Geoffrey with the sword in the scabbard. After a ritual amount of chanting, in the twinkling of an eye (or even less) the sword is out of the scabbard, slices clean through the cucumber without even touching Geoff, and is back in its scabbard. So fast that even standing on the spot I can't see it happen. One of the most impressive demonstrations we've ever had in the studio. No wonder that when they call for Robert Hall – also equipped with a cucumber – he doesn't look too keen. They make him lie on the floor and wield the sword high in the air bringing it down with great force on the unfortunate cucumber – but miraculously stopping just short of Robert.

It's at this point that the programme ends – with much relief. Poor old Robert looks terribly pale. And I feel deeply for him as he walks out of the studio to be greeted by the news editor: alas, no praise for his courage and coolness, merely: 'Can you meet the crew at eight-thirty tomorrow outside the Mechanics' Institute Liversedge?'

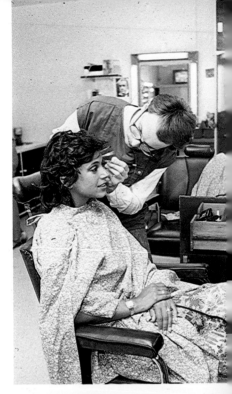

The four questions I am most frequently asked are: 'Who's the most interesting person you've ever interviewed?' 'How long have you been on *Calendar* now?' 'Wouldn't you like to be a producer?' and finally, 'What qualifications do you need for a job like yours?'

The answers are simple. 'I don't know.' 'Fifteen years, man and boy.' 'No', and 'I don't know.'

On the last one, I remember getting a letter from a schoolboy from Huddersfield. It ran as follows:

GIVE US THE TOOLS AND WE WILL TRY NOT TO MESS IT UP . . .

Dear Richard,

For some time now I have been giving serious consideration to my future career. I feel that the best way I can make a contribution to life in the latter half of the century would be in the media. A job like yours seems to be ideal. You have the opportunity to expose social evils . . . to cause action to be taken to help the less privileged members of our society, to cross-examine our leaders and elected representatives. Above all, you have the ability to impart a little pleasure to the lives of thousands of lonely people. So that is why I would like to be a TV interviewer. Could I therefore ask you if you need 'O' Level Maths?

The answer was – no. At least this particular TV interviewer didn't get it in spite of two attempts!

But you do need qualifications. At least two. To be able to read, and to be able to hear. This is because there are two essential tools of the trade – the life support system for a TV presenter.

The earpiece

It looks horrible. It consists of a plastic button attached to a wire. Then a transparent hollow plastic tube about six inches long which culminates in a moulded pink blurb and a hook like a miniature shepherd's crook. The blurby thing fits into your ear – some people have them specially moulded – then the shepherd's crook fits neatly over the top of the ear. The whole apparatus looks revolting – as though it should be more use in a hernia operation. But once neatly ensconced in the ear, the full live action drama of everyday life in the control room is available to you. You can hear what is known as 'talkback'. You often get more than talk.

The vision mixer casually strikes a match to light up right in front of the talkback mike. Immediately your ear is on fire – someone's struck a match right inside it. Try it. (Or rather don't – unless you've a fancy for barbecued eardrums!)

Or at a critical moment in an interview, Councillor Hardup is making his most important point in your right ear. The phone rings in your left. Someone answers: 'London line coming up on remote three' says a voice. Loudly. 'Say again!' say the sound department. 'Thirty seconds to London' says the PA.

'Clear camera two to the monitor,' says the director.

'How long left on the interview?' says the producer.

'We've lost gen lock!' shrieks the technical supervisor.

'Where's the London interviewee?' casually asks the PA, looking at an empty chair in the London studio . . .

'Wouldn't you agree?' says the councillor in the studio. 'I don't know,' I think to myself. I haven't heard a thing. It's far more interesting in the control room.

Of course the earpiece can be fun. I remember the interviewer taking on distinguished journalist Paul Johnson. There was Paul having a go at everything and the interviewer valiantly challenging every point. In the box, a freelance director. It was his last day, which was just as well. At each question thrust at Johnson he was giving a running commentary in the control room.

'That's it Geoff! . . . Cut to one . . . that's a goodie – you've got him there . . . cut to three . . . oh *yes*, what a question! . . . cut to two . . . give a two shot, three . . . No Geoff – you let him off there, come on now . . . in the final thirty seconds . . . get him on the closed shop . . . go on, go on . . . that's it . . . yeeess! Clear cameras and cut to one.'

It was, as I said, his last day.

THE CALENDAR YEAR

The autocue

This is where reading ability comes in. (Don't worry – it's all in capitals and not joined up.) But as everyone knows, nobody remembers all the news. You read it off the autocue – a cunning mirror device which lets you read the script off the front of the camera while all the time you're looking straight into the lens, so you come over at home open-faced, sincere, concerned, articulate, charming and a real clever clogs. People can even turn the pages of their script on the desk without looking down.

That's the skill. But beware of becoming a slave of autocue. You'll be able to recognise the symptoms. Glazed eyes darting from left to right (or right to left as the viewer sees); head inclined slightly back as if in awe (hence awetocue?); never looking down – as if you're up Blackpool Tower with vertigo; *don't* look down – if you do you won't find your place on the script, and if you try to look up again you'll have lost your place on the autocue. And then the race develops.

The autocue girl runs the script through according to your pace. At least that is the theory. But suddenly she's fractionally ahead of you. You race to catch up . . . she hears you going faster and speeds up herself. And then the race is really on – who's going to get to the end of the piece first, her or you? If she does she can go home . . . She generally wins.

It's always advisable to check the autocue before transmission. The script is typed on to a long thin roll which is then fed under a closed circuit camera and then to monitors on the actual studio cameras. And typing errors do happen.

Here are a few examples . . .
From the opening of a political programme:
'Hell! MPs went back to Westminster after the Easter recess . . .
'The Secretary of State for Social Services Mr Norman Flower was is Leeds today . . .

Of course, the earpiece comes right inside your ear. Even the waxiest of ears still hears something. But with the autocue you've actually got to be able to see it. And that does funny things to people's vanity.

'Come closer', pleads the short-sighted presenter as the cameraman edges right up to his knees ' . . . damned if I'll wear specs', thinks the presenter, ' . . . won't look half as good.' What he doesn't know is that a camera close in causes distortion – a large long thin nose, jowls down the cheeks, high rounded forehead and pointed chin. Still, it's better than wearing glasses – isn't it?

Since we came on the air there has certainly been no shortage of news in the region. Remember the tragedy of Lofthouse Colliery, with miners trapped underground, and a four-day search which found them dead. The chemical plant at Flixborough, exploding on a Saturday afternoon – nearly wiping out two villages and killing fifty people. The spy case of Nicholas Prager, who sold RAF secrets from Finningley to the East. Other court cases – the long-running Poulson affair, the curious affair of Lord Kagan, the Helen Smith inquest.

The Hull fire-raiser, the Black Panther – who, after months of hunting by police in the Midlands, turned out to be living in Bradford. And another Bradford man, the subject of the biggest news story of all – Peter Sutcliffe, the Yorkshire Ripper. Then the

PUTTING IT ON THE MAP

summer of 1982 brought the grisly story of Barry Prudom, killer of three people, including two policemen, ending in a shoot-out in the market town of Malton . . .

And then there have been the ongoing news stories. The development of the Selby coalfield – soon to be the biggest in Europe. The mighty Humber Bridge, the longest single-span suspension bridge in the world. The Harrogate Conference Centre, the cost of which has trebled and left Harrogate ratepayers reeling at the shock of their rate increases. The continuing horror at the activities of the committee of the Yorkshire County Cricket Club.

And sadly, all the while, the erosion of the traditional industries in the area. The fishing industry has been killed off. Rusting hulks now lie in Hull St Andrew's Dock, formerly the hub of European fishing. In West Yorkshire, hundreds of fine stone-built mills, that once clattered with the sound of looms and echoed to the persistent chug of the steam engine, now lie idle, deserted and forlorn; each year sees this once proud industry plunged deeper into depression. And steel in Sheffield and Scunthorpe – the industry began to collapse there in the early eighties as both the BSC and the private companies battled for survival against foreign competition and a depressed home market. And with the decline of the major industries – the various ancillary activities associated with them died off too . . .

And yet, the region is not dead, nor even sleeping. It is very much alive. It is criss-crossed with motorways, new factories and industrial estates. New industries; chemicals, electronics, computers, tourism, have been developed and are flourishing.

This changing picture has been observed and recorded by the *Calendar* team over the years. And coverage of these stories has run alongside the permanent and predictable side of life in Calendarland. In the coming pages are chronicled some of the more delightful aspects of life here – events which happen for the most part every year.

The fact that these events happen, where they do, year in, year out, is both impressive and reassuring; comforting that whatever modern life may throw at us, people will continue to organise and take part in such events. Take the Fell Race at Burnsall, where as a mere mortal you stand aghast and amazed as men who look like fellow mortals, only thinner, exhibit superhuman stamina, and, you think, a touch of madness, as they pound up the fell and charge their way down again in less than fifteen minutes. Or the Yorkshire Show . . . because it's more or less the same every year – or the more eccentric events like the Gawthorpe coal carrying championships. It's good to have them there – every year. And while *Calendar* cannot cover each of these events each time, most of them, over the years, have featured on the screen. And so, what follows is a permanent record of some of the fixtures in the *Calendar* year. No one knows the region and its events better than Maurice Colbeck – and we have already seen, from his photographs in *James Herriot's Yorkshire*, how well Derry Brabbs captures the spirit of a place in his photographs.

The result is a compendium of Calendarland, in words and pictures – a celebration of the area we live in and love.

The Year Begins...

Mankinholes
Open Air Swim

Nearest Sunday to New Year's Day
– early afternoon

At Lee Dam, Lumbutts, near
Todmorden.

There is parking space in the open,
near the dam, but police
restrictions on certain areas, so
it's best to get there early.

No charges, but a collection is
made.

In the swim at Lumbutts

An icy rain begins to blow across
Lee Dam, a moorland pool set
amid the Pennine hills at
Lumbutts, near Todmorden, as we
wait for the swimmers to appear.
It pits the uninviting surface and
drips from the surrounding trees.
Ragged grey clouds obscure the
watery sun. Only the
imperturbable sheep in the
sloping, oddly-shaped fields are at
home here today, and the Persil-
white duck that sails calmly along
without the slightest idea that its
peace is soon to be rudely
disturbed.

This is the Sunday nearest to
New Year's Day and it seems
incredible that any sane person
would enter that forbidding pool
except on pain of death or the
promise of a different sort of pools
winner's reward! But obviously
something is about to happen, or
what are the other bystanders
waiting for? Why are cars lining
one side of the narrow lane which
leads down to the dam, and why is
further parking prevented by
yellow cones placed by the police?
Why are groups of people still
sauntering to the dam from the
Top Brink pub and from the Youth
Hostel up the road at the hamlet
of Mankinholes?

The swim is timed for 2 p.m., but
the crowds have begun to gather
long before that – motivated
by . . . what? Admiration for the
courage of the swimmers? Or
because they enjoy the
comparative warmth – *warmth*? – of
a grandstand view from the bank
of the dam?

The rain seems to be getting
even colder – 'It could easily turn

to snow', says one optimist. Not
that the most ferocious blizzard
would deter these swimmers from
performing their New Year
immersion (though it might well
send the onlookers scurrying for
shelter). N**othing** deters these
swimmers – some years they have
to build a fire on the ice before
they can enter the frigid depths.

Excitement quickens as the
swimmers appear! An incredible
assortment of human beings is
waiting on the bank, some wearing
bathing trunks, some disguised as
St Trinian's girls in school
uniform, carrying tennis racquets
and displaying goose-fleshed
expanses of thigh decorated with
suspenders. Some of the men are
just as hairy-chested and robust-
looking as you'd expect; others are
mere slips of lads the wind might
blow over. But they all look a good
deal more cheerful than the
muffled, scarved and overcoated
folks who huddle around the bank
trying to pretend that the freezing,
driving rain isn't dropping off their
ears and running down their
noses. These are the ones whose
ancestors no doubt delighted in
ducking the odd witch or two; they
are waiting for the squeals of
agony which will arise when those
nearly nude bodies, in varying
shades of pink, white and purple,
make contact with the water.

Suddenly, they're in! And the
incredulous derision of the crowd
turns to admiration and perhaps a
kind of envy. These incredible
beings are actually *in*! How *can*
they do it? Admittedly, no sooner
are some of them in than they are
out again. But even if they do no
more than totally immerse
themselves for a second or two, we
timid mortals on the bank regard
them with a wondering, if
uncomprehending, respect.

Chivalry – or something –
allows the ladies to be first in.
But soon the lads, dozens of them,
are swimming the full 90-yard
width of the pool, climbing on to
the diving board on the other side
and fearlessly re-entering the
glacial depths head-first, thus
deepening the inferiority complex
of the onlookers, who by this time
can hardly claim to be superior
even in numbers.

For every year the heroic band
of swimmers seems to grow.
This time there are 86, an increase
of 18 on the year before. Usually
they sport an assortment of
costumes, but apart from the
Belles of St Trinian's, who have
travelled all the way from Grimsby,
and the almost inevitable 'JR',
complete with stetson and outsize
cigar, the only 'costumed' entry
appears to be a lady bearing an
anti-bomb-symbol on her bosom
and the initials TND, denoting
that her heroic sponsored swim is

being made on behalf of the Todmorden Nuclear Disarmament Group, for which she raises twenty pounds in ten minutes.

Equally high-minded are two animal rights campaigners from the Pennine Animal Liberation League. The Animal Liberators do rather better, raising over fifty well-earned pounds: they might have earned more but one of them has to leave the water when she finds she can no longer breathe.

The whole incredible business began years ago when Todmorden wanted to raise money for swimming baths. By the time the baths were an accomplished fact, the unbelievable New Year swim had apparently become a habit; though nowadays the main object is to raise money for Todmorden Carnival, which is why the prizes are presented by the Carnival Queen. There are sections for 'the local lads', who live within five miles of Todmorden, as well as a men's open section which is won by a competitor making his twenty-first swim. Eighteen women and girls have competed and there is surely a poetic justice in the fact that the prize goes to Mrs Miriam Slater, wife of John Slater, owner of Lee Dam, who has loaned his pool for the event.

Notwithstanding all the heroism, only £80 has been raised for Carnival funds; yet the organisers declare they are delighted with the result. After all, as they acknowledge, it has not been the best of days for the event. At 37 degrees the water is positively summery, without even a splinter of ice to gratify the sadists who are suspected to form the hard core of the crowd. People, the organisers tell you uncomplainingly, can be 'quite cruel' – happiest when the ice has to be broken before anyone gets a toe wet. These organisers are nothing if not progressive: always on the look-out for something new, as if the horrific swim were not attraction enough. It's been suggested, for instance, that the swimmers should first take part in a fell race to the starting point. Or that 'a celebrity' might boost their charitable efforts . . . So who'd be a celebrity? Seems there's something to be said for being just an ordinary mortal after all – and keeping your feet dry.

Blessing the Plough

Plough Sunday (first Sunday in January)

Cawston, Norfolk.

Cawston is a small village 20 miles north-west of Norwich on the B1145 between Aylsham and Bawdeswell. Plenty of parking on the roadsides.

The Haxey Hood Game

6 January (12th day of Christmas) 2.00 p.m.

Haxey is a small village in Humberside, 3 miles south of Epworth, 9 miles north-west of Gainsborough.

The game is some 600 years old. It starts at the town cross in Haxey. Parking in the streets of the village. Accessible to anyone who wants to go and watch.

Boggans and bellicosity

Even before the petrol engine made the streets perilous for pedestrians there were certain days in the year when frail, faint-hearted souls would have been well advised to stay indoors. Those were the days when mass ball games were played at many places in England, Scotland and France. Shrove Tuesday proved a popular occasion, but any opportunity might be seized upon

for these vigorous encounters – saints' days, Christmas, Easter, or even a local wedding day.

Often it was a simple contest between the two halves of a village, town or parish, but there were variations. It might be a case of married men against bachelors or wives versus spinsters. Rules were largely conspicuous by their absence and sometimes as many as two thousand people (divided into several teams) would take part. Occasionally there were contests on horseback.

With the standardisation of ball games in the nineteenth century many of the games began to die out, but one that has survived is the 'Haxey Hood', a ferocious encounter reminiscent of the Eton Wall Game, which takes place on 6 January every year at Haxey near Scunthorpe in Humberside. In this game it is not a ball that is fought for from end to end of the parish, but a 'hood' made of rope encased in leather. At the outset of the

contest this is thrown into the crowd, from which point on it is a free-for-all, with every player doing his best to carry the hood to his own part of the parish. At the end of the day, the hood finds its way to one of the local pubs, where it remains for the ensuing year. Heroic thirsts are assuaged and the rousing notes of the traditional Boggans' Songs which preceded the fray fill the air once more.

Three teams from the villages of Haxey and Westwoodside, near Doncaster, join battle, sometimes in the snow. Each team carries the honour of a local pub – the Carpenter's Arms at Westwoodside, and at Haxey, the Duke William and the King's Arms.

Masters of ceremony at the event include the Lord, the Chief Boggan and the Fool, identifiable by their ornately decorated headgear. At the Haxey village cross the Fool makes a speech, undeterred by the fact that he is

being ceremonially 'smoked' with burning straw.

Before the game proper begins, practice hoods are thrown into the crowd just to warm things up; after that it's the real thing. The only rule, announced by the Fool at the start of the game, is: 'If you meet a man knock him doon but don't hurt 'im.'

As with every worthwhile old custom, there is a suitably romantic account of its origin. Sometime in the fourteenth century, so they say, Lady Mowbray, the Lady of the Manor, lost her hood. She must have been very fond of it, because when it was found for her by villagers, she rewarded them with a gift of land. Since then the event has been celebrated annually by the Haxey Hood Game.

Goathland Plough Stots

Afternoon of the first Saturday after Plough Monday, which is the first Monday in January

Ancient sword dance through Goathland which is on the North York Moors, about 7 miles south-west of Whitby.

No entrance fee.

Free village car park in Goathland.

Awd Betty
and the Vikings

The snows of January may lie feet thick on the ground and a piercing wind threaten to blow away this entire village high on the North York Moors, but the Goathland Plough Stots will still dance on the Saturday following Plough Monday.

On Plough Sunday they take their 'plough', a miniature replica these days, to church to be blessed – 'It's t' only time the vicar can get us all to church!' – and the following Saturday (work makes this more feasible than Plough Monday) they dance, emerging before 10 a.m. from the village green reading-room, their headquarters, to face the cold wind and the utter indifference of the Goathland sheep. These animals claim the village commons as their own and tolerate visiting humans only as a source of hand-outs, though feeding them is frowned on by their owners. But even the sheep seem to accept the Plough Stots as part of the scenery, hardly raising their heads from grazing as the men in their smocks of pink or blue and their red-striped trousers perform the time-honoured rituals to the music of two accordions.

The dancers form a circle. Linking their 'swords', specially made of spring steel, they form archways with them and step under and over them, not without difficulty at times for these are 'big lads', cast in the mould of the North Yorkshire ploughboys who performed the same dance in days gone by. In those days they took a full-size plough with them and anyone refusing their demands for money would have his garden ploughed up as a reward for his meanness.

The present-day villagers have no fears of such vandalism, perhaps because they readily contribute to the collecting boxes thrust before them by one of the dancers, or by the small boy who accompanies the team with the same constancy as the little brown and white dog which clearly considers itself an honorary member of the team. The money covers the teams' expenses and any left over benefits the lifeboat service.

Before long there are two teams circling the village and as they dance, their chairman, Mick Atkinson, explains in his lilting North Yorkshire accent that the teams' gyrations are based on 'a Viking fertility dance brought over by the Norsemen', who had the somewhat drastic idea of beheading their most beautiful slave girl as a sacrifice to the gods. At this point Mick has to break off the conversation to double as the beautiful slave girl, or so at least one presumes as he stands in the dancing circle with his head surrounded by the interlocking blades. Since the present-day dancers would not dream of beheading their chairman (much less a beautiful slave girl) he returns safely from the circle to continue his history of the dance.

The coming of Christianity, it seems, not only robbed the event of its gorier elements but provided the grand finale to the dance when the interlocked swords, now forming a 'star' in commemoration of the Star of Bethlehem, are raised aloft by one member of the team.

You soon stop counting the number of times the accordionists embark on their lively repertoire – 'Pop goes the Weasel', 'Cock o' the North' and other ditties that make your toes tap to their rhythm and might almost tempt you into joining the dance yourself if you didn't know it was harder than it looks. If Goathland men seem to find it easy, that's probably because they're brought up to it. 'Every man 'n this village can dance,' they tell you. They may not be able to dance as soon as they can walk, but they soon start learning at the village school.

And not all of them are men – or so it seems! A large lady, modestly veiled and wearing a green dress, approaches with a collecting box, and acknowledges contributions in a gentle soprano: 'Thank you, sir . . . Thank you . . .' It's chairman Mick Atkinson, alias Awd Betty, and before long 'she', too, has joined the dance. Betty is one of those characters – another is Old Isaac – whose origins have long ago been forgotten.

The Plough Stots' sword dance may date back a thousand years, but the custom as we know it is perhaps only 150 years old. It lapsed after the First World War but was revived in 1921 by Mr F. W. Dowson. And though it was suspended again during World War II, it was revived once more in peaceful times. It will doubtless continue as long as the village itself, for Goathland and the Plough Stots are surely inseparable.

Precisely what the Plough Stots signify it is hard to say. The word *stot* presents no problem: it means 'a three-year-old bullock', and it was no doubt also applied to the young men of the village on the assumption that they themselves

were as strong – and possibly as stupid – as bullocks!

Long before Plough Sunday became a date in the Christian calendar, men danced and made a hullabaloo at this time of year. The object in the earliest times was to drive away evil spirits from the land and thus ensure a good harvest. Hence the echoes in the Plough Stots of an ancient play re-enacting the age-old battle between good and evil.

With the coming of Christianity, the Church took over the ancient rites and gave them a new meaning: instead of a half-fearful, half-blustering attempt to frighten the demons, the purpose now was to ask God's blessing on the land in the year ahead. But the rustics were reluctant to abandon the fun and games which had enlivened the bleak winter days for as long as anyone could remember. So, after the prayers, farm lads would seize the newly blessed plough and trundle it about the village, accompanied by clownish figures whose names would vary from area to area.

Plough Monday festivities seem to have occurred all over the country at one time, but they were especially popular in the North and Midlands. They were apparently at their peak in the eighteenth century and contemporary writers record the goings-on with a kind of bewildered fascination tinged with disapproval – 'On this day,' wrote T. Row in *The Gentleman's Magazine* in 1762, 'the young men yoke themselves and draw a plough about with Musick, and one or two persons, in antic dresses, like Jack Puddings, go from house to house, to gather money to drink. If you refuse them, they plough up your dunghill. We call them here the Plough Bullocks'.

T. *Row* was the pseudonym of the antiquary Samuel Pegge of Derbyshire, whose account squares very well with the revived festivities of Goathland. Writing in 1777, one John Brand describes north-eastern customs which included a Fool wearing skins and a hairy cap, with 'the Tail of some Animal hanging from his Back'. Whatever the regional differences, all the customs seem to have had money as their ultimate objective.

John Brand was in little doubt that the Plough Monday pranks had their origin in the Festival of

Fools, which used to be held on and around New Year's Day, regardless of the Puritans' disapproval. At one time, it was the custom for the participants to wear white and to elect the prettiest girl in the village to sit at the head of their table. She was always called Bessie.

Sadly, as those more innocent days passed into history, the custom degenerated. The part of Bessie, the Plough Monday Queen, was then played by a man wearing 'drag' (at Goathland, for instance, beautiful Bessie became Awd Betty). By the end of the century, all too often the custom was perpetuated only by half-drunken men with blackened faces, who would roam the streets demanding money and frightening the children, the old and the timid. With the coming of more respectable times, the ancient custom virtually died out – but happily, not at Goathland, where it seems determined to last for ever.

Horn Day

Ripon.

Five days are officially known as 'horn days' and these are Candlemas, Easter Monday, Rogation Wednesday, the Sunday after Lammas and St Stephen's Day. The Sergeant at Mace is then entitled to wear the horn and he walks in front of the Mayor in the ceremonial processions held on these days and to the Cathedral services. Best to park in the market place.

The horn is also blown by the official hornblower at 9.00 p.m. each evening in the market place.

Cradle Rocking Ceremony

Sunday nearest 2 February

Church of St Mary, Blidworth, Nottinghamshire.

Blidworth is a colliery village about 6 miles south-east of Mansfield. A baby boy is baptised in the morning and the rocking ceremony takes place in the afternoon. Nearest car park is in the nearby pub yard.

Pancake Races

Shrove Tuesday

High Street, Ely, Cambridgeshire, 11.00 a.m.

Between the Dower House and the Market House, Winster, Derbyshire, midday.

Thorpe Abbots, Norfolk (in fancy dress) midday.

Shrovetide Skipping

Shrove Tuesday, 2.00 p.m.

Foreshore, Scarborough.

Starts near the harbour, on the south side of Scarborough, and proceeds along the Foreshore towards the Spa. Possible to park on the Marine Drive, or near the Spa; no parking on the Foreshore.

Skipping fever

Anyone travelling on the foreshore road in Scarborough on Shrove Tuesday might be forgiven for thinking the population had gone suddenly mad. For stretched across the entire width of the road are long ropes with which everyone in sight seems to be either skipping or waiting to have a go!

Scarborough residents, however, and students of folklore show no surprise. It happens every

year and has done tor as long as anyone can remember. Furthermore, although the Scarborough custom may be particularly inescapable – especially to motorists in a hurry – it is by no means unique; people used to skip at this time of year in various parts of England.

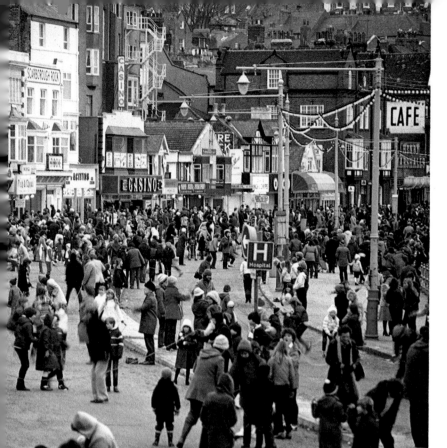

turning the ropes while the women skipped. Then the war came and the skipping ended . . .

Whatever the reasons, long may the ropes of Scarborough turn!

Ringing the Pancake Bell

Shrove Tuesday

Scarborough.

The 'curfew bell', which used to hang in the entrance to St Thomas the Martre Hospital, is rung at 12.00 noon as a signal to begin frying pancakes. The bell is now housed – and rung – in the town museum.

Shrovetide Football

Shrove Tuesday, 2.00 p.m.

Ashbourne, Derbyshire.

Starts in the car park near the Green Man Hotel. Open to onlookers, this is a free-for-all with two teams and no real rules.

Ashbourne is on the A52, 7 miles west of Belper, 10 miles south of Buxton and 12 miles north-west of Derby. The large town car park is used for the football match, so it's best to get there early to find street parking.

What, you may ask, started it? There's a rather plausible theory that it used to serve as an opportunity to break in new ships' hawsers, but if so, why was the custom practised in inland places as well? It is more likely that skipping, like other energetic Shrovetime customs – cock-fighting, pancake racing, street football – provided a chance to indulge in high-spirited fun before Lent put a damper on things.

Just *when* Scarborough started to skip is hard to say, but they were certainly doing it over a hundred years ago on the beach. Then for some reason it became the custom to use the foreshore road instead.

It begins, like many other similar customs, with the ringing at noon of the Pancake Bell – no longer from the parish church but now from the Rotunda Museum. Then, from about two in the afternoon, the Scarborough population – or its most active elements – appears to converge on the foreshore.

Bunches of children, mothers and their offspring, move like purposeful lemmings in the direction of the North Sea,

carrying ropes that leave no one in any doubt what their purpose is. And fishermen do take part, whether or not their purpose is anything as serious as breaking in new hawsers. Perhaps that's just an excuse.

If you must visit Scarborough on Shrove Tuesday, better take a skipping-rope, or at least enter into the spirit of the thing! The police usually close the foreshore to all but essential traffic; should you somehow find yourself sharing the road with the skippers, be cheerful and patient: awkward customers have been known to have their cars rocked! After all, Scarborough has not kept its skipping for centuries just to have the custom disrupted at the whim of a bad-tempered motorist.

It seems a pity that such a cheerful and energetic custom has not survived in all the other places where people used to skip. For instance, there was skipping on Good Friday (Long Rope Day) in Sussex, and at various places in Cambridgeshire. In Cambridge itself, skipping went on all day, with breaks for meals, at Parker's Piece, the traditional venue. All the family took part, the men

Spring

Spring Events

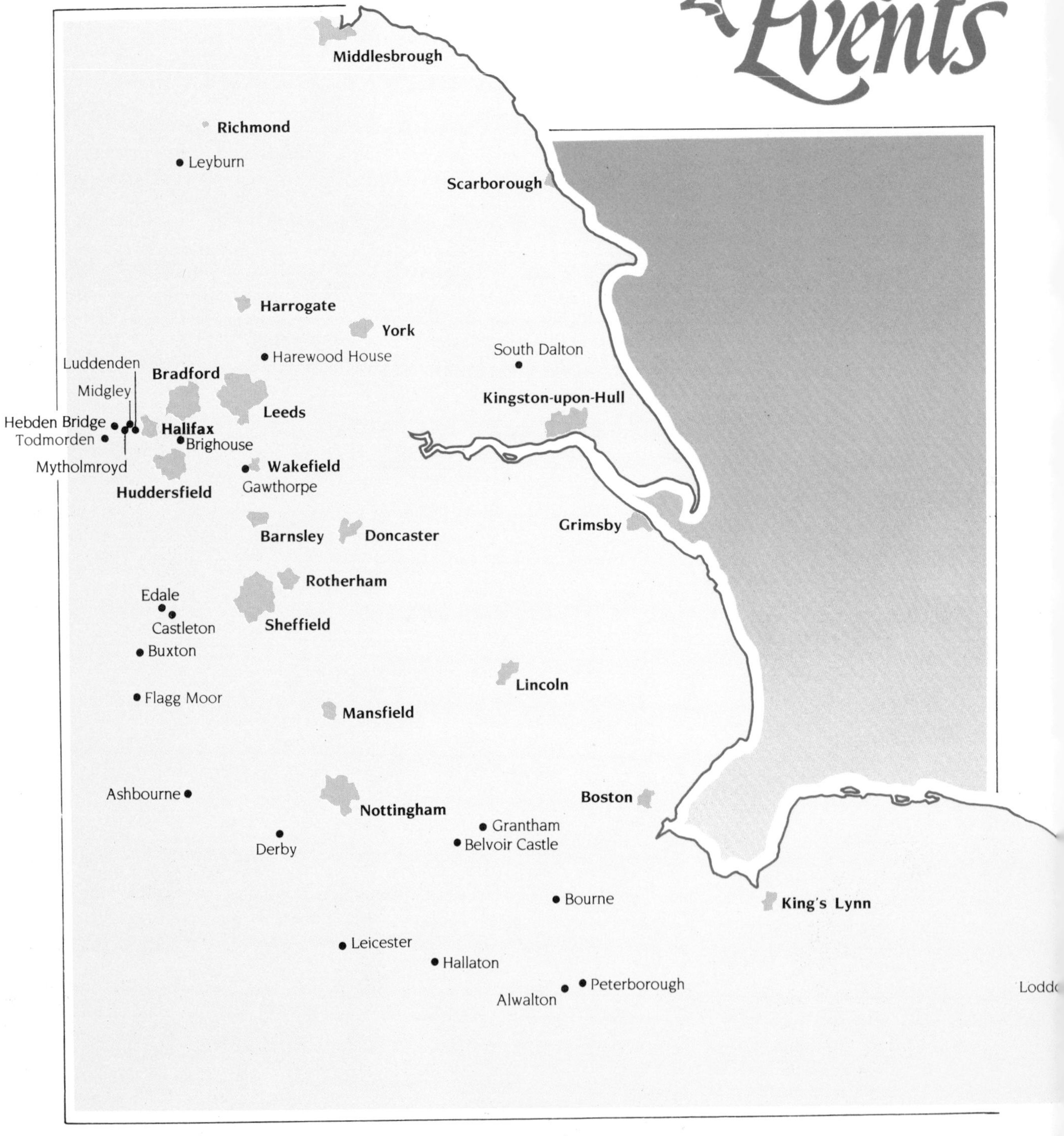

Middlesbrough

Richmond

• Leyburn

Scarborough

Harrogate

York

• Harewood House

South Dalton
•

Luddenden

Midgley

Bradford

Hebden Bridge

Leeds

Kingston-upon-Hull

Todmorden •

Halifax

• Brighouse

Mytholmroyd

Wakefield

Huddersfield

Gawthorpe

Barnsley

Doncaster

Grimsby

Rotherham

Edale
•

Castleton

Sheffield

• Buxton

• Flagg Moor

Lincoln

Mansfield

Boston

Ashbourne •

Nottingham

• Grantham

• Belvoir Castle

Derby

• Bourne

King's Lynn

• Leicester

• Hallaton

Alwalton

• Peterborough

Lodd

The Shire Horse Show

Saturday, mid-March

East of England Showground, off the A605, Alwalton, near Peterborough.

This is the biggest national heavy horse show in the country and entrance for competitors is restricted to members of the Shire Horse Society. Open to the public; there is an entrance fee which includes admission to the Showground parking area.

Mintex International Car Rally, York

3-day rally in late February

Begins 10.00 a.m. on Friday at York racecourse and continues to Harewood, Ingleby, Cropton, Pickering, Staindale, Dalby Forest and Oliver's Mount. Finishes at York racecourse, 4.00 p.m. on Saturday.

There are car parks and refreshments at Harewood and York.

Lincoln Music Festival

Early March – two weeks' duration

Central Methodist Church and Church Hall, High Street, Lincoln.

The High Street is the main road through Lincoln and the Church Hall is at the Newark Road end. There is a large pay and display car park at Tentercroft Street, which is nearby.

The Festival is open to the public. There is a small entrance fee each day or you can buy a season ticket.

Wensleydale Tournament of Song

Usually the third week in March

Methodist Church, Leyburn.

The heats of these competitions are open to the public and tickets can be obtained at the door. There are two winners' contests in Wensleydale School.

Leyburn is on the main road between Bedale and Hawes. Parking space in Leyburn market place.

Kiplingcotes Derby

Third Thursday in March

Starts at South Dalton and ends at Kiplingcotes Farm.

This is a horse race over the Wolds. To get there by car head for Market Weighton and then take the road to Driffield and Middleton-on-the-Wolds. The course crosses this road about 2 miles from Market Weighton. Take the lane on the left, which leads to Warter, and park well down the lane, beyond the finishing line. There is plenty of room. Around 10.30 a.m. the horses canter from here to the start point at South Dalton and race back – 4½ miles.

The oldest horse race in the world

The Yorkshireman loves horses, which perhaps explains why he has so often been accused of stealing them. 'Shake a bridle over a Yorkshireman's grave and he'll get up and steal your mare', they used to say. (A gross slander, of course, which no doubt originated the other side of the Pennines.) Not surprising, then, that in addition to staging some of the oldest horse fairs in England, the county makes an even more striking equestrian claim to fame. At Kiplingcotes (whose very name sounds like the rattle of hooves) is held the oldest horse race in the world. Or so they say in the horse-loving East Riding.

It all began, according to tradition, in 1519 when the local nobility wanted to see how well their horses had survived the winter. No such justification exists these days, but the race goes on. At midday on the third Thursday in March a white flag, waved by a villager, signals the start of the race from Kiplingcotes Station, near Market Weighton. The course of the race follows the path of a Roman road between Market Weighton and Middleton-on-the-Wolds and covers four and a half miles of rolling Wolds.

The rules, read out by the Clerk of the Course at the winning post (where the weigh-in also takes place), are few and simple. Horses of any age may compete 'to carry horseman's weight, ten stones, exclusive of saddle, to enter at the post before eleven o'clock on the morning of the race'. If the rider should weigh less than ten stones, extra weight can be added in the form of stones from the fields carried in a bag round the waist. The winner is awarded a twelve-inch high silver cup – the Jean Farrow Trophy – given by the first woman ever to win the race; Jean Farrow's triumph came in 1939, since when female riders have often won. In addition to the trophy, the winner receives the interest on a sum of money invested for this purpose in the time of Henry VIII. But it is possible, in financial terms, for the second rider home to do better than the winner – the runner-up receives all the entrance fees, which may well amount to more than the interest on the investment. What matters most, of course, is being first home.

Standing by the side of the lane that leads to the thatched-cottage village of Warter, the winning post bears the traditional date of the first Kiplingcotes Derby (as it is now universally called). The earliest authentic record of the event at *Kibling Cotes*, however, states that the race was first run, not in 1519, but in 1555.

Which date is right? Well, if any man was an authority on racing in Yorkshire, it was the late Major J. Fairfax-Blakeborough, author of what appears an endless list of books on the subject. His *magnum opus* was probably the definitive *Northern Turf History* and here, if anywhere, we might expect to find the truth. Alas for tradition! The Kiplingcotes Derby, states the Major, was established in 1619. If he's right, that venerable winning-post is wrong by a century. And he has a measure of support, for Thomas Langdale in his *Topographical History of Yorkshire*, published in 1822, asserts that the race began in 1618. Langdale provides us with further details. The event began, he says, when Lord Burlington, along with 'five noblemen, nineteen baronets and twenty-five gentlemen of the

county of Yorkshire', fifty men in all, contributed between them 365 shillings, the interest on which provides the winner with his – or her – prize money.

Daffodil Day

On one or two Sundays around Easter

Langley Park, near Loddon, Norfolk.

Langley Park is 3 miles north of Loddon, off the A146 going towards Lowestoft. It is a public park and there is usually a fête and a procession including floats. Plenty of parking space near the park.

Pace Egg Play

Good Friday, 9.30 a.m. – 4.00 p.m.

Hebden Bridge area, West Yorkshire.

The Midgley version of a traditional play to welcome the spring is performed by boys of Calder High School.

St George's Church, Mytholmroyd, 10.00 a.m.; Holme Street, Hebden Bridge, 11.00 a.m.; St George's Square, Hebden Bridge, 11.30 a.m.; Midgley Bus Terminus, 2.00 p.m.; Luddenden, 3.00 p.m.; outside the White Hart, Todmorden, 4.00 p.m.

Sweet eggs and strong beer

> Room, room, brave gallants, give us room to sport –
> For in this room we wish for to resort
> Resort and repeat to you our merry rhyme,
> For pray you remember, 'tis Pace-Egging Time.

Thus, with great gusto and bravado, begins the Pace Egg Play performed on Good Friday in the streets of the Hebden Bridge area by boys of Calder High School. The play is the Easter version of the Old Mumming Play found in many parts of England and often performed at Christmas. Beyond that, its origins are far from clear. Certainly it has been performed in the Calder Valley for a great many years, as some of those who once acted as children still recall.

For months the boys (girls seem never to have taken part) would be tutored by their mothers, who lavished great care on the costumes to be worn by such colourful, if rather mysterious, characters as St George, Slasher, the Doctor, the Black Morocco Prince and Tosspot. Today, wearing colourful smocks adorned with rosettes, with hats trimmed with paper flowers and wielding wooden swords, the boys revive the old pageant, which, on the surface, might appear to have little to do with Easter, though it contains strong elements of death and resurrection.

THE CALENDAR YEAR

Enter St George, who boasts of his valorous deeds and is promptly challenged by Slasher:

I'm a valiant soldier,
Bold Slasher is my name.
With sword and buckler by my
    side,
I hope to win the game,
And for to fight with me, St
    George,
I see thou art not able,
For with my trusty broadsword
I soon would thee disable.

St George is speechless –
almost . . .

Disable! Disable! It lies not in
    thy power.
For with my trusty broadsword I
    soon will thee devour.
Stand back, Slasher, and let no
    more be said,
For if I draw my glittering sword
    or spear,
I'm sure to break thine head.

Slasher, with equal modesty, dismisses St George's threats, asserting that his head is made of iron and his body of steel, while his hands and feet are of knuckle-bone.

They cross swords and St George, predictably, draws first blood. He struts around the ring triumphant as any wrestler on television, while the Fool cries out for a doctor. The doctor arrives and declares his fee to be ten pounds –

But, Jack, if thou be an honest
    man, I'll take only five off thee.
Fool (*Aside*)
You'll be wondrous cunning if
    you get any!
(*Aloud*) Well, how far have you
    travelled in doctorship?

Doctor
From Italy, Titaly, High
    Germany, France and Spain,
And now I'm returned to cure
    disease in Old England again.

This case will present little difficulty, we gather, for the doctor claims he can cure

The itch, the stitch, the palsy
    and the gout.

If a man has nineteen devils in
    his soul,
I can cast twenty of them out
I have in my pocket crutches for
    lame ducks
Spectacles for blind hummer-
    bees and pack-saddles for
    broken-backed mice.
I cured Sir Harry of a nang nail
    almost fifty-five yards long,
So surely, I can cure this poor
    man.

Here, Jack, take a little out of my
    bottle,
And let it run down thy
    throttle,
And, if thou be not quite slain,
Arise, Jack, and fight again.

The Doctor's bottle has the desired effect. Slasher rises and, summoned by a trumpet call, goes his way in search of new battles.

Act Two finds St George as boastful as ever –
'Twas I that fought the fiery
    dragon,
And brought it to the slaughter,
And by those means I won
The King of Egypt's daughter.

This time another challenger appears, the Black Prince of Paradine. He is despatched by St George with his customary ease. Soon the father of the Black Prince

– the King of Egypt, no less – arrives in search of his son and, finding him slain, calls upon Bold Hector to avenge him. To do him justice, St George seems hesitant to perform further slaughter. He warns

Bold Hector, do not be so hot,
For here thou knowest not who
    thou's got.
'Tis I can tame thee of thy pride,
And lay thine anger, too, aside.
I'll inch thee and pinch thee as
    small as flies,
And send thee overseas to make
    mince-pies,
Mince pies hot, mince pies cold,
I'll send thee to Black Sam
    before thou'rt nine days old.

They fight and Bold Hector retires, wounded. The last character to appear is 'th' Old Toss Pot' –

He's a gallant old man,
And he wears a degree.
He's a stick in his hand,
An' he wears a pig tail,
An' he takes his delight
In drinking mulled ale.

Finally Toss Pot speaks (or rather sings) for himself –

I've some eggs in my basket
    although I appear,

'Eggerpecting' [expecting]
   sometime to come in for my
   share.
Although I am ragged.
And not so well dressed,
I can kiss some bonny lasses
   As well as the best.

He then performs his essential function, collecting coppers from the crowd. Meanwhile the other players sing the traditional Pace Egg song, as they beg for money, 'sweet eggs and strong beer', just as their forebears did at the houses and farms of the district. Today, however, the proceeds go to charity.

The late Mr Harry Greenwood, who published one version of the play in his *Memories* (Arvon Press, Hebden Bridge, 1977) had to rely on his memory for the words, for he knew of no written script – it was all handed down, he said, from generation to generation. However, other investigators have discovered printed versions of the play dating from the 1800s.

On Good Friday, recalled Mr Greenwood, after they had toured the district performing the play and collecting perhaps five shillings each, the boys would walk to Todmorden Fair, spend their money, then walk back home. So whatever other reasons might exist for the performance of the play, it obviously provided pocket money which was not easy to come by in any other way. Furthermore, it offered something to do in the early spring, for preparations, rehearsals and costume-making began perhaps two months before Good Friday.

The psychological and historical reasons for the play may perhaps never be fully known, though we need not look so far to find the connection between eggs and Easter. The early Christians saw the egg as a symbol of resurrection and even before Christianity eggs played a part in the Spring Festival in many countries. A more cynical-sounding explanation is that eggs were not eaten during Lent, so when Easter came, people had more eggs than they knew what to do with.

The original Easter egg was an

ordinary farmyard egg, which was coloured by various means, sometimes with dyes, sometimes by boiling it wrapped in the brown outer skin of an onion, which turned it an attractive brown or yellow. The term 'Pace egg' is probably derived from the fact that Easter is called the Paschal Festival because of its links with the Jewish Passover. In various parts of the world the eggs, having been first hard-boiled, are rolled down hills until they break and then they are eaten. The idea is to keep your egg whole as long as possible. Sometimes they are cracked together in the same manner as conkers.

Whatever the original reasons for Pace-egging, it has provided lots of simple fun for a great many years. We are fortunate that the

boys of Calder High School have revived the tradition and made it so much their own.

Pace Egg Play, Brighouse

Easter Saturday

Brighouse Children's Theatre perform the Brighouse version of this traditional play, as they have done since 1950. A collection is usually made afterwards.

Halifax Shopping Precinct, 9.45 a.m.; Piece Hall, Halifax, 10.15 a.m.; Mirfield Library forecourt, 11.00 a.m.; Brighouse Town Centre, 11.30 a.m.; New Street Shopping Precinct, Huddersfield, 12.00 noon.

THE CALENDAR YEAR

Siamese Cat Show

Easter Saturday

Sun Pavilion, Valley Gardens, Harrogate.

The event is open to the public but there is an entrance fee.

No car park, but there is a reasonable amount of parking space in nearby roads. Usually restricted to 2 hours, free parking.

Egg Rolling, Bunker's Hill

Easter

Bunker's Hill, near Derby.

Bunker's Hill is a popular walking spot between Duffield and Quorndon, both being small villages north of Derby. Best to park at Quorndon, which is nearer, and walk to Bunker's Hill.

Chapel-en-le-Frith Morris Men

Easter Sunday

Edale, Castleton and Buxton

Open air dancing; open to the public; usually includes a collection; parking in the villages.

Chapel-en-le-Frith Morris Men are active all summer throughout Derbyshire.

'Hunt the Outlaws', Belvoir Castle

Easter Sunday and Monday

Belvoir Castle is 7 miles from Grantham, on the A607.

The event is open to the public, young and old alike, and there is an entrance fee which covers the castle and the event.

Free car and coach park.

Leeds Musical Festival

Biennial, odd years; time of year varies, but usually between April and October.

The Leeds Musical Festival is a large-scale event which takes place in a wide range of venues; Leeds Town Hall, Leeds Parish Church, Leeds Playhouse, St Anne's Cathedral and the Grand Theatre are all involved. To underline the stature of the event the programme tells us that 'Leeds bids fair to be regarded as the most musical city of Britain outside London'. A theme is usually chosen to give the Festival unity; there are also fringe events and a film programme. A souvenir programme giving full details is normally available from Barkers, the Headrow, Leeds.

Free parking near all venues in the evening, subject to police regulations.

Bottle Kicking and Hare Pie Scrambling

Easter Monday

Hallaton, Leicestershire.

The Hare Pie Scramble is usually followed by the Bottle Kicking and both take place on the rising ground at Hare Pie Bank, which is on the outskirts of the village on the Cranoe Road past the church.

Hallaton is a village 15 miles south-east of Leicester near Market Harborough. Usually room to park in one of the fields. This is a big event which attracts many onlookers.

World Coal Carrying Contest

Easter Monday

Starts at the Royal Oak, Owl Lane, Gawthorpe and ends at Gawthorpe Maypole.

Duration 4½ mins.

Gawthorpe is a small village near Ossett in West Yorkshire. Parking in the village.

The world coal carrying contest

At the century-old Bee Hive Inn in Gawthorpe one day in 1963 Amos Clapham, President of the Maypole Committee, was leaning on the bar lost in his own thoughts when in burst one Lewis Hartley in exuberant mood.

'By gum, owd lad, tha looks tired!' declared Lewis, slapping Amos heartily on the back. Whether because of the force of the blow or because of the words that accompanied it, Amos was just a little put out.

'Ah'm as fit as thee!' he told Lewis. 'If tha doesn't believe me, get a bag of coil on thi back and I'll get one on mine and Ah'll race thee to t'top o' t' wood!' (Coil, let me explain, is West Riding for 'coal'.) While Lewis digested the implications of this challenge,

Fred Hirst, Secretary of the Gawthorpe Maypole Committee (and not a man to let a good idea go to waste), raised a cautioning hand.

"Old on a minute,' said Fred and there was something in his voice that made them listen. "Aven't we been lookin' for summat to do on Easter Monday? If we're goin' to 'ave a race, let's 'ave it *then*. Let's 'ave a coil race from the Royal Oak to the Maypole.'

Thus was born the World Coal Carrying Contest, which every Easter Monday lifts the village of Gawthorpe out of obscurity and into the headlines. No event in the Olympic Games could stimulate more enthusiasm than this annual contest of stamina and muscle.

Gawthorpe is a tough little place, lying between Dewsbury and Wakefield where the Yorkshire coalfield merges into the heavy

woollen district. The nearest pit is closed now, but hard work is still so much a tradition here that the residents can scarcely have enough of it! Hence the yearly battle to be King of the Coal Humpers – or Queen, for in these liberated times the ladies, too, have joined in the game.

They are let off rather lightly. All they have to do is run from the bottom of Gawthorpe High Street to the Maypole on what remains of the village green carrying a 10 kg bag of coal. But no-one complains, for they add a feminine touch where it is least expected and who would quarrel with that? Incidentally, when the Coal Carrying Contest began in the early '60s, there was some talk about having a rolling-pin throwing contest instead. It may have been that the men were afraid the women might become too expert, but at any rate, the idea never caught on.

The main event, the men's contest, starts at Owl Lane from where competitors, each carrying 50kg of coal, have to run close on a mile (1012.5 metres to be precise) as quickly as possible before dropping their burdens at the foot of the Maypole.

Competitors come from near and far – even from America – and from a variety of occupations. You'd expect coalmen to make a good showing, but window-cleaners and farmers have done splendidly in past years. And it isn't necessarily the big men that win; ten and a half stone is considered to be a favourable weight for a competitor, provided his legs and lungs are strong. Training for the contest, of course, is most important; one former champion, a farmer, revealed that he had trained by running up and down hills carrying sacks of potatoes.

And the prizes? There are modest cash sums for the winners in both the men's and women's contests, as well as commemorative trophies and tankards. But when it comes to the additional prizes, much depends on who is sponsoring the event. A brewery might offer barrels of beer. the Solid Fuel Advisory

Service free vouchers for coal; there may even be a free holiday to be had.

There is glory for the winner and possibly an entry in *The Guinness Book of Records* – the current world record, incidentally, is 4 minutes 23 seconds – but what of those who do not succeed? There is, let me tell you, no sadder picture than that of the defeated coal-humper staggering the last quarter mile of the Gawthorpe course, uphill, weaving his way as best he can among the abandoned coal sacks that litter the course . . .

High Peak Point to Point

Easter Tuesday, 2.00 p.m. onwards

Horse race which starts at Flagg Moor, off the A515 between Ashbourne and Buxton. An official car park is set up at Flagg Moor, and there is a fee. Open access to the races.

East Midlands Orchid Society Annual Show

Mid-April, one day

Town Hall, Grantham, Lincolnshire.

Not always at the same venue. Small entrance fee and parking in the nearby pay and display car park.

World Dock Pudding Championship

Saturday of the third weekend in April, 10.00 a.m. to lunchtime

Community Centre, Mytholmroyd.

The 'pudding' is made locally from a type of dock unique to the area and a contest is held to judge the best.

Open to the public; small entrance fee; craft stalls etc. Huge car park at the Leisure Centre.

Harrogate Spring Flower Show

Thursday-Saturday, late April

Valley Gardens, Harrogate.

There is an entrance fee.

No car park, but there is a reasonable amount of parking space in nearby roads. Usually restricted to 2 hours, free parking.

Midland Area Brass Band Championships

Late April

De Montfort Hall, Leicester.

This is the qualifying contest for the National Brass Band Championships, which are always held in London. It is open to the public and tickets are available on the door. De Montfort Hall is in a park, quite near the University, and is accessible by car or bus from the town centre. There is a car park, and a huge field for parking beyond, but it is advisable to get there early. Parking is free.

The Championships are sometimes held in Nottingham.

Sound the trumpet!

Brass banding is a way of life in the North. From Belle Vue, Manchester, to Hardraw Force in Wensleydale – where the arpeggios vie with the music from the highest single drop waterfall in England and where the audience sits in a natural amphitheatre of grass and limestone – the cornet and trombone have been for generations the means of music-making by the common man. Here, Fred and Harry Mortimer are revered as patron saints of an artistic cult whose sturdy supporters could hardly be outstripped in dedication by the devotees of any other art.

It really began more than 150 years ago when workmen, who had precious little leisure and nothing to do in what they had, were formed into bands by local mill-owners and philanthropists. These were not the first bands. Centuries earlier, there had been the local 'waits', whose original purpose was to act as watchmen in castles, palaces and walled towns. Eventually they formed bands with uniforms, without which, under an Act of Elizabeth I, they were in danger of being regarded as 'rogues, vagabonds and sturdy beggars'. But the Municipal Reform Act of 1835 caused the waits to be disbanded, though many of them continued as church bands, a feature which had been forbidden under the Puritans.

'Banding' has not had it easy, and it was a good job its adherents were such sturdy souls! But they did have some help. Just about the time the waits bands were dissolved, some of the earnest Victorians who made it their purpose to prevent the devil finding work for idle hands decided that music had charms which could be employed in maintaining industrial peace. Such a one was Lord Brougham, a keen supporter of the recently founded Mechanics Institutes, who urged the inclusion of music in the curriculum as a prophylactic against vice, riot and debauchery!

The first of the new bands established to achieve this worthy end were not comprised entirely of brass instruments, but were combinations of various wind instruments. What is now one of the most famous, Black Dyke Mills Band, whose first notes were heard perhaps as early as 1816 in the village of Queensbury, near Bradford, was originally made up of brass and reed instruments. It was known as Peter Wharton's Band then and, happily for the members, one of their keenest players was a local mill-owner, John Foster. When the band fell on hard times, Foster attached it to his mill, changed its name and transformed it into a wholly brass ensemble.

Giants of the banding world were born in those days. Over in Lancashire, Besses o' th' Barn Band began life in 1818 as Clegg's Reed Band, but thirty years later became an all-brass band. By the 1840s reed instruments had been completely ousted – the brass band movement was born. It may well have played its part, along with Methodism, in preventing the kind of bloody revolution suffered in France.

British skill and invention (inspired, admittedly, by the Germans) played a part, too, in developing these instruments. In 1810, for instance, James Halliday inserted valves (or keys) along the length of a horn and thus produced a chromatic bugle,

which was to prove seminal in the evolution of brass instruments. Fourteen years later, after seventeen years of experimentation, John Shaw of Glossop, in Derbyshire, took out a patent for two varieties of brass instrument slide. There can be few better instances, perhaps, of the marriage of mechanical invention with artistic skill, than those which occurred about this time and which assisted the majestic onward march of the brass band as an artisan's art form.

The North of England, and particularly Yorkshire and Lancashire, is the spiritual home of 'banding' and surely Yorkshire must have a fair claim to pre-eminence. Not for nothing did Albert Modley, much-loved Yorkshire comedian, claim to be 't' best bloomin' blower in Briggus Brass Band', for Briggus (more correctly Brighouse and Rastrick) Band has few rivals and of those it has, Black Dyke, many times British Open Champion, is in the forefront.

The latter was undoubtedly first in the field, and its list of successes in the British Open Championship reminds you of the glorious days of Yorkshire cricket when the county side triumphed eighteen times in thirty-six seasons (we'll ignore the times they came second). Black Dyke first won the British Open as early as 1862, repeating this success the following year. They won it again in 1871, 1879, 1880 and 1881, after which came an unaccountable decade of unsuccess (you daren't use the word failure in connection with Black Dyke!) Normality was restored by the victories of 1895 and '96, and thereafter Black Dyke seemed to take the crown when they felt like it, allowing other bands a look-in to encourage them but at the same time making it clear who was boss. They won in 1899 with a little help from Verdi, who wrote the test-piece *Aroldo*. They did it again in 1902, when they gave Appoloni's *L'Ebreo* an airing. In 1904, and 1908 and 1914 they were victors yet again. Then, for twenty-one years, their name was missing from the trophy.

The arrival of a team of newcomers from Cheshire called Fodens, who had had the temerity to win the British Open at their first attempt in 1909 under the redoubtable William Rimmer, and then go on to take the Open and the National Championships the following year, must have caused some dismay in the Black Dyke ranks. Fodens won the Open again in 1912 and '13, though the Queensbury Band bounced back in 1914. The Cheshire band was also successful in 1926, '27 and '28 but Yorkshire was not to be balked for ever – reinforcements arrived in the form of the Brighouse and Rastrick Band, who were to dominate the contest in the years 1932 to 1934.

The arrival on the championship scene of this band from less than five miles away must momentarily have robbed the Black Dykers of their puff, but the two were certainly no strangers to each other. As long ago as 1857, a Brighouse Band (who were, at least spiritually, ancestors of Brighouse and Rastrick) took on Black Dyke at a contest at the Halifax Piece Hall but failed to beat them. Thus was born – though perhaps it was hardly realised at the time – the vigorous but respectful rivalry which continues today. By 1860 the Brighouse band was known as Brighouse and Rastrick Temperance Band. About twenty years later it changed from brass and reed instruments to all-brass and in 1928 assumed its present name. Fifty years later, in 1978, the Brigussers were again British Open Champions, though that success came towards the end of a brilliant decade for Black Dyke during which they secured the championship no fewer than five times. It seems to be in the nature of things for these two premier bands to run neck and neck and, indeed, both have been world champions.

But it would be less than just to ignore some of the other great bands which were born and have their being in the area. Collieries, as well as mills, have fostered Yorkshire banding. The winners of the 1922 British Open

Championships came from Carlton Main Frickley Colliery. That band was formed in 1898 as South Elmsall village band, and it only officially became a colliery band in 1905 when mining at Frickley was begun by the Carlton Main Colliery Company, a prosperous and far-sighted concern who gave the band so much encouragement and support that its reputation alone was enough to make working at Frickley a privilege much sought after by the musical miner. Just a few miles away are two other pit bands, Markham Main and Grimethorpe. In 1974 the latter shared with Black Dyke the distinction of being the first brass bands to take part in a Promenade Concert at the Royal Albert Hall.

Other famous Yorkshire bands are that of the Hammonds Sauce works at Shipley and Yorkshire Imperial Metals (or Yorkshire 'Imps'). Since the latter was formed in 1936 as the Yorkshire Copper Works Band it has

changed its name twice, but its musical consistency has varied little since the 1950s when it attained first rank status. In 1970 and 1971 it won the British Open Championship at Belle Vue and in 1978 secured the national title.

Brass banding points out Cyril Bainbridge in *Brass Triumphant* (Frederick Muller, 1980), has an affinity with professional football in its metaphors, its divisions, promotions and relegations. Even the silver trophy awarded at the Finals in London, in an atmosphere reminiscent of a Wembley Cup Final, rather resembles the F A Cup. Players and conductors are 'transferred' frequently (though without the astronomical fees involved in football) and the efforts of a champion band and its star performers draw the support of fans with all the enthusiasm of their soccer counterparts on the terraces.

Just as the movement has matured musically, attracting in

the present century the interest of such composers as Holst, Elgar, John Ireland, Sir Granville Bantock, Dr Herbert Howells, Sir Arthur Bliss and Ralph Vaughan Williams (besides entering *avant-garde* fields), so it has broadened socially, outgrowing the old 'cloth cap' image to attract a fellowship drawn from many backgrounds but united in its dedication. Most remarkable of all, as evidence of their musical acceptance, has been the appearance of brass bands at leading musical festivals and the 'Proms'.

There are estimated to be about 3,000 bands and 100,000 bandsmen in Britain today, and the British way of 'banding' has now begun to attract interest in the USA and Canada, as well as on the Continent. As we look ahead, several factors seem to promise an even brighter future for this movement which has progressed so surely during a century and a half. The patronage of employers, on which the earliest bands relied heavily, has in some cases broadened to become large-scale sponsorship by commercial concerns which sometimes support not just a single band but entire contests. Recording, broadcasting and television have all played their part in popularising brass band music, but surely most important of all has been the growth of school and youth brass band music. With the reservoir of youthful talent thus provided, brass banding can hardly fail to continue its triumphant progress.

Running Auction, Bourne

End of April

The auction takes place at Queen's Bridge in Bourne. Two boys race 100 yards out and back and the bidding for Whitebread Meadows, which is let each year, takes place at the same time. Organised by local auctioneers.

Bourne is on the A15, west of Spalding and north of Stamford.

Summer

Summer Events

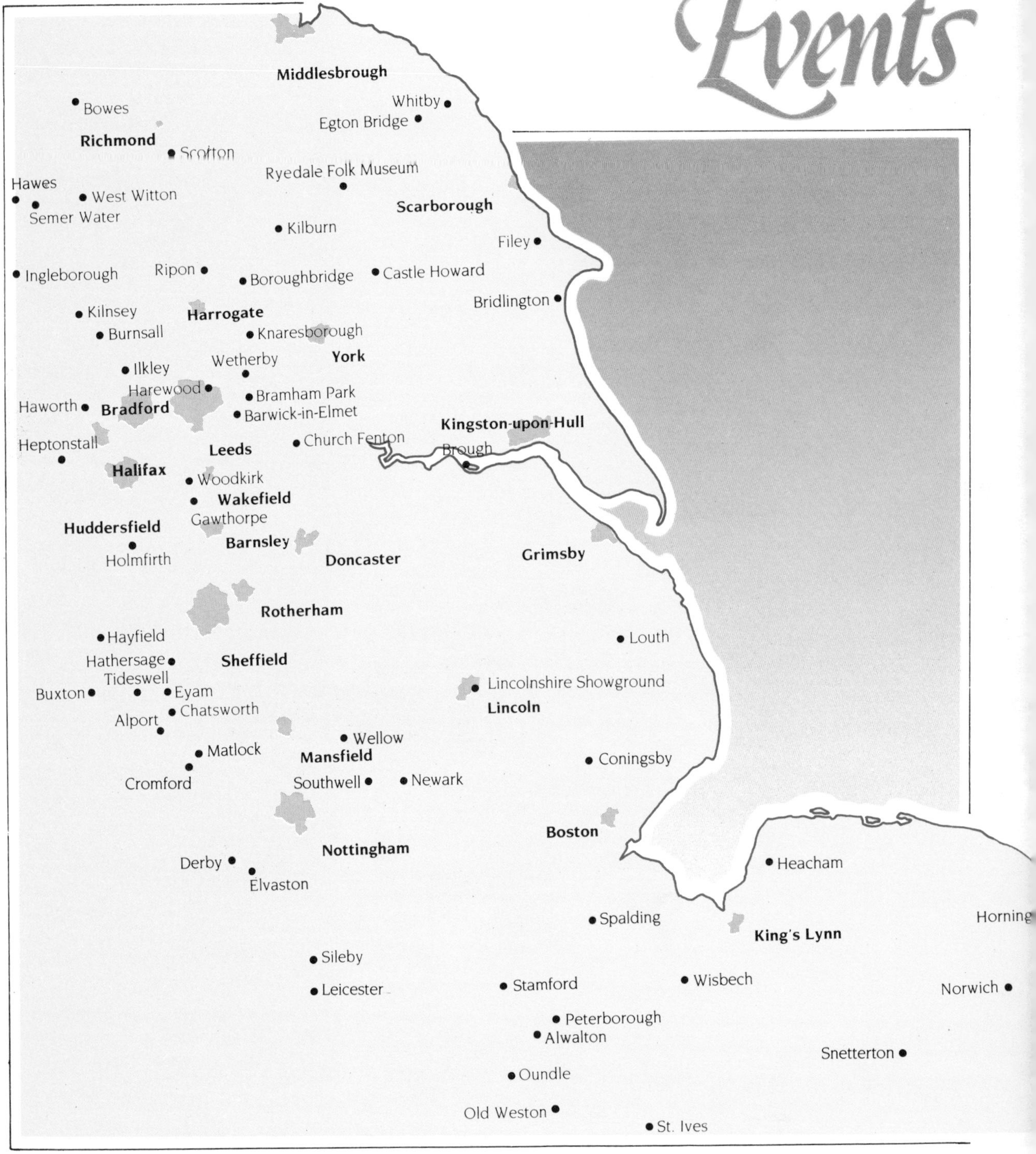

Middlesbrough

Bowes

Whitby

Richmond

Egton Bridge

Scotton

Ryedale Folk Museum

Hawes

West Witton

Scarborough

Semer Water

Kilburn

Filey

Ingleborough

Ripon

Boroughbridge

Castle Howard

Bridlington

Kilnsey

Harrogate

Burnsall

Knaresborough

Wetherby

York

Ilkley

Harewood

Haworth

Bradford

Bramham Park

Barwick-in-Elmet

Heptonstall

Church Fenton

Kingston-upon-Hull

Leeds

Brough

Halifax

Woodkirk

Wakefield

Huddersfield

Gawthorpe

Barnsley

Holmfirth

Doncaster

Grimsby

Rotherham

Hayfield

Louth

Hathersage

Sheffield

Tideswell

Buxton

Eyam

Lincolnshire Showground

Alport

Chatsworth

Lincoln

Matlock

Wellow

Cromford

Mansfield

Coningsby

Southwell

Newark

Boston

Derby

Nottingham

Elvaston

Heacham

Spalding

King's Lynn

Horning

Sileby

Leicester

Stamford

Wisbech

Norwich

Peterborough

Alwalton

Snetterton

Oundle

Old Weston

St. Ives

Gawthorpe Maypole Celebrations

First Saturday in May

Gawthorpe, West Yorkshire.

The procession, with military band, starts from the centre of Gawthorpe, at the village green, and proceeds to Ossett and back.

Plenty of parking in the village. Gawthorpe is close to Wakefield and is easily accessible from the M1.

Gorky comes to Gawthorpe

Although it is a matter of conjecture as to how long there has been a maypole in the village of Gawthorpe, it was certainly there in the latter part of the nineteenth century, for there are accounts of it having been cut down and taken away by the 'Streetsiders', inhabitants of a neighbouring area. After a pitched battle between the culprits and the men of Gawthorpe, it was recovered and re-erected in 1875 on the village green where it stands today, an over-sized barber's pole, crowned with a weathercock.

They will tell you in Gawthorpe that the maypole brings good luck to the village. It certainly seems to provide the local community with a focal point for its various educational, social and fund-raising activities. Research into the origins of the maypole has stimulated an interest in local history and you are quite likely to hear stories from the villagers about the Viking chieftain, Gorky, who sailed to these parts by way of the River Calder (and from whom the village might have derived its name); or about Adam Adamson who died from a broken neck when he fell down a pit shaft as long ago as 1399 (coal being part of village life then as now). You might also hear about the origins of the Gawthorpe Maypole Celebrations which have been held every year for over a century.

Today, as always, the high spot of these celebrations is the procession – a magnificent affair that goes on for miles. You'd never dream that a village of only 4,000 inhabitants could mount it. There's the military band, followed by the May Queen and her attendants; civic dignitaries and church leaders; past May Queens and Maids of Honour; Maypole plaiters. Then there are the entrants in the various competitive classes – Motor Vehicles Industrial, Decorated Motor Vehicles Non-Industrial, Fancy Dress (for adults and children), Fancy Dress on Horseback, Decorated Bicycles, Vintage Cars and so on; there are a score of classes at least, most of them competing for trophies as well as money prizes that add up to hundreds of pounds. There are also gymnastic and dancing troupes, including the Maypole Dancing Team who have been training in the village school for all their intricate variations of ribbon plaiting – The Barber's Pole, The Gipsy's Tent, The Spider's Web.

After the procession comes the Old Folks' Tea and treat –

They luv their owd fowks theear, ya see,
They're honoured and respected

writes an anonymous Gawthorpe laureate in the official programme of the event. And after that, for those with any energy left, there is, of course, the Feast or fun fair.

These festivities are now organised by the Gawthorpe Maypole Committee which was initially set up to raise money for the annual Old Folk's Tea and Treat. Since then its scope has widened to encompass the running of social events and general fund-raising in the village. Cecil Hitch, President of the Maypole Committee, told me. 'We're carrying on a tradition that maintains the local spirit. Gawthorpe is one of the best villages in the country for raising money. We cater for the community as a whole and if any of our local organisations need money for special equipment, or any other sort of help, we'll be delighted to do whatever we can.'

In 1962, the Maypole Committee had the opportunity of buying its own field for £600. It acted without hesitation and today the Maypole Field, as it is

known, provides the venue for bonfires and firework displays, gymkhanas and whatever else the Maypole Committee can think of to enliven village life.

Newark Round The Houses Race

First Sunday in May

Ladies start 2.30 p.m.
Men start 3.00 p.m.

Run by Newark Athletic Club. The race starts in London Road Car Park, which is near the market place in the centre of Newark, goes on a six-mile circuit of the town and ends back in Baldertongate.

There is a car park near to the start point; non-members are not usually accepted.

Spalding Flower Parade

Saturday, early May, in the afternoon

The procession, with floats, starts from the Halley Stewart Playing Fields and follows a 5-mile route through town.

Parking in the town centre.

Tulips by the million

Six million tulip heads, arranged in dazzling designs by an ingenious floral artist. That is the basis of the Spalding Flower Parade, held annually on a Saturday in early May. Since it began twenty-five years ago the themes have varied from television fantasies, like the Muppets, to rocket ships. Whatever the theme, the emphasis is on fun! The mile-long parade of twenty or so floats starts from the town centre and on its five-mile journey through the streets of Spalding is accompanied by perhaps a dozen colourful marching bands from many parts of Britain.

For months before the parade, much hard work has gone into its preparation. Float making, for instance, is an art form in itself. After the designer has translated his idea into a colour wash drawing, a blacksmith and a strawing expert spend months making a framework in steel and straw that must not only reproduce every detail of the intricate design but also be strong enough to support the float riders – and there can be quite a few of these, for a float might represent anything from a railway train with passengers to a 'sea-going' float characterising Maritime England.

The reason for all this magnificent display is not far to seek. Spring in the South Holland district of Lincolnshire is made glorious by the wealth of bloom in the bulb fields around Spalding. First the daffodils flower, usually in early April, then, during the last two weeks in April and the first week in May, the tulips are in bloom. The commercial object in growing them, however, is to produce bulbs rather than flowers. And because tulips without a

developing flower produce better bulbs, a few days after the flowers appear, the tulips are beheaded. Which might look like wanton destruction, were it not for the fact that the carefully garnered tulip heads bloom again so gloriously in the Flower Parade.

The procession of floats and bands usually sets out at 1.30 p.m. from the Sir Halley Stewart Field in the town centre and travels through the streets to Springfields Gardens, from where it returns to its starting point. Since the town roads are closed to traffic before the start of the parade, visitors should arrive in Spalding by 11 a.m.

During 'Tulip Time', churches in Spalding and some of the surrounding villages are beautifully decorated and in many church halls meals may be obtained.

To get the very best from the occasion you might arrange to arrive well before the great day and tour the fields by following the signposted 'Rural Rides' of fifteen to twenty-five miles through the wonderfully fertile area where the bulbs are grown. Here visitors will not only find the daffodil and tulip fields, but they may be sure of a welcome at village flower festivals.

From March, maps showing the Rural Rides may be obtained from Spalding's Tourist Information Centre at Ayscloughfee Hall in Churchgate, where daily advice can be had on where the best fields of flowers are to be found.

Derby Arts Festival

First three weeks in May

Majority of events take place in the Guildhall and the Cathedral in the centre of Derby. Tickets usually obtainable at events; central car parks. Extra events (Scottish dancing and an art exhibition) take place in March.

Pageant of the Horse

First Sunday after May Day holiday

Held at Doncaster Racecourse on Leger Way, near Doncaster Common and the airport, in a residential area to the south of Doncaster.

Traditionally the event is free.

There is a car park at the race course.

Hardraw Force Brass Band Festival

Second Sunday in May, all day

A regular nineteenth-century event which has been revived recently.

The Festival takes place in a natural amphitheatre by Hardraw Force Waterfall, which is accessible through the George and Dragon pub. Nearest town is Hawes.

Pay at the pub to get to the Waterfall. There is a car park.

At least as old as the Clinton Arms is the Olde White Hart. Age has wrought changes here, too, for during its long career the hostelry has been shop as well as inn; now fully restored, it presents a fine example of careful conservation.

Newark has long been centred on its market, whose symbol, the superb market square – one of England's largest – is paved with stones long ago unloaded as ballast by ships sailed here from northern lands by fair-haired Scandinavians. Those medieval seamen had to lighten their vessels or their keels would have dragged on the bottom of the

Newark and Notts Show

Early May

The Showground, Winthorpe, Newark, Notts.

The Showground is on the A46 between Newark and Lincoln. There is ample parking in the Showground car park and the charge is by the day. There is also an entrance free for the show.

Showplace for a county

One agricultural show may be much like another in essentials, but the locations vary delightfully. Bustling Newark-on-Trent takes a modest pleasure in the fact that, out of all Nottinghamshire, it is chosen to be host to the county agricultural show. The event indeed includes Newark's name in its title – it is the 'Newark and Notts' show, held every year in early May on Newark's permanent

showground, just outside the town.

Newark, as English as a morris dance or a game of bowls, is called the 'Key to the North', though it could lay equal claim to be the 'Gateway to the South'. Travellers in either direction still recognise its name as that of a halfway mark, as they did in the stage-coach days whose traces the town still bears.

One of Newark's oldest inns, the Clinton Arms, was a coaching house as long ago as 1494. Inns rarely change their names, but old age can alter all – before it held its present name this one was called the Kingston Arms and, still earlier, the Cardinal's Hat. From its balcony Gladstone addressed the solid citizens of Newark, sparing no oratorical effort as he fought to win their support.

CHAIN LANE

shallow river Trent. And tradition tells that the shrewd citizens of Newark knew how to make good use of the Northmen's throwaway cargo.

Fringeing the square, neighbour to the Clinton Arms and the Olde White Hart, is the proud town hall which John Carr of York, the 'Architect of the North', built in 1773, and the half-timbered Governor's House that was home to the Governors of Newark during the Civil War.

Throughout the conflict, Newark was a staunch Royalist stronghold. Never defeated, the town surrendered only at the King's insistence when he was taken prisoner at nearby Kelham. The Newark garrison left the town with full military honours whilst Cromwell ordered the fortifications to be dismantled. Happily, this command was never completely carried out and although time has also taken its toll of the building, a comprehensive conservation programme has now ensured the castle's future.

Dickens, who went everywhere and never failed to make some quotable and, if possible, outrageous comment about it, was asked in 1857 to be Newark's M.P. He replied that 'no consideration on earth' would induce him to join 'such an incoherent assembly'.

Newark apparently managed very well without the Great Inimitable. Its various industries flourished – notably smock-making, clock-making and printing. S. and J. Ridge of Newark printed Byron's poems on a wooden press which may be seen in Newark Museum along with a pipe presented by the poet to John Ridge.

From 1804 to 1806 Byron's mother lived in neighbouring Southwell, linked since 1974 with Newark to form a new and large authority. So it is impossible now to talk of Newark and forget Southwell, which remains a town in its own right, with its own Norman minster, the Cathedral Church of St Mary, and even its own river, the little Greet which runs to join the Trent.

And it still has Burgage Manor where Byron's mother lived while her son was at Cambridge, and the historic Saracen's Head Hotel, another coaching inn, whose story dates from the Wars of the Roses. Charles I 'slept here' and you may see his actual bedchamber.

Southwell is also a country town, renowned for the Bramley apples and roses it grows. Inevitably, then, it has its own agricultural show, held on a Saturday in August since 1953, and there its true nature as a country market town is demonstrated, just as Newark's true character is shown week by week at its Wednesday cattle market, but even more so at the Newark and Notts Agricultural Show, when it plays host to visitors from the whole county and beyond.

Hayfield May Queen Celebrations and Procession

Saturday nearest 12 May, afternoon

The procession begins at Hayfield School. Hayfield is a village on the A624 mid-way between Glossop and Chapel-en-le-Frith in the Peak District.

Free parking in the village.

Lincoln Vintage Vehicle Society Open Day

Sunday afternoon in mid-May

Held at the Depot on Wisby Road, Lincoln, about 3 miles out of the city centre. Easily accessible by road. Admission is usually free and there are trade stalls etc. There is a car park.

MG Owners' Motor Rally

Mid-May, one day

Elvaston Castle Country Park, Borrowash Road, Elvaston, Derbyshire.

A static show, with manoeuvres: cars are judged according to condition. Open to the public, small charge for the car park.

Elvaston Castle is six miles south of Derby and accessible from the M1, A52 and A6.

THE CALENDAR YEAR

Penny Hedge Planting

Usually on Ascension Eve
(mid-May) at 9.00 a.m.

Harbour Side, Long Church Street,
Whitby.

A ceremonial planting of twigs in
Whitby Harbour to withstand a
certain number of tides.

Yowers and yethers

There's no longer any *need* to plant
the Penny Hedge at Whitby on
Ascension Eve, for reasons which
will emerge as its story unfolds.
But they still plant it, because
people expect it and visit the
upper harbour at 9 a.m. on the
east side of the old Yorkshire
fishing town just to see it done.
And how can you disappoint
people who have got up early
enough to do that, especially
when most of them are on
holiday?

What they see might well seem
utterly meaningless! Three men
make their way to the harbour.
There is nothing unusual about
their dress; they are sensibly
wearing gumboots with which to
cross the harbour mud, but one of
them carries a horn and the
others, bundles of branches and
hazel stakes. Then, as the
hornblower looks on, the other
two hammer the stakes into the
ground and weave the hazel
wands among them to make a
rough fence. That finished, a blast
is sounded on the horn, after
which the hornblower cries, 'Out
on ye' three times.

That, as they say, is it. The Penny
Hedge, or Horngarth, has been
planted for another year and the
three men return solemnly to the
harbourside, leaving the
onlookers to speculate about the
meaning of it all.

It began, according to legend,
on 16 October 1159, when three
local men were hunting the boar
at Eskdaleside, near Sleights, a
few miles inland from Whitby.
They were – again according to
legend – Ralph de Percy, Lord of
Sneaton, William de Bruce, Lord
of Ugglebarnby and a freeholder
of Fylingdales called Allatson.

The three were hot on the trail
of a fine wild boar when the

animal rushed for shelter into the
cell of a hermit, one of the
fraternity based on Whitby Abbey.
He rose from kneeling before the
altar in his cell just long enough to
bolt the door, then resumed his
prayers.

Furiously, the hunters, balked of
their quarry, battered on the door
while the hermit ignored them
and the wounded boar licked its
wounds. Finally, under the
hunters' determined onslaught,
the cell door collapsed and the
three men rushed in, killed the
boar and ran their boar staves
through the hermit's body. He was
discovered, still alive, and taken to
Whitby Abbey. There, just before
he died, he told Abbott Sedman,
that he forgave his murderers – on
one condition: 'upon Ascension
Eve' the culprits, and eventually
their descendants, should build
on the river shore at Whitby a
hedge which would withstand
three tides. Should it fail to do so,
their lands would be forfeit to the
abbey.

The terms of the penance are
remarkably precise. The hedge
was to be built of 'yowers and

yethers' cut with a penny knife in a
specified wood then carried on the
wrongdoers', or their proxies',
backs to the place appointed.
There, after the performance of the
task, 'the Officer of Eskdaleside'
was to blow his horn and call 'Out
on ye' three times and the
penance would be accomplished.
And that has been the custom
performed for many years by a
local family.

But according to the terms of
the penance, should it ever be
made impossible by a 'full sea' the
duty need be performed no more.
Until recently this had never been
known to happen, but in 1981
happen it did, so the wrongdoers
were absolved at last and the
hermit could rest easy in his grave.
Perhaps he rests all the easier
because he knows that he has
given the Yorkshire coast one of
its most colourful and enduring
customs; because, rather than
accept the dispensation, the
present-day owners of the land
concerned carry on the custom for
the benefit of tourists.

What is the crowd really
watching? It seems a pity to knock

60

holes in an attractive legend, but as long ago as 1770 a Whitby historian declared that none of the characters in the story had actually existed, at least at the supposed time and under the names given to them in the legend. Nor was there a chapel on the site of the hermitage until nearly a hundred years after 1159. So how did the custom originate?

Some say the hedge may have started as a fish weir built at the start of the salmon-fishing season, but another name for the structure erected on the beach is the 'Horngarth', which may be derived from 'Thorngarth' and probably refers to the sort of fences or hedges once serving as boundaries for the land cultivated by tenants of Whitby Abbey. At the annual sounding of the horn, it has been suggested, the tenants were required to make good any damage to their fences or perhaps to the fences protecting the abbot's personal property.

When the practice became obsolete some abbot may have been reluctant to forgo his rights (as often happened in similar cases) and the story of the hermit could have been invented to justify the continuation of a custom that lent dignity to the ecclesiastical landlord. Why (if the story is true) did the dying monk choose Ascension Day Eve, which falls thirty-eight days after Easter Sunday? Did he perhaps know that the building of the fence was unlikely to be prevented by high water on that day, and that therefore the penance was due for a long, if not an indefinite, run? If so, he need hardly have been so precise, for thanks to the tourists, his penance seems likely to continue anyway!

Dicing for Bibles

Whit Tuesday, 12.00 noon

Parish Church, St Ives, Cambridgeshire.

St Ives is a small town east of Huntingdon and north-west of Cambridge. Dice are thrown and bibles awarded to twelve children under twelve. Plenty of parking, including the library car park, near the church.

Wharfedale Music Festival

Third week in May
Ilkley.

Most events take place in the King's Hall, near the railway station, and tickets are available from the Information Desk in the library on Station Road. There is a free car park next to the station.

Kindly commendations

According to Yorkshire folklore, it was the congregation of a West Riding chapel visiting Ilkley on their annual trip that first sang Yorkshire's tribal chant. Improvising to the hymn tune 'Cranbrook' as they bowled happily along in their charabanc, they added stanza to stanza to tell in lugubrious terms the story of the young man who was rash enough to go courting bare-headed on Ilkley Moor. Everybody knows the tune they sang even if they don't understand the words – they say there is an Icelandic version which, to the English southerner, is only slightly less comprehensible than the original. This is the song which became universally known during the First World War and which unites Yorkshiremen the world over at least as effectively as The Red Flag unites Socialists. It is, of course, On Ilkla' Moor Baht 'At.

Given its links with such a cultural event as the birth of the county anthem, Ilkley is surely the obvious first choice for an event like the Wharfedale Music Festival. The town has a decorous, cultivated air. No longer need it smart beneath the snubs of visitors like a Dr Richardson who, in 1709, found it 'a very mean place . . . chiefly famous for a cold well, which has done very remarkable cures' especially in cases 'arising from late hours, the abuse of liquors' . . . and so on. And Ilkley is unquestionably in Wharfedale, often considered the loveliest of the Dales, though many of those competing have been known to come from foreign parts like Colne – and that's in Lancashire!

The only way to get the full flavour of the Wharfedale Music

Festival (or indeed of any other of its remarkable kind) is to travel fearlessly with one of the choirs, ready to share the agonies of anticipation, the thrills of victory and, if the worst happens, the pangs of defeat. Which is why I found myself at Rothwell School, somewhere between Leeds and Wakefield, almost the only male among a coachload of highly vocal females in a variety of ages, shapes and sizes.

The Rodillians, they call themselves, a name explained by the fact that this much-respected ensemble was first formed of pupils of Rothwell Grammar School. Today the net for talent is more widely cast, but rehearsals are still held at the school and the choir is still run by its founder, Joyce Blakey, who taught there until she retired. How shall I describe her? Commanding figure? Benevolent despot? These are the clichés that spring to mind. Joyce ('Miss Blakey', still, to many of her 'girls') is a perfectionist who demands nothing less – and often rather more – than her girls are able to give her. But that's how she gets the results that win the Rodillians fame both here and abroad.

'Is everybody here?' demands Joyce from the front of the bus (in a voice which clearly threatens detention for anyone who isn't). Heads are switched back and forth and absences are dutifully reported. Some of the girls are already wearing their red ankle-length dresses, a present from *She* magazine, donated after one astute and dedicated chorister had written to the fashion editor requesting ideas for a new choir costume. Others carry their 'uniform' in hold-alls, planning to change on arrival at Ilkley. The mood in the coach is cheerfully confident. The girls (aged anything up to sixty-five) are hoping to look around Ilkley and do a bit of shopping between test pieces. They cast a weather eye at the moody mid-May sky while waiting for the last stragglers, who have to brave Miss Blakey's stare as they tumble into the coach, laden with apologies, explanations and shopping bags.

THE CALENDAR YEAR

We're off . . . the coach creeps through the school gate on to the road and everyone sits back with the sense of pleasurable anticipation that reminds you of bygone school trips. This sort of nostalgia could well be a reason why Joyce's girls, most of whom have families and homes to run, attend rehearsals faithfully and allow themselves to be drilled and bullied into something as close to perfection as will satisfy 'Miss Blakey'. She's not easily satisfied, but when she is, her smile comes as a worthwhile reward even to the most recalcitrant.

So, for a large part of this Saturday, the girls are virtually back at school and loving it, especially, perhaps, since they don't have to stay there. It's a way of stepping out of the present for a few hours with the comforting knowledge that the present is waiting for them when the time comes to return to it. It's the female equivalent of 'banding' – a single-sex world where girls can be girls for a while and where the odd male among them is fair game for leg-pulling if he doesn't keep his head down and avoid entanglements.

It seems a long drive to Ilkley, to the King's Hall and the two churches that are in use for the multitude of competitive classes . . .

Come to Ilkley if you sing, whether it's Folk, Gilbert and Sullivan, light opera, grand opera, or oratorio; whether you sing solo or in a group, to an organ or a piano accompaniment; whether you are over sixty or under thirteen. If you tootle the flute or manipulate the mandolin; if you play in a band or an orchestra; if you write poetry or simply recite it, then come to Ilkley! And, if you're lucky and the adjudicator likes your performance, you may go home with a prize. It's quite possible, of course, that you won't, for adjudicators are the most unpredicatable of creatures – in the eyes of the competitors, at least.

Ilkley at last. We disembark and since we are well in time, we go into the Winter Gardens for a look at some poetry. Displayed on

boards down the middle of the hall are the prize-winning entries in the poetry section. There are poems from all over the North – love poems, reflections on Science and Art, on simplicity, hatred and sacrifice, as well as a poem on 'Mi Grandad'.

But we must enter the King's Hall now to compete in Class 128: Madrigal Groups for the Thackray Memorial Trophy . . . We don't win. Goaded, perhaps, by a feeling that we've let Miss Blakey down, we gird up our girdles and launch with some determination into Class 138. This time we do win, and are awarded the Ilkley Gazette Trophy, last won by the Rodillians ten years before. The adjudicator's kindly commendations restore the air of mutual approval between the choir and its conductor.

And so, bearing our spoils, we say farewell to Ilkley and Wharfedale and head for Rothwell and home, conscious that, in leaving the Music Festival, we are leaving a different world. Year after year since 1906, when the festival was founded, competitors have rehearsed with utter dedication week after week, perhaps to have their efforts rewarded with a trophy, or at least to hear them assessed by the olympian adjudicators, whose kindest comments are often reserved for those with the lowest marks. Here, if nowhere else, is a world where trying counts. All who are involved in it belong to an artistic freemasonry for whom 'the Festival's the thing'.

The welcome printed in the programme says it all:
In these days of economic uncertainty and high unemployment it is indeed a matter of great satisfaction to the organisers to present another festival rich in scope and variety, evidence enough of the continuing interest shown by competitors, parents, teachers and schools . . .
We warmly welcome all those who come to listen or participate . . . ENJOY THIS FESTIVAL . . .
That, as they say, is what it's all about.

Ilkley Literature Festival

Spring Bank Holiday Week, biennially (even years)

Up to eight different events each day, featuring a wide range of modern writers. The King's Hall, Winter Gardens and Ilkley College are the main venues. There is an entrance fee for most events, usually between £1 and £5. Programmes are available before the event with full details and a map.

Tickets available from the Festival Office.

Books baht 'ats

Even if Ilkley's name were not eternally enshrined in Yorkshire's tribal hymn, it would still seem the appropriate heart of Yorkshire. Unpretentious, yet utterly sure of itself, it is shown in one local guide-book as sitting at the very centre, not just of Yorkshire, but of Britain itself. Around it, circles of

dots are drawn to indicate the distances from Ilkley to other, less blessed parts of the world. Within thirty miles of this nucleus are Bradford, Leeds and York; within ninety, Nottingham, Chester and Newcastle; and so on. Only the limit of the page, it seems, prevents the loyal cartographer bringing the entire globe within Ilkley's orbit.

Ilkley, as such guide books claim, has 'a unique situation' – at the heart of Wharfedale yet within easy reach of the county's great centres of population. It has probably been a holiday resort of some kind since the first Roman soldier at the garrison of Olicana dabbled his tired feet in water from chalybeate springs on the moors. Yet it has never, I submit, become another Harrogate.

Harrogate, with its cosmopolitan air, its 'Kursaal' and French Weeks, seems fashion-conscious and almost dilettantish compared with Ilkley, set between

the hard-living farmers of the Dales and the work-grimed centres of industry like Leeds and Bradford.

The 1974 Reorganisation of Local Government won few cheers from Yorkshiremen, but by chance or design the planners seem to have got it right when they re-located Harrogate in the 'New County' of North Yorkshire and left Ilkley in what they now called West Yorkshire, the heir and successor to the great workaday West Riding that used to be, with its mills, its coal and its steel.

J. B. Priestley, Phyllis Bentley, the Brontës – such names remind us that Yorkshire is undoubtedly a literary county, even if choral singing still vies with brass banding as the principal art form. The West Yorkshire ground is thick with aspiring writers. They meet in ardent groups for mutual criticism, admiration and the soaking up of know-how from visiting scribes with any degree of

achievement; they patronise literary lunches and demand that authors autograph books for them; they fall on literature festivals as travellers lost in the desert might fall upon oases.

At Ilkley's cultural water-hole they drink and, presumably, are satisfied, for the draught is well-suited to their West Yorkshire tastes. Here is a literature festival with its sleeves rolled up, with workshops to start the day and a do-it-yourself challenge glinting in its eye.

The first Ilkley Literature Festival was mounted in 1973 by a small band of enthusiasts headed by Michael Dawson, former Director of the Yorkshire Arts Association and himself an Ilkley resident. (Almost incredibly, at that time the only other festival devoted entirely to literature was Cheltenham's.) The essential aims were to help writers and readers to meet, and increasingly to appreciate each other. Its guiding principles could be summarised as follows:

a) To promote enjoyment and understanding of literature and of those arts or crafts which in any way use or touch upon literature and the written word.

b) To make literature and writers accessible to the public.

c) To encourage writers through the promotion of their work.

d) To stimulate debate about the position of literature in our society.

The Festival, which was at first biennial, was financed by dedicated fund-raising as well as by grants from the District Council and the Arts Council (after 1973 by the Yorkshire Arts Association). Mounted with courage, originality, enormous enthusiasm and a high degree of professionalism, that first Festival set a daunting standard. Deservedly, it was an instant success.

The programme included a personal appearance and reading by W. H. Auden, a lecture on Dickens (The Yorkshire Television Lecture) by Angus Wilson and a symposium on women and literature. A three-day extramural

course on 'Literature and Revolution' was sponsored by Leeds University. There was also the world premiere of a new play entitled *Thunder* by Richard Crane, an account of the tragic lives and deaths of the Brontë siblings – 'a full-blooded drama about a family whose lives were every bit as compelling as the lives of the characters they created . . .'

The concern to gain the interest of children was apparent in the first Festival, although a talk by John Rowe Townsend on 'Contemporary Children's Literature' was announced as being 'mainly for parents'. There was an exhibition of children's books, together with demonstrations of new teacher-reading machines and publishers' displays, at which several children's writers appeared.

Evidence of how things can change in ten years is provided by the presentation of the 1982 children's events which were

announced as 'Your end-of-term treat!' and which included a fancy dress parade – 'Come dressed as a character from a book' – as well as more serious matters, such as an essay competition for secondary and upper schools on 'How I would improve life in the twentieth century' and a very successful writing workshop for young adults, run by two poets and two novelists.

The names of some of the more eminent participants in the Festival during the years since its inception provide a guide to the consistently high standard attained – Conor Cruise O'Brien, Marguerite Duras, Lord David Cecil, Melvyn Bragg, Anthony Thwaite, Alan Sillitoe, Charles Causley, Malcolm Bradbury, Barbara Ineson, Michael Rosen. Premières have included *Ludd* by J. Mackendrick and *Cave Birds* by Ted Hughes. Nor has the Festival confined itself too narrowly to literature but has staged

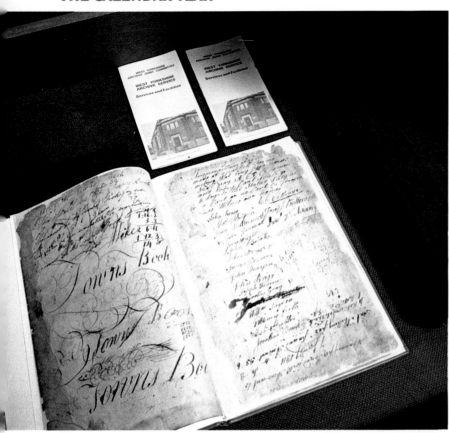

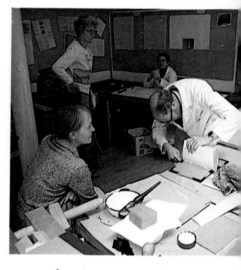

exhibitions of works by Sidney Nolan, the Australian painter-poet, and of Michael Ayrton's sculpture and drawings.

Since the first Festival in 1973, which listed in its programme 'Folk in Pubs', a daily Easter Fair, Street Theatre and a Puffin Tea Party, there has always been in existence the light-hearted fringe of events which have leavened the literary lump and engaged the interest of the man in the street – in Ilkley's case, the stroller on the Grove, Ilkley's elegant high street.

In 1982 June Oldham, Ilkley novelist and children's writer who, from the outset, had been associated with the Festival, took over from Michael Dawson as its director. For the first time, only one year had elapsed between festivals. With only a year to prepare, her first Festival was a resounding success, ample reward for her obvious energy and determination.

How does a new director set about preparing her first Festival programme? One of her innovations was the 'Up Stage'

studio theatre in the Winter Gardens, already home of the Festival Club. 'Up Stage' was to be the setting for lunchtime, afternoon and evening poetry readings, lectures and late-night events, as well as for the sort of spontaneous discussions that June Oldham clearly hoped would become a feature of future Ilkley Festivals.

Another of her aims was to seek to involve people in the highly technical business of modern book production – after all, those who are not involved in publishing or printing tend to see books as objects which are mysteriously born of a single mechanical process; you put the author's manuscript in one end of the machine and collect the complete bound and jacketed volume from the other! But, as the display of past and present printing equipment at the Festival Club demonstrated so well, books are the product of a variety of operations. Visitors were invited to try their hands at phototypesetting – the modern

way of setting a manuscript – as well as being able to watch calligraphers perform their antique craft and book-restorers demonstrate methods of preserving and repairing fine old volumes.

One advantage of holding a literature festival in Ilkley is that you need not go far to find your stars. Jilly Cooper, herself a daughter of Ilkley, had already appeared. The net for the 1982 Festival was cast a little wider to encompass Hull, where Philip Larkin, one of Britain's leading contemporary poets, is Librarian at the Brynmore Jones Library at Hull University. But the organisers hit a snag! Larkin is notably reluctant to appear at festivals. So, nothing daunted, June Oldham commissioned a programme to be presented by Platforms Theatre on 'Philip Larkin's Blues and Other Colours', paying skilful and dramatic tribute to Larkin's poetry, as well as involving his interest in jazz.

Since the 1982 Festival had a woman at its helm for the first

Maypole Dancing

Spring Bank Holiday Monday,
2.00 p.m.

Wellow, Nottinghamshire.

Maypole dancing takes place on
the village green. Space to park on
the roads or in the pub grounds
opposite. Wellow is a village south
of Ollerton on the A616.

Barwick in Elmet Maypole Raising

Spring Bank Holiday Tuesday,
every three years

The Maypole is taken down on
Easter Tuesday, repainted and
'raised' at Spring Bank Holiday.
A big occasion with lots of
spectators, and the pubs are open
all day.

Takes place in front of the Black
Swan and usually a field is opened
for parking.

Barwick in Elmet is north-east of
Leeds on the A1.

East of England Motor Show

During the fourth week in May

Held at Lilford Hall, Lilford Park,
Oundle, near Peterborough
(on the A605 between Oundle and
Thrapston). Open to the public;
the entrance fee is a fixed charge
per car rather than per person.

Orange Dole

Late May, 2.30

Sileby Churchyard, Sileby,
Leicestershire.

This is an ancient custom which
takes place on the Sunday School
Anniversary. There is an
anniversary service after which
200 oranges are handed out under
the Cherry Tree in the Churchyard.

Sileby is between Loughborough
and Leicester, off the A6. It is only
a small village and it is possible to
park at the vicarage.

time, it was not all that surprising
to find Mary Scott, Eva Figes,
Carmen Callil and Olwen Wymark
discussing 'The Women's
Movement and Literature'.
They surely discussed Woman's
place in Literature – and possibly
decided that place was in Ilkley!
It's a sobering reflection that a
present-day Ilkley Romeo might
well be wasting his time
'a-coortin' Mary Jane on Ilkla'
Moor baht 'at' – she'd probably be
so much happier talking books at
the Festival . . .

The Director of a festival of such
scope requires more than artistic
expertise, necessary though that
may be, and one of June Oldham's
aims is to find new sponsors to
ensure the Festival's continued
expansion and improvement.
The list of sponsors so far involved
contains household names from
Yorkshire as well as from wider
fields. Long may they, and others,
continue to attract more visitors
to Ilkley at festival time for their
delight and enrichment through
literature.

Richmond Annual Meet and Carnival Weekend

Saturday – Monday, Spring Bank
Holiday weekend

In and around Richmond.

Open to the public, parking space
in the centre of Richmond.
Church Service and Veteran Car
Rally on Sunday; Fancy Dress
parade on Monday; other events
on the cricket fields.

Derbyshire Well Dressings

There are well dressings throughout the summer all over Derbyshire. Precise dates are available early in the year from Derby Tourist Information Office.

Tissington
Mid-May
Etwall
Around second weekend in May
Wirksworth
Around last weekend in May
Middleton by Youlgreave
Late May/early June
Monyash
Late May/early June
Ashford in the Water
Late May/early June
Litton
Late June/early July
Tideswell
Late June/early July
Youlgreave
Late June/early July
Bakewell
Late June/early July
Buxton
Mid-July
Pilsley
Mid-July
Stoney Middleton
Late July
Bradwell
Late July/early August
Eyam
Late August/early September
Wormhill
Late August/early September
Hartington
Mid-September

Painting in petals

For a few days each spring or summer the streets of grey stone villages half hidden in the Derbyshire hills shake off their customary modesty, deck their streets with flags and embark on their annual festivals, a frequent feature of which is well-dressing.

The actual date of the custom varies from place to place. At Tissington, for instance, the ceremonies take place on Ascension Day. At Wirksworth the appointed day is Whit Wednesday, while at Wormhill the wells are dressed in August, as they are at

Eyam, the famous Plague Village, where the Townend and Townhead wells are the focal point of services and processions.

Well-dressing was once practised over most of Britain. It has probably persisted so long in Derbyshire because limestone country is not rich in springs and the presence of a well was therefore all the more highly valued. The custom, or a version of it, has been practised in many parts of the world and dates from pre-Christian times, but whereas a Himalayan version may amount to no more than the hanging of fragments of coloured cloth on bushes surrounding a mountain spring, the Derbyshire custom takes such a distinctive form that visitors are attracted from far and near. Like many another colourful and attractive custom, however, it fell into abeyance and might well have died. Now it flourishes perhaps more strongly than ever.

At Wormhill in the nineteenth century, well-dressing was the

occasion of great rural enjoyment. Tents and booths were erected, sports were held, and the ravine where the spring was located echoed with the sounds of revelry. In the unaccountable way of such things, the custom at Wormhill lapsed for a century or more until it was revived in 1951, Festival of Britain year.

Fortunately, the secrets of the craft had survived in other villages, such as Tideswell, whose well-dressers lent their expertise. First, a boarded wooden framework is prepared, which takes the form of six units – the picture board, border board, 'mantelshelf', headboard and two 'dollies'. Each of these is covered with a one-inch layer of wet clay. To this is applied the paper on which the designs have been drawn. These are then pricked into the clay with a dressmaker's spiked wheel and the paper is peeled off, leaving the design traced in dots on the clay.

The next step is to colour in the

outlines using only natural materials such as grow in the gardens, fields and hedgerows of the district. They may be reeds, beans or berries from holly or rowan trees. Once the outline is complete, the filling-in begins. And here, flowers, mosses or berries are employed with skill and artistry, but never, *never* at Wormhill will you see such intrusions as coloured wools or metal foil!

Experience has shown which are the best flowers. They vary as widely as the voluptuous hydrangea and the humble buttercup, while parsley, too, comes in handy.

The themes illustrated vary, though there is usually a Biblical connotation. When well-dressing was first revived at Wormhill, the picture pricked in the clay was a Nativity scene. In 1982, Maritime England Year, the theme celebrated the men who 'go down to the sea in ships and occupy their business in great waters' – particularly the Royal and Merchant Navies, the lifeboat service, the fishermen and Britain's naval heroes. Hence the

central panel depicted St Olave's Church, with its Trinity House Chapel (Trinity House being the authority responsible for our lighthouses and pilotage service). A wartime Mediterranean convoy was shown in the lower panel, and also featured were the crests of the Royal Navy and Trinity House, the aircraft-carrier HMS *Hermes*, a lighthouse, a sailing-ship, and a scene on the deck of one of Nelson's men o' war during the Battle of the Nile.

Some say that the Romans introduced well-dressing when they built shrines over mineral springs and scattered flowers on the water as an offering to the appropriate deity. When the Romans left, the custom seems to have lapsed and during the dark ages it disappeared altogether.

At Tissington it was revived in the early seventeenth century as a thank offering for the immunity of the village through a plague epidemic and for the fact that, during a period of drought, the local wells had never run dry. An old woman is said to have hung garlands over the village wells, but the development of the forerunner

of the floral artistry we see today, with its amazingly brilliant pictures on clay-covered boards, did not appear until about 1818 and then the first attempts were simple geometrical patterns. Gradually, over the years, a remarkable local art-form has developed.

The link with disease, first noted at Tissington, seems to have been a feature since early times. Just as pilgrims now immerse themselves in the water at Lourdes, so people once bathed in the Derbyshire springs, drank the water or threw pins into it in the hope of improving their health and preserving their sanity.

THE CALENDAR YEAR

Boar's Head Morris Dancing

Throughout the summer

The Boar's Head Morris Men perform at various venues including the Piece Hall in Halifax town centre.

There is a free, long-stay car park at Wade Street, behind the R.S.P.C.A. and a short-stay car park behind the town hall. There is usually either a collection or a fee for Morris Dancing events.

Chatsworth Angling Fair

Sunday, end May, 9.30 – 5.30

Chatsworth Park, Edensor, Derbyshire.

Fee for the Angling Fair which does not admit you to Chatsworth House. Parking in the grounds.

Oak Apple Day (or Garland King Day)

29 May, 10.00 a.m.

Castleton, near Tideswell, Derbyshire.

Horseback procession followed by a silver band.

The parade, commemorating the Restoration of King Charles II to the throne in 1660, begins at a different Inn in Castleton each year. It proceeds to Spittle Bridge, then around the village to the market place, and ends at St Edmund's Church.

Castleton is in North Derbyshire, near Sheffield.

Mayor's Sunday, Boston, Lincs

Late May, early June

Parade starts at 'Boston Stump' (the Parish Church) at 11.00 a.m. and goes through the centre of town. It arrives at the Assembly Rooms at 12.00 noon.

Easy to park in Mayfair – the broad main street – but get there early. Car parks in the town centre.

Antient Scorton Silver Arrow Contest

Usually held during May or June

This event is always held in Yorkshire, but not necessarily always in Scorton. Contact Richmond Tourist Information near the date for further details. Scorton is a small village off the A6136 south of Richmond. There is also a gold tournament.

The bonhomie of bowmen

The antient Scorton Silver Arrow traces its pedigree back with absolute certainty to 14 May 1673 when twenty-two archers competed on the village green at Scorton, near Richmond in North Yorkshire, and Henry Calverley emerged the winner.

One imagines it to have been a day when the May sun shone, when *bonhomie* and good sportsmanship prevailed. So much so indeed that the twenty-two bowmen declared, 'We must do this again!' And they did – again – and again – and again. What's more, they're still doing it and will probably continue until the twang of the last bowstring is drowned by the Crack of Doom.

After that they'll no doubt set up their targets in the Elysian fields and continue shooting with no change in the rules except, perhaps, a rather stricter and more serious enforcement of the ban on swearing. (On reflection, perhaps they'll stop imposing fines for profanity since there will be no poor in heaven – or so one presumes – to benefit from the contents of the swear-bag.)

The rule against swearing was drawn up, along with a handful of others, at that very first contest of 1673. Having proved himself the best archer, Henry Calverley was automatically elected captain and thus empowered under the rules to nominate the venue for the next contest – just as winners have been doing down the centuries and still do today.

The society has a complete list of such winners from that first meeting, including, by the way, a fair sprinkling of 'Revs'. To what extent they contributed to the swear-bag is not, alas, recorded, nor whether 'Dear me, missed again!' merited a fine.

There are in the record occasional blank years and even a long hiatus between 1798 and 1809, but generally speaking, only pestilence or a world war has been allowed to break the sequence. And during most of the playing years many of the same trophies have been competed for, most notably the original Silver Arrow itself – well, virtually original. It was broken, according to legend, in the early 1700s when an Oxford undergraduate, in the irresponsible way of some such, tried to shoot the 'antient' projectile from a bow and broke it, whereupon it was repaired and remains the society's most treasured relic. According to the Assay Master, the tail is made of sixteenth-century silver and the fore-part seventeenth-century silver.

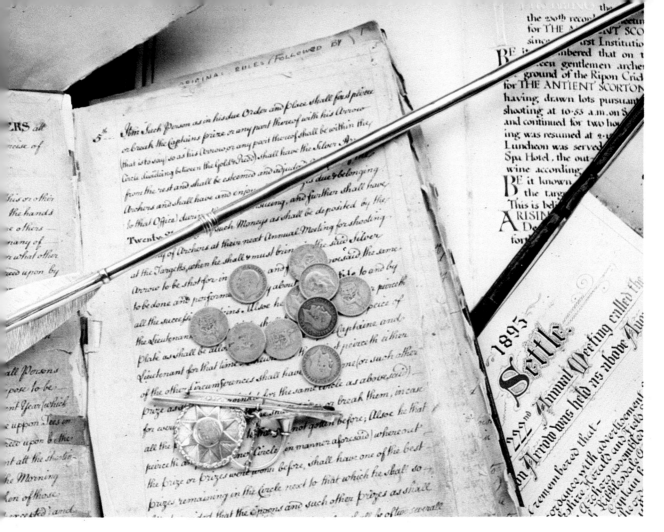

No one knows where the priceless projectile came from. One legend hints at a connection with Roger Ascham, who taught Queen Elizabeth I to shoot, and also wrote a treatise on archery. He lived not far away at Kirby Wiske. And they do say that Henry Calverley himself begged the silver dart from the ne'er-do-well son of a local landowner, turned out for being found in bed with one of the house-maids. If all the poor lad owned was this highly negotiable piece of silver, it seems unlikely that he would have parted with it so readily, but that's the story, and Calverley is said to have presented it to his fellow archers as their principal trophy on 14 May 1673. (But they are, on the quiet, rather a leg-pulling lot! So could it be that in his presentation speech Henry told some high-flown tale which, down the years, has come to be revered as fact?)

However it came to them, the arrow is won by the first man at each annual meeting to strike an inner gold at one hundred yards; he thereby becomes the Captain. Since each archer has only two shafts to loose at each end, there is no chance to make practice flights and so assess the effects of the wind and the peculiarities of the field. Having placed a lucky shot in the winning spot, the new Captain might be rather taken aback to find that he had not only the privilege of choosing the venue for the next event – it can be anywhere within the pre-1974 Yorkshire boundaries – but is also responsible for organising what can fairly be termed the whole shooting-match.

His task is made less onerous by the appointment of the Lieutenant, who achieves that rank by being the first man to strike the red (or at any rate, achieve runner-up status). He, too, has a trophy, an elegant bugle which he has to sound (with varying degrees of success) to signal the 'Commencement of Shooting' at the next meeting,

along with other burdens of office. At lunch, traditionally taken at 'a local ordinary', it is the Lieutenant's duty to read the minutes of the previous meeting.

Also amongst the so-called 'Scorton Group' of trophies is the horn spoon, lined with silver, which bears the warning, in Latin, 'Don't laugh at me, my friends'. And really, there's no reason to, because its winner also receives all the money left at the end of the day's shooting. Another trophy, the Wilkinson Sword, donated by Wilkinsons the cutlers, is awarded for the greatest number of hits by a longbowman. Not all competitors, you see, are armed with the sort of weapon which gave us victory at Crécy and Agincourt. Modern bows, 'with all the technical gubbins', as one archer put it, are allowed, but not crossbows or compound bows.

The sword is also named the Ben Hird Memorial Trophy, for it commemorates one of the best-loved of the Scorton

veterans, who died in 1976.
Ben first won the Scorton Arrow as a lad of nineteen in 1900, though the sight of his crude equipment was almost enough to make some of the stuffier members demand that he should quit the field without releasing a shaft.
There was by no means universal delight when Ben, the stripling nobody with his home-made bow, ended the day as Captain. But they had to get used to him, for Ben was to be a lifelong Scorton archer; never again was he the captain but with each succeeding year the audience for his reminiscences grew.

A second group of trophies comprises the Thirsk Insignia, given to the society by Henry Peckett on behalf of the Thirsk Bowmen in 1884, and for this, competition is restricted to Yorkshiremen. There is the Arrow Belt and Quiver, won by the highest scorer; a Bugle, awarded for the highest number of hits; and a silver medal for the best gold. Then there are the Subscription Prizes and the silver Philips Cup. Half the money collected at the meeting goes to the man scoring the best gold. So if the best gold also happens to be the first gold of the day, the archer can take home not only the Silver Arrow and the Philips Cup but 50 per cent of the sweep as well!

Apart from such minor perks, the event is untainted by commercialism. Fixing the entry fee is a simple matter of estimating the cost of the event and dividing it by the number of entrants. Recently that has averaged about eighty, though in 1930 there were only three and a few years later no more than eleven. Love for tradition is moderated by a recognition of what is practical. As the Clerk to the Council of Captains, Major Crees, told me rather regretfully, 'If we limited it to longbows we'd get about ten'.

Great stress is laid on 'the spirit of Scorton'. 'It's essentially,' the Major explained, 'an occasion for enjoyment. Even the rules make it plain that one is there for an enjoyable day's company.'
Contestants at Scorton shoot at

100 yards two ways' – that is, with a target at each end. They use a four-foot target with a three-inch black disc as an 'inner' gold at the centre of the gold, which has a diameter of nine inches.
Contestants pick a card at random for position, then at 10.30 a.m. the Lieutenant sounds his bugle and shooting begins. Starting with the Captain and the Lieutenant, each man shoots two arrows each way; at 1 p.m. lunch is taken; the annual meeting follows, after which, at 3.30 p.m. shooting is resumed, still at the rate of only two shots per man, and continues until 5.30 p.m.

For every colour hit, the contestants are paid a nominal reward from the kitty – two shillings for a gold and one shilling for a colour. The archer 'scoring' a white has to put a shilling *into* the kitty. A shilling? Yes. The Scorton Archers will have no truck, if they can help it, with these new-fangled decimalised denominations of coinage.
('It used to be sixpence up to 1981 said Major Crees, who assiduously collects shillings for this express purpose.)
But what of those who *miss*? Ah, they serve to demonstrate the splendid sportsmanship of the Scorton event. There is, naturally, no prize for them, but no penalty either. 'It would be grossly unfair, explains the Major, 'to the longbowmen.' And incidentally, despite the growing fashion for bows fitted with 'technological gubbins', the longbow is gaining popularity fast.
Sportsmanship? The term is hardly adequate! Members are put on their honour to keep their own scores, which they report faithfully to the lady scorers in their tent midway between the targets. Only once was there an attempt at cheating. It happened at Harrogate, of all places.
Needless to say, that archer will never shoot again for the Scorton Arrow.

On the whole the harmony of the event is rarely ruffled.
There was, admittedly, an occasion in the 1970s when the award of the Arrow was the subject of dispute. But such

disagreements are soon settled by the Council of Captains, formed in 1967, when it was felt that things at this generally free and easy event were getting rather too casual. There was, for instance, the time when a competitor failed to return the trophy he had won the year before. Naturally, he was sternly sent back home to fetch it . . . 'from Lancashire,' added my informant bleakly.

Doubtless he'd forgotten it and doubtless there were no hard feelings; for the Scorton men refuse to take their sport too earnestly. In orthodox target archery nowadays, 'they're so bloody serious you daren't even cough,' I was told. In the Scorton competition, however, you have to concentrate regardless of the sounds of enjoyment coming from all around. And don't think, if you're the sensitive type, that the swear-box will protect your ears. On the contrary, the fact that it's all in a good cause encourages a bit of playful over-emphasis – 'What's that you said? You'd better not say *that* again!' And of course he does, someone joyfully shouts for the judge, and there's a little bit more to hand to the local vicar for the poor of the parish. Since the vicar is always approached in advance and invited to share in the socialising, he's unlikely to refuse the cash as immoral earnings!

As chivalrous as the traditional Robin Hood, the Scorton Archers make no secret of the fact that, where the Silver Arrow is concerned, woman's place is in the scoring tent or, in the case of the Captain's Lady, presenting trophies at the end of the shoot. They have no fear, either, of an invasion by single-breasted, bow-toting Amazons, since 'women don't shoot at 100 yards,' they tell you rather smugly. In any case, the Scorton men are by no means convinced that the ladies can swear well enough to maintain the Scorton tradition. Which just goes to show what nice old-fashioned things they are. But just to prove that this is no anti-feminist group, a ladies' competition has been introduced for the Ascham Arrow.

Traditionalists to the backbone, the Scorton archers treasure the parchment – now in the County Council archives at Northallerton – that records their foundation. Most of it is illegible to unaided twentieth-century eyes, but it certainly bears Henry Calverley's signature. Also highly valued is the fine cloth on which the prizes are displayed. It was embroidered by an ardent supporter, Marjorie McCree of Slaidburn. Then there is the society flag, as well as sashes and special badges presented by the first American to win the contest. An illuminated record of each contest is executed on handmade parchment by the nearest college of art.

A message of loyalty has always been sent to the Sovereign. In 1977, when the Queen Mother was in the Scorton area, she was prevailed upon to visit the society and was so fascinated that she outstayed her scheduled time – though certainly not her welcome.

War can still be waged with arrows. But now we call them missiles and launch them from submarines. So in an age like this, the bow, so deadly within its own small scope, is not only an item — sometimes highly developed – of sporting equipment, but a martial museum-piece as well. In the eyes of the Scorton bowmen it is both, although they probably prize it most for its traditional associations. They would dearly love the contest to continue indefinitely in its time-honoured way, but even archery may have change thrust upon it. 'We shall have to think of permitting the compound bow one day,' said Major Crees. Let's hope they never stoop to allowing anything so damnably foreign as the sort of crossbow used in William Tell's time to shoot apples off small boys' heads!

Whatever their weapons, long may the Scorton archers continue their custom with its delightful blend of playfulness and solemnity. Long may their swear-box enrich the parish poor, and the Captain's lady hand out the trophies. Perhaps they are preserving more and better things than they know . . .

Spring Show of the Swaledale Sheep Breed

Thursday, late May

An all-day event.

Held on open moorland next to the Tan Hill Inn, the highest pub in Britain. The nearest town is Bowes and the Inn is at the top of a steep minor road off the A66, west of Bowes. Likely to be an entrance fee; parking nearby.

Harden Moss Sheep Dog Trials

Saturday and Sunday of the second or third weekend in June

Harden Moss Farm, Greenfield Road, Holmfirth, near Huddersfield.

Open to the public. The sheep dog trials take place on the moors above Holmfirth. Take the A635 out of Huddersfield towards Greenfield and Harden Moss Guest House is on the right-hand side. There is a parking ground for which a charge is made.

This is a big local event and is usually well signposted.

Men, dogs and sheep

Come rain, snow, blistering sun or hurricane, the sheepdog trial, it seems, must go on. Only fog, which would obviously render the whole thing pointless (if not impossible), is seen as a just cause for abandonment. Even so, driving rain and wind are nearly as unfortunate since they reduce the audibility of call and whistle and the shepherd must then 'talk' to his dog with his hands.

Television enables people who would hardly know a Swaledale sheep from a Suffolk to become familiar with the setting and atmosphere of a sheepdog trial. The silence, as the exasperating sheep positively refuse to understand what is required of them by the patient, intent dog (surely demonstrating the meaning of 'dogged'!), combines elements of sport with a ritual whose solemnity is unbroken until a ripple of applause unites man and dog, performers and audience, in an almost palpable sense of achievement.

First, a group of sheep is turned into the arena at the far end of the course, something under half a mile from where the handler stands with his dog. The sheep look as lost and uncertain as unwilling entrants in a talent contest, nervous of what may be demanded of them. They needn't worry – they're only required to be themselves!

The trial begins with the Outrun, during which the handler sends his dog to run in a great, widening pear-shaped curve behind the sheep. Away speeds the dog like a bullet, soul and being bent on fulfilling the command. Nobody in our cruelty-conscious age, which waxes furious about circuses, battery hens, and sometimes even show jumping, ever levels a charge of cruelty against those who train sheep-dogs. It never occurs to them, because you have only to watch a collie in action to see an animal fulfilling its essential nature, even though it does so at the behest of man and for man's benefit. Here is as good an example of 'symbiosis' as the fungus and alga which together compose lichen, or the bird which fearlessly picks the teeth of the crocodile! But nobody deducts points from *their* performances as the judges might do in a sheep-dog trial should the dog fail to run far enough, run too far, or need to be redirected by his frustrated master (who probably adds a few unofficial signals under his breath).

Now the Outrun is completed and the dog is in position behind the sheep. This is stage two, the Lift, and it lasts only long enough for the sheep to become aware, without panic, of the presence of the dog. The dog must 'persuade' the sheep to move towards the handler in as straight a line as possible. And if I were a dog, I would wonder why the job had to be made harder by the presence of two hurdles between which the little flock must pass!

Two more pairs of hurdles face the dog on the Triangular Drive, the third leg of which brings the flock into the shedding ring, a mid-field area marked out with sawdust. Here, one (in the case of a 'Single'), two, or more marked

sheep must be separated from the rest.

Finally there is the Penning, in which the sheep are driven into a small enclosure. If only one dog is being used, the enclosure has a seven-foot wide gate, but there is no gate at all if it is a Brace or Doubles event in which two dogs are run simultaneously. In the latter case, the dogs work the sheep together until they reach the shedding ring where the flock is divided into two, with one dog penning and guarding its own half of the flock while resisting (or so the handler hopes) all temptation to lend a paw to its partner.

Both the men and the dogs who perform these miracles of communication and discipline are of a special breed, found in many parts of Britain, speaking many different dialects, and yet, in a sense, one language. Up in the

Dales or the Lakes you may still hear a shepherd counting sheep by the old traditional method – *yan, twan, tethera, methera* instead of one, two, three, four. You can find it, with local variants, in Wales or wherever there are hill farmers.

Theirs is a hard calling. Only men in love with such a life could face its rigours in some of the bleakest country in England, the South Pennines. Winter is early to arrive and loth to leave these moorlands, where even the rough grass has 'all on' to suck life from the cold, sullen, tree-starved land. So men and dogs and sheep join forces to scrape a living.

These men are hardly garrulous. On the moors, there's no one to talk to but your dog and conversation with him tends to be limited to necessary commands – 'Come by!' . . . 'Away to me' . . .

'Away here' . . . 'That'll do, lad'.

The dog expects little more from the man it sees as leader of the pack. Without a thought for the shepherd's reasons, he finds utter fulfilment in making his master's timid, woolly, perverse charges do his bidding.

Here the dogs have names like Moss and Jaff and Mirk and Glen, names as short and unmistakable as the commands which send them streaking across the moor to outflank a straggler. No one watching an expert dog controlling sheep by its eye and its almost hypnotic presence, close enough to touch a sheep's nose, would insist that artistry was a human prerogative.

Once England's wealth depended on sheep – hence the Woolsack which is still the Lord Chancellor's seat in the House of Lords. Sheep are bred all over

Britain, but it is in the uplands of Northern England, Scotland, Wales and the West Country that shepherding calls for, and gets, the best that dedicated men and their dogs can give. And that best is demonstrated most clearly at the sheepdog trial.

These trials could be called the social events of the shepherd's year, but there are more rigorous get-togethers, such as the occasion of the annual winter 'gather' when the sheep on the moor in the region of the quaintly named Isle of Sky – nothing to do with Scotland – are taken into pens at Wessenden Lodge, where some will be dipped, some restored to their rightful owners after being sorted out by ear clippings and ruddle marks, and some returned to the moor to be mothers of next year's lambs.

High on the more northerly moors, where Yorkshire, Cumbria and Durham meet, is Tan Hill Inn, reputedly the highest hostelry in England and part of Yorkshire until the reorganisation of 1974 edged it into Durham.

Scottish and English drovers, taking sheep and cattle on the old trail from Brough to Reeth, ate and drank at Tan Hill and few hostelries can have been a more welcome sight than this oasis in a desert of endless moorland. Sometimes, in winter, Tan Hill's walls have meant the difference between life and death to those cut off for weeks by sudden snowfalls. In 1963 the inn was isolated for seven weeks by drifts sometimes fifteen feet deep. This is a place where winter never really admits defeat. Snow has been found here in June and August; frost and ice have been visitors as early as September.

Whatever the weather (and it's often bitter), Tan Hill comes into its own on the last Thursday in May when it hosts the annual Swaledale Sheep show. 'The Swaledale Royal', they call it, these men for whom it is a grand occasion of reunion. As music from a Dales village band echoes on the crisp moorland air, the Tan Hill Inn does a roaring trade.

York Festival and Mystery Plays

In June, once every four years.
Usually held in Museum Gardens, Museum Street, York.
Tickets available from the office at 1 Museum Street, York. They are usually offered to York residents first, then put on general sale. There is a car park around the corner in Blake Street and a long stay car park in Marygate. Failing that, plenty of car parks around the castle walls.

Madam, I'm Adam . . .

Walk about the ancient city of York as Festival time approaches, talk to the folk in Stonegate or The Shambles, and you will find a new liveliness, an air of expectancy – and plenty of comment about the Mystery Plays and the Festival. Perhaps not all the comment will be favourable, but that in itself is evidence of interest. A pub landlord seems chiefly interested in whether or not licensing hours will be extended; a university student feels there should be more 'continental gaiety' in the city at Festival time; another wants more modern jazz. You will probably not go very far before your questions about the Festival are answered with the words 'I'm in it – I'm "Eve"' – or Martha, or Pilate's son, or Lazarus.

The entire Festival, held every four years, lasts about three weeks during the latter half of June and the beginning of July. In that time it covers a wide enough range, you might think, to satisfy everybody. There are exhibitions in the various galleries, colleges and gardens, and services, concerts and recitals in the Minster, the Guildhall and many of the historic churches in which the city abounds. There are plays at the Theatre Royal; fireworks, perhaps, on the river Ouse, with appropriate Handelian accompaniment; and, since we are after all in the North, there is brass band music without which, for some visitors at least, no Festival would be complete.

Past Festivals have featured open-air opera, street theatre, puppet shows and dance troupes giving performances in many of the city streets, by the river and by the city walls. You might think this a hazardous venture in England, even in midsummer, but the Festival organisers are nothing if not optimistic.

At the heart of the Festival is the York Cycle of Mystery Plays, through which the medieval past that seems to permeate the very stones of the city springs into new and vivid life. The plays are enacted in the Museum Gardens, where the white limestone ruins of St Mary's Abbey form a perfect backcloth for this pageant of life and eternity that was once presented on the pageant wagons as they toured the city. In these ingenuous plays, earth, heaven – and even hell – meet and overlap. God himself is the first to speak, announcing, from a specially erected stage or, as in 1980, from the top of the ruins, his plan for the creation and redemption of mankind. And out of the huge cast of well over a hundred, comprising archangels and devils, Adam and Eve, the apostles and other characters from the Gospels, only one is usually a professional actor – the man who plays the central role of Jesus. The other parts, just as in 1397 when King Richard II visited York to see the plays, are largely played by the citizens of York themselves. They are enthusiastic amateur actors, who rehearse conscientiously and are word-perfect long before the first night. (Although if they are not, they are unlikely to be fined for their short-comings as were their medieval predecessors.)

Even when the stage is at its fullest, there are almost as many unseen participants off-stage – a wardrobe group, for instance, of perhaps thirty. In earlier times, dress must have presented few problems since much of it – at least in the case of the common mortals – was contemporary; only a few of the costumes were specially made and brought out annually for the great occasion. The Eve of today probably wears a body stocking; her forebear would have simulated nakedness with white leather. (In the same way

that men played female parts during Shakespeare's time, so medieval audiences would invariably have watched a man play the part of Eve.)

There are also property mistresses and assistants, the musical director, the movement director and the lighting designer, as well as corps of assorted stewards, including the 'cushion stewards' whose offerings are no doubt highly prized during the three hours the audience spends sitting on the tiered wooden seats. Even three hours, however, is little enough time, for into this have to be concentrated performances which would require a whole day to stage in full.

In the medieval past every self-respecting town of any size was proud to stage its mystery plays, in which the various guilds – the Barkers and the Tanners, the Armourers, Girdlers, Nailers, Bakers, Cordwainers, the Goldsmiths, who presented the Adoration of the Three Kings, and the Butchers, whose play was about the Crucifixion – vied with each other in the gusto with which they each performed their own scene as the pageant wagons stopped at pre-ordained points in the town. When King Richard watched the York Plays on Trinity Thursday in 1397, he was of course given the place of honour, a royal box opposite Holy Trinity Priory gateway in Micklegate.

Of the many medieval mystery plays once current in England only a few complete cycles have survived, such as the Wakefield and Chester cycles. Beverley, Norwich, Newcastle and many other places had their own plays as well, but none of these has survived. York's plays, too, might easily have been lost, or at least severely edited, for they were frowned upon by the Protestant clergy. Despite the fact that they had been a much-loved part of the city's life for over two centuries, the Corporation ordered in 1560 that the script be 'perused and amended'. Fortunately this process, inspired by the Archbishop, Edmund Grindal, took about ten years, and the overhauling of the plays,

projected for 1597, never took place. Instead, Edwin Sandys, who by this time was Archbishop, discreetly took possession of the book and when the citizens demanded to know when the plays would be performed again, made tactful excuses. They were not, in fact, to be performed again until they were revived in 1951 as part of the Festival of Britain celebrations. Since then they have been a central feature of the York Festival. (The great manuscript of these plays is now secure in the British Museum.)

Despite the passage of the years, the action of the plays – at times touching, amusing and awe-inspiring – absorbs modern audiences as thoroughly as it did their medieval ancestors. Much of the language is still understood with little difficulty by today's largely northern audiences. Only when the dialogue would be quite incomprehensible is it changed, and then by the substitution of words which would not be out of keeping with the rest of the script's late Middle English northern dialect.

But even without words, the spectacle itself would be gripping, from the first play depicting the Creation of the Angels and their Fall (traditionally performed by the Barkers' and the Tanners' Guilds) to the final production, the Last Judgement (which used to be the contribution of the Guild of Mercers). Between these opening and closing scenes we are shown the Creation, Temptation and Fall of Man; the Annunciation; the birth of Christ, and the visits to Bethlehem by the Shepherds and the Kings. Episodes enacted in Part Two include the entry into Jerusalem, the Last Supper and the agony and arrest of Christ in the Garden of Gethsemane. In Part Three the drama reaches its climax with the trials before Caiaphas and Pilate, the procession to Calvary, the Crucifixion, Resurrection, Ascension, and the Last Judgement, when the devils come into their own with great enthusiasm, dragging the damned away to the fiery, smoking mouth of a visible hell!

In addition to the performances in the Museum Gardens, the custom at most Festivals since 1965 has been to revive the medieval practice of presenting plays on wagons. The single play chosen is enacted at the west or east front of the Minster, and then again at King's Square, which was one of the original medieval stations. An authentic note is usually struck at the start with the reading of the fifteenth-century proclamation and with the sounding of a fanfare of trumpets. Between performances the wagon, laden with cast, rumbles to the next station along Low Petergate, part of the old pageant route.

A river play, too, is sometimes performed at one or two places on the river bank, to which the cast – once drawn from the Guild of Fishers and Mariners – are carried by boat.

Who pays for all the spectacle and drama? Today, although much help is received from commercial undertakings and organisations, such as the Arts Council, the Yorkshire Arts Association and the City Council, the Festival is run by a limited company. At one time, when the York Mystery Plays were the responsibility of the Mayor and the Corporation, payment was a highly contentious matter,

especially when several guilds combined to put on one play. A special tax called 'pageant silver' helped to pay for the productions – and a good deal else, one assumes, for it was still being collected two centuries after the plays had ceased! It seems strange that the citizens continued to pay this tax; perhaps they cherished the hope that the next year, or the year after, their beloved plays would be performed once more. They would no doubt have been astonished to learn that another two centuries would pass before the plays were acted again.

Scarborough Fair

First week in June

Carnival groups, majorettes and bands perform during the week throughout Scarborough in addition to normal entertainments. Open air venues; free. Parking on the Marine Drive, North Bay, and the Spa. Further information from Scarborough Tourist Office tel. 72261.

Nottingham Festival

Usually the first two weeks in June

A wide range of arts, music and outdoor events. Main venues are the Old Market Square and the Playhouse. There is a water spectacular at Victoria Embankment and hot air ballooning. Also a fringe festival.

Tickets at individual events, from the box office in the Victoria Shopping Centre or from the mobile ticket office in the market square. Plenty of multi-storey car parks.

Vintage Commercial Vehicles' East Coast Run

Early June

Hull to Bridlington.

A morning start from East Park, on Holderness Road on the east side of Hull. Arrives afternoon at the Spa, Bridlington.

Easy to park in the streets off Holderness Road and watch the start.

Midland Counties Country Show

Saturday and Sunday, early June

Cromford Meadows, on the A6, just south of Matlock in Derbyshire.

There is an admission charge each day, which also gives access to the showground car park.

The Midland Counties Show began as a horse show. The bias is towards country pursuits, rather than agriculture, and the show features hunting, shooting, fishing, gun dogs and police dog handling competitions.

Lincoln Water Festival and Mayor's Carnival Procession

Saturday and Sunday in early June

Brayford Pool, Lincoln, which is in the city centre, at the bottom of Steep Hill, about 20 minutes walk from the Cathedral.

No entrance fee, but there are collections, raffles etc. There is a multi-storey car park nearby in Lucy Tower Street.

Lincoln Wine Festival

One week in mid-June, during normal licensing hours

Cornhill, Lincoln town centre

Open to the public; there is no entrance fee. Plenty of car parks round about.

The *Lincoln Water Festival*, held in early June, is linked with the *Lord Mayor's Procession*. The Festival takes place at Brayford Pool, Lincoln, and the route of the procession is from South Common to High Street.

A week later the *Lincoln Wine Festival* is held during normal licensing hours at Cornhill, Lincoln. It began with a group of enthusiasts forming a Lincoln section of the German wine club based in Lincoln's twin town, Neustadt. The German Festival takes place in October, at the end of the grape-picking season. Wine for the festival is brought over from Neustadt and the festival is open to the public.

Knaresborough Bed Race

Second Saturday in June

Parade through the town centre around 1.30 p.m. followed by a race to and from Cunningham Hall around 4.00 p.m.

Pay and display car park near the market place.

Church Fenton SSAFA Air Display

Second Sunday in June

At RAF Church Fenton, which is between Tadcaster and Sherburn in Elmet off the A162.

There is a large car park, and admission is charged on entry.

Winged wonders

At the other end of the scale from the mighty Vulcan, one of the best-loved of the older warriors at a recent RAF Church Fenton Air Display was an immaculate Tiger Moth. Forty years old, it had served with the RAF from 1942 to the end of the war. What happened to it after that is not entirely clear, but three years before it appeared at Church Fenton it had been found earth-bound and derelict in a barn in Northern Ireland. Shipped to England by Austin Mercer, a Cleckheaton businessman, it was rebuilt by David Fenton of Hornet Aviation,

Brayton, near Selby.

The Tiger Moth joined other veterans – a Lancaster Bomber, a Spitfire, a Hurricane . . . even a German Messerschmitt – no longer enemies, though they recalled an earlier conflict. Even they were not the oldest aircraft on show. There was a Blackburn B2 built fifty years before and ever since then preserved by British Aerospace at Brough.

The RAF, the Navy, the US Air Force, as well as civilian pilots, played their breath-taking parts; there were amazing aerobatics from the Phantom and the Jet Provost; the Royal Marines and the RAF Falcons performed free-fall parachute displays. The incomparable Red Arrows appeared truly to dice with death as their intricate, lightning formations criss-crossed the throbbing sky.

A very Yorkshire product at this Yorkshire event was the ultra-modern Slingsby T67A

two-seater aerobatic trainer, developed at Kirkbymoorside. But there could be little doubt that the true star of this particular air show was the awesome Vulcan, whose giant triangular wing had brought terror to the Argentines and hope to British Forces when it darkened the South Atlantic sky during the Falklands conflict.

But this is not a warlike event. Nor, though the crowd of 35,000 were in the usual Church Fenton holiday mood, was it in any sense frivolous. The object of its organisers and its sponsors, the *Yorkshire Evening Post*, was to raise money for the Soldiers' Sailors' and Airmen's Families' Association and in this they succeed to the tune of many thousands of pounds.

The Northern Horse Show and Country Fair

Sunday, mid-June

Grange Park, Wetherby.

Grange Park is about 2 miles south of the A1 Wetherby roundabout and the show is always signposted. There is a free car park and a reasonable entrance fee.

This highly popular event, held at Grange Park, Wetherby, in June, combines equestrian and rural events with popular crowd-pullers, such as dog agility competitions, hot air balloons, and paraplegic events including riding for the disabled. The show is run entirely by voluntary effort and is held in aid of the British Paraplegic Sports Society (the sports movement for the paralysed). It was first organised in the 1960s under the inspiration of the Earl and Countess of Swinton (the Countess is herself partially paralysed as a result of a riding accident and is the show's Paraplegic Sports Director).

Although it was not originally intended to be held annually, being meant as a single fund-raising event for the building of the sports stadium at Stoke Mandeville, the success of the first show clearly called for its continuation and it has since been held every year. Given good weather, the event can command attendances reaching five figures. Consequently it has raised many thousands of pounds for the Paraplegic Sports Society.

Barnaby Horse Fair

Tuesday nearest 11 June,
afternoon

Near Horsefair.

Horsefair is a street in
Boroughbridge named after the
ancient fair which attracts
travelling people from all over the
country. Boroughbridge is a small
town and the fair is easy to find.
Parking in the streets.

Long live the horse fair!

Bargaining as a fine art is still
practised in England, even in
these computerised days of
supermarkets and check-outs, but
you will probably have to go to a
traditional horse fair to see it at its
best. These events persist in spite
of all attempts to regularise them
out of existence, and the reason
for their survival is probably the
sheer vitality of the British horse-
coper, a man as impervious to
change, it seems, as he is to insult.

'What?' demands an intending
purchaser incredulously as a price
is quoted. 'For *that* spavined,
wall-eyed, three-legged brute? If I

drove that I'd be had up for
frightening the women and kids.
An' serve me right!'

'What about this one then?'
says the vendor, unperturbed, as
he invites inspection of a horse at
the end of the line of bored and
weary quadrupeds.

'You know as well as I do,' says
the horse-buyer, 'that if you
moved that one, *or* the one at
t'other end, the rest of 'em 'ud fall
down flat.'

A time-worn joke, perhaps, but
it's just the sort of straight-faced
contentious badinage that has
been exchanged for centuries.
A would-be buyer expresses
outrage at the price asked for a
donkey. Equally indignant, the
owner retorts, 'Nay man, if you
took it to Scarborough you'd get
the price back three times over in
one afternoon.'

The trading is not always so
vociferous. Sometimes it is done
almost in a whisper. Cheque
books are noticeably absent:
some sales are conducted by an
auctioneer, but mostly a roll of

notes changes ownership after the
traditional striking of hands
between buyer and seller has
signalled that a sale has taken
place.

There's a single-mindedness
about horse-traders which makes
it advisable for mere pedestrians
to be wary. Ponies and horses are
galloped up and down by boys to
show their paces. Performances
between the shafts of carts and
traps are similarly demonstrated
and it pays not to get in the way.
If you do get kicked, don't expect
sympathy – expect instead to be
accused, in the most colourful
language, of upsetting the horses.

If you tire of looking at horses,
there's probably an escapologist
or a fire-eater to divert you, or
novelty sellers or a refreshment
stall, or the invariably fascinating
gipsy tents and caravans. At any
rate, you are unlikely to be bored
at one of England's remaining
horse fairs, whether it is held at
Appleby in Cumbria, Lee Gap near
Wakefield, or Barnaby Fair in
North Yorkshire.

THE CALENDAR YEAR

Barnaby Fair has been held at Boroughbridge for three hundred years, on or around 11 June, St Barnabas' Day. 'Barnaby bright, longest day and shortest night' the locals still say in that old-fashioned country way of reducing everything to rhyming couplets (though since the calendar was changed in 1752, the longest day has been 21 June). Saint's day or not, the occasion is not universally welcomed. There have been those, indeed, who consider the fair a curse and who have done their best to persuade the powers that be to stop 'this annual nuisance', as they are inclined to call it.

Now this may seem rather surprising in a place which clings as tightly to its history as Boroughbridge. The town is situated on the river Ure, six miles south-east of Ripon. In the days of William the Conqueror, when the road to the north was diverted to cross the Ure, the point chosen for the crossing was given the name 'Burgbridge'. The huge stone 'Devil's Arrows' were old even then. Aldborough, nearby, was once the site of Isurium Brigantum, a Romanised city of the Brigantes, the Celtic race that once ruled Yorkshire. You may still see a fine Roman pavement here, and there is an excellent museum of Roman remains.

I won't pretend that Barnaby Fair goes back to Roman times, but it is certainly old. I remember talking long ago to an old resident of the town who recalled for me her memories of bygone fairs and the uproar that used to flare up among the travelling folk . . .

'They used to fight and get drunk and they'd think nothing of using iron bars on each other. Blood used to flow, I can tell you! You just locked your doors and kept out of the way. And the men selling horses would tether them to the door handles and we used to put seats out for the men . . . In the evenings they would sit on their caravan steps and play their fiddles and dance. But, no, I certainly wouldn't like the fair to be stopped.'

Nevertheless, there are those

who would: farmers complain that horses damage crops and hedges and that gipsies create nuisances by camping on unauthorised sites for weeks on end, using Boroughbridge as a base for visits to the horse fair at Appleby.

The street where the caravans once parked and the horses were galloped is still called Horsefair, but modern traffic has long ago ousted the fair folk. For some years the fair was held in a field beside the auction mart, but the 1982 fair took place in a field behind a car park off the main street, a venue sanctioned by Boroughbridge Town Council. It was the fifth site since 1976, when 85 of the 1,500 electorate of Boroughbridge voted 2–1 in a referendum to have the fair's 300-year-old Royal Charter rescinded.

Harrogate Borough Council was unmoved. So the fair goes on, and gipsies and tinkers and horse-copers meet as they have since the fair was first held in 1682.

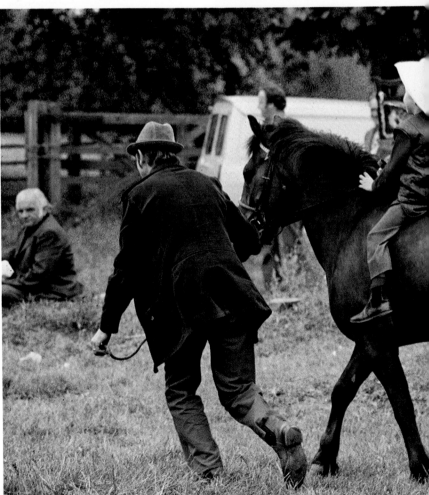

Newport and District Agricultural Society Annual Show and Gymkhana

Second Saturday in June

Common Lane, South Cave, Brough, Humberside.

South Cave is north of Brough, on the A63 between Howden and Hull. There is an entrance fee and a car park.

Hunt the Outlaw, Sherwood Forest

Second week in June and at appointed times throughout the summer

Sherwood Forest, Edwinstowe, Mansfield.

A free event for children at a set meeting time. Parking in the Edwinstowe car park area.

Sherwood Forest is 17 miles north of Nottingham on the A614.

Midsummer Celebrations at Ryedale Folk Museum

Third Saturday in June

Ryedale Folk Museum is in Hutton-le-Hole which is a small village some 30 miles north of York, near Kirkbymoorside on the North York Moors. It is an open air museum with traditional exhibits.

There is an entrance fee and one can park in the centre of the village and walk.

Corn dollies and cruck houses

Wander into Hutton-le-Hole in Ryedale on the third Saturday in June, and you could be forgiven for thinking that you had strayed into the past.

For this is the day when old Ryedale comes vividly to life at the Ryedale Folk Museum. And though May Day is now weeks past, don't be surprised if you see the children capering round the maypole.

But there is much more here than games. This may be your chance – a rare one – to watch experts working at a variety of time-honoured crafts. The blacksmith, making his anvil ring and demonstrating his legendary strength of arm, could hardly be more of a contrast with the lacemaker, quiet, patient and dextrous as she produces a delicate beauty with her 'pillow' and bobbins. Here, too, is the corn-dolly maker, cunningly fashioning figures and ornaments from the yellow stalks which seem so malleable in his practised hands. No longer is the dolly believed to embody the Corn Spirit that must be protected through the winter to ensure next year's harvest. But it surely plays its part in reminding us that even in these technological times we depend on the sun, the soil and the harvest for our survival.

Spinning and weaving, coopery, wood-carving, stone dressing and besom-making . . . All these skills are still alive and well and may be studied at this splendid museum which is well worth visiting at any time. Indeed, the word 'museum', as popularly understood, hardly

conveys a true impression of this group of early dwellings and farm buildings, typical of those once seen in the North Yorkshire valley of the river Rye, one of the most beautiful parts of the North York Moors National Park.

Covering some two-and-a-half acres, Ryedale's is very much an open-air museum. Entering by way of the former cowhouse door and the stable, along a well-kept path between smooth green lawns, you pass from one reconstruction to another. A number of the buildings, three of which have been transported here from nearby villages, have thatched roofs.

One of the most interesting is the Cruck House from Stang End, which was dismantled in 1967 and reopened the following year. Typical of yeomen's houses of the period, it shows the features of cruck construction employed in many old farmhouses hereabouts: the walls were built around a framework of beams arranged in the form of a series of three capital 'A's', but the 'A' has two cross-pieces formed by the collar beam above and the tie beam below; the uprights are known as the crucks and where they meet at the top they are joined by the 'saddle'.

Other re-erected houses include a thatched cottage from Harome, with 'Yorkshire sash' windows typical of the eighteenth century, and locally made cooking ranges, one of them designed to burn peat or turf. One room of the cottage is fully equipped as a dairy. Also from Harome is the fine manor house, again cruck-framed with the biggest crucks so far found in North Yorkshire. Then there is the Crofter's Cottage opened in 1977 – not a reconstruction, this time, but based on archaeological evidence. This is the sort of house lived in by the North Yorkshire crofter from about the thirteenth century – just one room for family and animals together. Houses like this were found by Canon Atkinson, author of the classic *Forty Years in a Moorland Parish*, when he first came to Danby, as a young priest in 1847. 'Smoke-filled hovels' he called them, and so they must have been in some cases, though the better examples, like this one, were built high enough for the smoke to rise above the occupants before it filtered out through the thatch (there was no chimney).

One of the most prized exhibits is a unique reconstructed glass furnace of the type introduced to Britain by refugee Huguenot glass-workers in the sixteenth century. It is no wonder that the museum regards this exhibit with special pride and affection, for it was discovered – in 1969 – by one of the museum's trustees on land actually belonging to another. Discovering it, however, was easy compared with the task of excavating and transporting it across the moors to the museum. Once the furnace had been excavated (with expert help from Leeds and Sheffield Universities), many drawings were made and photographs taken, and the stones, some of which weighed over half a ton, were carefully treated, then reassembled in the form seen by visitors to the museum today.

Important though it is, the glass furnace is just one among many fascinating reminders of Ryedale as it used to be – with its superstitions (witness the 'witch posts') as well as its crafts and farm implements, and its Victorian dress.

If this place were haunted it would surely have the happiest ghosts in Yorkshire. They would be craftsmen like George Tomlinson, joiner and wagon builder, whose beautiful patterns in wood were followed by the blacksmith a century or so ago. Or we might meet John Reynolds, cabinet-maker, whose inlaid tool chest containing 300 tools was given to the museum by a descendant. The tools and notebooks left behind by the cooper, the clog-maker, the tanner, the ropemaker, the tinker and the farrier make us feel we know them still.

Lincolnshire Show

Wednesday and Thursday, late June

Lincolnshire Showground, 3½ miles north of Lincoln on the Lincoln to Brigg Road.

Entrance fee and car park.

Heptonstall Festival

Usually a Saturday at the end of June

All-day festival, with a procession after lunch, music, craft stalls etc. Open to visitors. There is a small free car park in Heptonstall and it is usually possible to park above the village and walk down.

Heptonstall is a village sited above Hebden Bridge in West Yorkshire. Hebden Bridge is on the A646 between Halifax and Burnley.

Coiners and conservationists

For the last ten years, anyone visiting the hilltop village of Heptonstall on the South Pennine Moors near Halifax on the last Saturday in June could be forgiven for thinking he had wandered into a fairy tale. He might, for instance, find Heptonstall suddenly and magically transformed into a seaside town — as it was in Maritime England Year, 1982. Seaside posters splashed the old stone walls with colour. Genuine Heptonstall rock was on sale; lifebelts hung around Weaver's Square; there were donkey rides; and in the church a sailing boat formed the centrepiece.

For this last June Saturday is the occasion of the Summer Festival founded by their former vicar, Peter Calvert, who is quite unnecessarily modest about his achievement. 'It's not an event on a large scale,' he points out, but 'a pleasant and entertaining day which shows the good things of village life'.

Indeed, it does so in a remarkably topical fashion. In Jubilee Year, the village suddenly became populated with kings and queens in a pageant of

royalty; in the Year of the Child, children of the world in national costumes appeared in the ancient streets, while in other years a time-slip effect has been provided by retelling, in vivid pageantry, the story of the village itself.

Though the parish church inaugurated this annual event, the vicar stressed it is very much a community affair, 'with entertainment for everyone'.

In the ruins of the old church of St Thomas à Becket, the Festival starts with an open-air communion service. During the

morning there is a coffee morning in the church hall, but the village is really *en fête* during the afternoon when over a hundred adults and children dress themselves to reflect whatever theme has been chosen for that particular year.

And after the pageant there are stalls and side-shows to visit, run by local organisations. In the spacious modernised interior of the church there are entertainments as there were in bygone days before churches became all too easily equated with boredom. And at the rear of

the church the festival theme is repeated in an exhibition, with posters, artwork from local schools, and probably relics of Calderdale's history, provided by the local Museums Service.

In Weavers' Square at the village centre, the band which has led the procession plays during the afternoon, sharing musical honours with the Riverside School Choir from Hebden Bridge at the foot of Heptonstall's steep hill. There are mummers, Morris Men, street theatre, dance groups . . . on this day the dour-looking

village devotes itself with true Yorkshire thoroughness to the business of enjoyment, for villagers and visitors alike.

Even without its festival, Heptonstall would cast a unique spell from its hillside setting above Hebden Bridge. If ever a place was haunted, surely this stone village with two churches, one a dramatic ruin, ought to be 'alive with ghosts'! For instance, its churchyard contains not only the graves of medieval priests but the body of 'King David' Hartley, chief of the Cragg Coiners, hanged

on 28 April 1770 for his share in 'the yellow trade', as it was called.

The coiners clipped the edges from gold coins, then melted down the clippings and used these to cast new coins. This practice reached such scandalous proportions that a customs and excise inspector, William Deighton, was sent from London to track down the gang. Deighton was ambushed and murdered for his pains, and though King David himself had not fired a shot, he was nevertheless hanged for counterfeiting, a crime which in those days was considered almost as heinous as murder.

Perhaps it was a sense of civic shame that caused Latin to be used when Hartley's burial was inscribed in Heptonstall Church records. In English the entry reads: *1770 May 1st: David Hartley, of Bell House in the township of Erringden, hanged by the neck near York for unlawfully stamping and clipping a public coin.*

'King David's' grave, which is simply headed *David Hartley, 1770*, is found by counting twelve stone slabs in a straight line from the porch of the old church, then two spaces down to the left.

Relics of the coiners, among other village memorabilia, are to be seen in the Old Grammar School, now a museum. The school was endowed in 1642 with money left for the purpose by a remarkable scholar and tutor, the Reverend Charles Greenwood. An average of fifty to sixty boys were studying at the school in 1824, but in 1889 its scholastic life ended after 250 years and it became a branch of the Yorkshire Penny Bank.

pebbles, concrete, floor flags from old dwellings and granite setts is the only one of its kind. Completed in its present form in 1967, the square was designed by Noel Singer, a local architect. A mullioned window, preserved in its stony guardianship, was saved from destruction when a seventeenth-century house was knocked down; an ancient well trough also survives.

If stones could speak there would surely be some ghostly whispers in the breezes that wander over these stones at dead of night.

But if it's ghosts you're after, try a midnight vigil in Chantry House where, during renovations, a spectre appeared at a long-hidden doorway. Here, surely, is a house ready-made for a horror-film set . . . Gravestones and coffin lids are built into its very fabric! Best (or worst) of all, human bones have a way of cropping up here and there — which is not surprising when you consider that part of the building was once a charnel-house, piled high with skeletons.

What a place to have sheltered in on the night of the great storm of 1847 when the west face of the old church tower collapsed! Patched up, the old church, whose fifteenth-century tower stands on a thirteenth-century base, served the villagers until 1854 when the present church was built and its predecessor was left in picturesque desuetude . . . if indeed it can be called picturesque: John Wesley, who preached there five times, called it 'the ugliest church I know'!

Perhaps Wesley was reflecting with some pride on his own essay in chapel-designing at Heptonstall — an octagonal structure, reputedly the oldest Methodist church in the world still in continuous use. The shape caused problems when the time came to fit a roof: Wesley had to have it made in Rotherham and carried in sections over hill and moor by horse and cart. In the heyday of Methodism, over a thousand 'scholars' in the care of seventy-two teachers and four

Showing themselves to be ahead of their time as conservationists, the bank kept the old place virtually as its pupils had known it. Even the desk at which the boys had laboured over their lessons (when they were not carving their initials in the black oak) was left unchanged, as were the open fire grate, the flagged floor, the headmaster's clock, and many of the old school-books. In 1954, when the bank had no more use for the building, it was taken over by the local authority.

Beside the churchyard, the cloth hall, now converted into cottages, recalls the days of the handloom weavers. The development of Halifax as a cloth market, culminating in the opening of the Piece Hall with its 315 rooms in 1779, probably helped to make this hall redundant.

Appropriately enough, the former cloth hall is quite close to Weavers' Square, once the site of handloom weavers' cottages and now the setting for what has been called a unique 'museum' of stone. It may well be that this collection of local cobbles,

Royal Norfolk Show

Two days in the fourth week in June

Showground, Dereham Road, New Costessey, Norwich.

The Showground is about four miles from the city centre on the A47 towards King's Lynn. This is an agricultural show with an entrance fee and a very large car park. Buses from the city centre.

Lincoln Mystery Plays

Late June/early July for a fortnight

The Mystery Plays are usually performed once every four years and take place outside the cathedral.

Tickets available from the Tourist Information Office, Castle Hill, Lincoln. Park in town or in the multi-storey car park in Lucy Tower Street, 20 minutes' walk away.

Rose Fair

July, one week

St Peter's Church and Gardens, Wisbech, Cambridgeshire.

There is a procession on Saturday with a different theme each year. It starts at the Council Chambers and proceeds through town. Strawberry teas are served in the Church Gardens throughout the week. Large free car park near the church, which is in the centre of town.

Haworth Rush-bearing Service

July

Parish Church, Haworth, West Yorkshire.

The Parish Church is in Church Street, at the top of Main Street. Plenty of parking space nearby, including the Parsonage Museum car park.

superintendents frequented this place.

So rich a heritage there seems to be in Heptonstall, especially since its situation has helped to preserve much of the old village intact, yet really we know only a little of its long history. Is it true that the Romans had a station here? The name of the village is Anglo-Saxon but somehow Heptonstall escaped inclusion in the Domesday Book. Like many another place it suffered a great plague, in 1631, and over 200 years later there was the famous storm which caused so much damage.

However, not everything in the village is of the very distant past. To enter the church for the first time is to receive a surprise (or a shock, depending on your attitude). For this church interior is probably the most 'modern' thing about Heptonstall. A legacy left for the purpose enabled the old Victorian furnishings, badly affected by dry-rot, to be cleared away and replaced by a light and open-plan interior with the altar no longer almost hidden from the worshippers by a screen. But the old, eleven-sided font used to baptise Heptonstall folk since the thirteenth century, still keeps its place. And to bridge the centuries, other relics of the ruined church have found a home in the new: an oak table, an oak chair dated 1690, the church records and, above the door giving entry to the building, the royal arms of George III.

The centre of this unique village has now been declared a conservation area; we may hope that it is safe for many future generations to visit and see where, and perhaps how, some of their ancestors once lived.

Alport Castle Woodlands Love Feast

First Sunday in July, 1.30 p.m.

Alport Castle Farm, Derbyshire.

This is a religious event of great antiquity perpetuated by Methodists as a symbol of care and concern within the Christian Fellowship.

Participants usually start at Woodlands Methodist Church and it is half an hour's walk from there to the Farm.

Alport Castle Farm is accessible from the A57, east of the Snake Pass and Snake Inn, close to Ladybower Reservoir. There is an access road and parking.

Hathersage Gala

First or second week in July

School Fields, Hathersage, Derbyshire.

Hathersage is a village in the heart of the Peak District, about 8 miles south-west of Sheffield and 7 miles north of Bakewell. Parking space in the village.

The Gala Queen Crowning Ceremony takes place on Saturday at 3.00 p.m. and there is a procession through the village on the following Saturday. Events throughout the week.

Lincolnshire Rose Society Annual Show

Early July
Pennel's Plant Centre, North Hykeham, Lincoln.

This event is not always held at the same venue and it is advisable to ring Lincoln Information Centre (Lincoln 32151) for further information.

The event is always open to the public and there is a small entrance fee.

The Lincolnshire Rose Society Show has been running since 1970, when the society was founded. Hundreds of exhibitors compete in four major sections: one open to the public; one for Lincolnshire Rose Society members; one for members of the Royal National Rose Society; and one, an open section, for floral art. There is a class for new roses, bred by members of the Society, and these new flowers are sometimes taken up by commercial firms.

Holmfirth Art Exhibition

Three days at the beginning of July

Civic Hall, Holmfirth.

There is a free car park across the road from the hall, and a small entrance charge at the door. All proceeds go to Cancer Research. Most exhibits, ranging from oil paintings to marquetry, can be bought.

Bramham Horse Trials and Yorkshire Country Fair

Thursday – Sunday in early June

Bramham Park is off the A1, between Leeds and Wetherby. The Horse Trials are open to the public. The charge for the car park usually lets you into the fair.

Boots and saddles

The horse trials at Bramham Park (a splendid Queen Anne mansion set in gardens in the style of those at Versailles and surrounded by rolling parkland) are now one of the principal events of the equestrian year. Originally a hunter trial and one-day event, the trials, run under British Horse Society rules, became a three-day event in 1974, since when they have achieved national importance.

The three-day event is based on the training to which cavalrymen and their horses used to be subjected. When the three-day event was first introduced into the Olympic Games at Stockholm in 1912 it was, in fact, called the 'Military' competition.

Inevitably, the mechanisation of the army after the First World War caused interest to fade, but it never died completely. Then, in 1949, at the invitation of the Duke of Beaufort, a three-day event was held at Badminton; today this is the greatest annual competition of its kind in the world.

The horse-riding world quickly took the three-day event to its heart. The grounds of Harewood House, home of the late Princess Royal, were used for the purpose in the 1950s but in the '60s the event moved to Burghley at Stamford in Lincolnshire, seat of the Marquess of Exeter. In 1974, three-day eventing began at Bramham for north country riders, some of whose sights were set on the international events at Badminton and Burghley.

Held in June each year, the Bramham trials are open to three grades of horse and rider – CCA (international 'Friendly' introduced into the trials in 1981), Standard and Novice. There is also a National Trial for young riders aged between nineteen and twenty-one (added to the programme of events for the first time in 1982) and, of course, the enormously popular Hunter Show with sections ranging from Brood Mare in Foal, to Foals and Working Hunters. There are also show-jumping competitions that are not associated with the tests of the three-day event; they have various sponsors and prize money ranges from £35 to £2,400 per class.

The tests in the three-day event are in three sections – Dressage; Speed, Endurance and Cross-country; and Jumping. Until recent years, dressage was unquestionably the least popular, probably because it was the least understood. In fact, it might well be called the 'fine art' of horsemanship, for it is the training of the horse in obedience and suppleness and calls for total empathy between horse and rider. To quote from the Event programme, dressage is 'a series of Drill movements in a Riding School-type arena to prove that the horse, though ready to run for its life in the following tests, is supple and obedient as well as keen and fit. Calmness and control will be in the forefront of the Judges' minds.'

The object of the speed, endurance and cross-country test might appear to be self-evident from its description, but like so many equestrian matters, it is by no means as simple as it may seem. It is not the horse, nor the rider, but their partnership that is being tested. And that calls for no small degree of skill, for this second day of the event involves, first of all, trotting for about three miles on roads and tracks; then a steeplechase over two miles at racing speed; another session along roads and tracks for nearly five miles; and, finally, after a ten-minute break for veterinary inspection, just under four miles of cross-country with no fewer than twenty-six obstacles, some of which can combine as many as five elements. The very names of these obstacles are enough to inspire apprehension – the Tiger Trap, the Wolf's Stiles, the Knife Rack.

The show-jumping test, on the final day, needs little description, thanks to television. Its aim is to prove that following the rigours of the cross country phase the horse still has the suppleness and obedience to jump a clear round over a reasonably straight forward course.

For some years now a Country Fair has been held in conjunction with the horse trials. Organised by British Field Sports Society members, it presents a varied programme including pony club events, clay pigeon shooting, falconry displays, greyhound and lurcher shows, fly casting and gundog trials. Participation by the public is encouraged, so if you fancy you have an innate but as yet unfulfilled talent for such rural pursuits, you may well find you have the opportunity to show your prowess at Bramham.

schoolboys – is my favourite, at least while I am there. For it possesses in such abundance the sense of fun which you find only in the country. Village folk, it seems, can always find something to laugh about.

Kilburn, for instance, makes its annual Feast an opportunity to take the mickey out of the big towns, where pomp and ceremony all too often take precedence over fun and games. And that is why for more than 900 years they have elected their burlesque mayor and Mayoress here as a kind of lord and lady of misrule.

After the serious business of fining the local population for every possible and impossible reason, the Mayoress is given free rein to chase and kiss the village girls and any other comely wench who happens to be present. They never seem to object. After all, what could be wrong with a chaste embrace from the Mayoress? Especially when it's for charity?

Not everyone knows about Kilburn Feast, but there can be few who don't know about the White Horse, which overlooks the village from Roulston Scar, where it was first marked out in 1857 by the village schoolmaster and his class. Here, surely, is village life at its best . . . insisting, in the face of logic and geology, that Kilburn has as much right to a white horse as Uffington in Berkshire, despite the fact that Uffington's is based on chalk, and Kilburn's isn't.

It was Thomas Taylor, a Kilburn local boy made good, who first had the idea. Thomas had left Kilburn to make his fortune in London selling Yorkshire hams and bacon. But never did he forget his beloved Kilburn. So when he saw the famous prehistoric White Horse of Uffington carved in chalk on the downland, he couldn't help thinking how well a white horse would look on Roulston Scar overlooking Kilburn. That would *really* put his home village on the map.

Thomas wrote a letter to the local schoolmaster, John Hodgson, who was also a part-time surveyor, outlining his plan. After a visit to a racing stable

Kilburn Feast and local costume frolics

Saturday to Tuesday of the weekend following 6 July

Events include a foot race to the White Horse; open-air service in Kilburn square; Lord Mayor's procession through Kilburn. There are also events in the cricket fields.

Kilburn is in North Yorkshire between Thirsk and Helmsley, south of the A170. Open to the public; most events are free; parking in the village.

White Horse and church mice

Through the main street of a Yorkshire village a giddy cortège is passing – it's the village's mayoral coach, a trap gaily decorated with flowers and drawn by a local lad. In the seats of honour are the 'Mayor' and 'Mayoress' of Kilburn, North Yorkshire, elected 'for a year and a day' and both, incidentally, men. His Worship wears top hat and tails, his consort, in

outrageous 'drag', is equipped with a truly impressive bosom (thanks to cunningly sited balloons).

'What's this?' demands the Mayor severely, looking over his shoulder at a car just behind the coach. 'We can't have this! I fine that driver 20p for following the mayoral coach!' And the motorist thus sentenced knows he must cough up or else.

A few yards further on the Mayoress draws his Worship's attention to a neat roadside cottage. A brief consultation follows. Then, 'Disgusting!' declares the Mayor, 'I fine that householder 30p for having net curtains'.

On Feast Day in Kilburn you can be fined for just about anything. But nobody minds, because all the fines go to charity.

All of which helps to convince me that it is in the villages where English life runs true and deep – and heaven help us if ever the villages vanish!

And of all the villages in Yorkshire, Kilburn – declared by somebody to be a village of

and set his pupils to mark out its lines on the hillside. It was to be 314 feet long and 228 feet high.

After the children had done their part, it was the turn of the village men. About thirty of them dug out the shape of the horse from the turf, then coated the new-born steed with lime. They stood back to admire their handiwork, never dreaming, on that day in November 1857, that they had set Kilburn a problem which would bedevil its inhabitants for generations to come – how to keep the horse white!

The natural colour of the rock on Roulston Scar is an unexciting dun. It is soft and friable and the site slopes at an angle of thirty degrees. Once the scrub had been cleared, there was nothing to stop the weather eroding the ground – which, of course, it did.

Maintaining the horse became a full-time job for the village. For many years an occasional coat of lime was the only whitening agent employed, but clearly more than that was needed. In more recent years, cement incorporating chalk chippings has been applied. And before that, Bob Thompson bought a pile of spent carbide to see how that might help to keep Kilburn's White Horse white. One way or another, Kilburn keeps its horse.

Thompson was one of the three trustees (the others were a farmer and the vicar) appointed to administer a White Horse fund. But quite apart from that, his name will be for ever linked with Kilburn. He was a woodcarver and furniture maker (of genius, some would say) and his signature, a mouse, became so well known that a letter simply addressed 'The Mouseman, England' found its way to Kilburn. The firm he founded is still operated by his grandsons in Kilburn, where great stacks of oak, seasoning in the North Yorkshire air, are his workaday memorial.

He has many more. In inns and churches and houses as far apart as London and the Hebrides, the little rodent that was his trademark can be found on beam or screen or choir stall; never very obvious, but certain to be hiding there somewhere if you are looking at a Thompson piece.

Thompson was born in Kilburn Old Hall in 1876. For a time he worked as a village joiner with his father, making coffins or repairing the local school. He was made an engineering apprentice but his heart had been given early to the English oak he saw growing around him. When he could he would escape to Ripon Minster, there to marvel at the fifteenth-century choir stalls carved by the adze of William Bromflet.

During the early years of struggle, Kilburn found a patron in the Benedictine Abbey and College at neighbouring Ampleforth. His first commission was for a memorial cross for the churchyard. After that, his services were called upon more and more and perhaps it would not be too much to say that the Ampleforth College Library represents his life's work as much as anything he did. 'My room,' he called it and he worked on it from the 1920s until just before his final illness began in 1955.

His other great memorial in Yorkshire is, fittingly, Kilburn's parish church of St Mary where the 'mouse' is present in strength – on lectern, pew and pulpit, on the case for the 'Breeches' Bible, and on the priest's stall in the chancel. There is also the chapel of St Thomas, refurnished as a memorial to the 'Mouse Man' in 1958, and there are even oak headstones in the churchyard.

Why did Thompson choose a mouse as his mark? It's said that he was working one day in a church when one of his workmen complained of being poor as a church mouse. Almost unconsciously Thompson found himself carving a mouse – it was destined to be the first of a distinguished and far-flung dynasty!

Stamford Festival

Around second week in July
Stamford, Lincolnshire.

Parade of floats starts in Broad Street at 2.00 p.m. on Saturday, and proceeds down the High Street. There is an outdoor Flea Market in Barnhill Street. Difficult to park in town on Saturday, but there is a large car park in Wharfe Road, near the Arts Centre.

Other events take place throughout the week; box office is often in the Arts Centre on St Mary's Street.

Pony club and push penny

For a week in July, Stamford celebrates its past and present with a week-long festival, the most public event of which is a grand parade of floats through the main streets of the old town.

From the recreation ground, along East Street, St Paul's Street, Broad Street and High Street, goes the colourful procession, expressive of some chosen theme, such as 'The world of sport and entertainment'. Local organisations vie with each other in presenting the most impressive spectacle and their efforts are judged, and the best of them rewarded, with due care and solemnity.

The sheer range of the events emphasises the richness of life in an English market town. A recent festival included a Cricket Week in Burghley Park (which was also the venue for Pony Club team games); Haydn's Nelson Mass; exhibitions galore of flowers, paintings and slides of Edwardian Stamford; a flea market; a street fair; a vintage car rally; and competitions for bowls, netball, water-jousting and bath-tub racing, during a Family Day on the green meadows beside the river Welland. And who would readily forget the World Pushpenny Championships run by the Stamford and District Pushpenny League?

Stamford is worth a visit at any time. It has the hospitable air of a place which has been a centre of social life for generations, especially in the Georgian days which fixed it in its present mould, with its theatre and Assembly Rooms (now an arts centre), and Town Hall. Other buildings echo earlier times, most notably Browne's Hospital, set up in the reign of Henry VII by a wealthy wool merchant, William Browne. The most splendid evocation of its architectural heritage, of course, is Burghley House.

Rush-bearing Ceremony

St Swithin's Church, Old Weston, Cambridgeshire

Sunday nearest St Swithin's Day (15 July)

Normal 6.00 p.m. service.
The church is near one end of the town and it is easy to park nearby. Old Weston is on the B660 west of the A1 and between Alconbury and Thrapston.

East of England Show

Mid-July

East of England Showground, Peterborough.

A very big event accessible from the A605, Oundle road, south-east of Peterborough. There is an entrance fee and a parking ground.

Coningsby Air Show

Mid-July, one day all day

R.A.F. Coningsby, Lincs.

R.A.F. Coningsby is about 18 miles south-east of Lincoln. Take the A158 from Lincoln to Horncastle and the A153 from there. There is parking in the field on the way in. An entrance fee is usually charged.

Great Yorkshire Show

Tuesday – Thursday, mid-July

Great Yorkshire Showground, Hookstone Oval, Harrogate.

Open to the public. There is an entrance fee. Free parking in the Showground car park.

The country comes to town

There is nothing like a visit to the Great Yorkshire Show to send your spirits soaring and bring a spring to your step! From the moment I enter that magnificent showground I have left my troubles behind – at least for a day. Even getting there holds few of the terrors of modern road travel. On entering the Harrogate area, traffic is neatly divided into Show and non-Show vehicles and from then on, coloured signs and experienced policemen shepherd you (to use an appropriate term) to your proper car park.

Here, for three days in mid-July, Yorkshire plays host to the farmers of Britain and to all who love the green and living world of the country. This is certainly Harrogate's, if not Yorkshire's, biggest annual event.

Visitors, many from abroad, flock to Harrogate; a recent 'gate' reached 129,000. They range from excited schoolchildren to specialists – like the beef expert here to cast a knowledgeable eye over the cattle. Cattle are perhaps pre-eminent among the livestock at the Show – indeed, the Great Yorkshire is now regarded as the best in the country for commercial beef, and has probably the finest display, as a ring feature, put on by any show in the country. A Texan visitor (immediately identifiable by his hat) was standing in the cattle lines, eyeing the enormous bulk of a magnificent Lincoln Red bull and murmuring 'That's some bull – *some bull!*' Admittedly, the Red was particularly striking, but he was still just one champion specimen among many. The Beef Shorthorn, the Aberdeen Angus, the Galloway, the Highland and the White-faced Hereford (which the American visitor would doubtless recognise as a breed long since 'naturalised' in the United States) are all represented by the very cream of their kind.

And still the stockmen primp and titivate their charges as painstakingly as if they worked in a West End beauty salon. A stockman with a scrubbing brush fluffs out the hairs of a mighty Charolais bull's tail until it resembles something you might see on a hat at Ascot. His curly-coated majesty seems utterly unconcerned.

Of course, other varieties of livestock, including the rarer breeds, are still well represented. For example, how many sorts of sheep do *you* know? Can you distinguish a North Country Cheviot from a Teeswater, a Lincoln from a Wensleydale, a Leicester from a Bluefaced Leicester? Did you realise that a Jacob ram, descendant of an ancient and distinctive breed that is mentioned in the Book of Genesis, sports four horns? More than twenty varieties of sheep are regularly exhibited, and every year sees an increase in the number of entries.

Horses and ponies are shown in perhaps a score of classes ranging from the heavyweights like Shires and Clydesdales to Yorkshire's own tried and trusted breed, the all-purpose Cleveland Bay, and from hunters and hacks to Arabs and the ponies – Welsh, Dartmoor, Dales. The star attraction for horse lovers will always be the Main Ring with its hunter riding events, show jumping, hackney championships, pony contests and a parade of magnificent heavy horses. In 1977, Silver Jubilee year, the Queen saw her own Cleveland Bay stallion, Mulgrave Supreme, take part in a Main Ring display by the Cleveland Bay Horse Society. These are the horses which, along with the Windsor Greys, draw the royal coaches.

There are also such excitements in the Main Ring as parachute jumping, four-in-hand coach displays to provide stirring reminders of past glories or a charge by lance-bearing mounted police – whether they are scarlet-jacketed 'Mounties' or the London Metropolitan! Bordering on the ring is the President's Lawn overlooked by the windows of the

President's Pavilion. The President presents proud veterans of the farming scene, in spotless best suits and a number sporting bowlers, with their long service awards from the Yorkshire Agricultural Society. At a recent Show there were ten of them – estate foreman, farm workers, estate joiner – each of whom had worked for the same family or on the same estate or farm for forty years or more. They each took away with them an engraved tankard, a certificate and a free pass to future Great Yorkshire Shows for as long as they live. And in the country that can be quite a time!

Compelling though the livestock exhibits may be, however, the visitor to the Show should on no account miss what might be called, without disrespect, the 'fringe' activities – such as farriery and wrought ironwork competitions. For the less well-informed on rural matters, I should explain that the term farriery refers to the blacksmith's craft, surely no longer to be regarded as a dying skill now there is such a resurgence of interest in horses generally – a skill which becomes an art when it enters the realm of wrought ironwork. This renewed interest in matters equestrian is faithfully reflected in the number of spectators who watch competitors demonstrating their skill in every branch of the craft. The top farriers use the age-old implements of their mystery – fire, iron and water – to shoe hunters, hacks and the magnificent Shires (a hazardous undertaking in the latter case, since a Shire may easily weigh a ton and must at all costs be dissuaded, however friendly or lazy it might feel, from leaning upon its attendant). The apprentices, meanwhile, demonstrate their skills in the making of shoes on an anvil whose shape has remained basically unchanged for centuries. But the smith is as up-to-date in some branches of his craft as he is traditional in others, hence the competitions in welding skill sponsored by farm machinery and welding companies.

In charge of these and other competitions is the remarkable organisation known as CoSIRA (the Council for Small Industries in Rural Areas). Its bucolic-sounding name should not be allowed to mislead; it is a highly enterprising group which joins with the Yorkshire Rural Community Council to put on displays of rural activities, ranging from stone-carving to small factory and workshop programmes of the type which both CoSIRA and the Community Council are keen to encourage in rural Yorkshire.

More than half the land in England and Wales is privately owned (a fact which is hardly likely to please everybody in this egalitarian age), and the owners of this vast acreage are represented by the Country Landowners' Association; they demonstrate their concern for the welfare of the countryside by means of exhibits at this and other shows.

Inevitably the Young Farmers are much in evidence. Their competitions and displays cover a wide range of activities – a three-course English breakfast made by boys, hat-modelling, handicrafts, stock judging, a safety competition, sweet making, bird identification, a farm machinery competition and a junior quiz.

And, of course, there are the perennial favourites – hand sheep-shearing, spinning, rope making, drystone-walling, cake icing and wine making.

Country folk, or at least the ones you meet in the show stands, are by no means the suspicious introverts they are sometimes made out to be. Nowadays they realise that if the countryside is to prosper, it must be understood and appreciated by the public at large, including town dwellers. So today 'catch 'em young' is the policy, the success of which is borne out by an exhibition of work by schoolchildren on themes such as agriculture and industry in Yorkshire at the North Yorkshire County Councils' Schools Centre – no longer just a teachers' refuge and a 'lost and found' for small children!

But it seems that everybody in these 'conservationist' days is concerned about the country, even those bodies which were once thought to be its greatest enemies. Ramblers may blench at the mere mention of the Yorkshire Water Authority and the Central Electricity Generating Board. How, they may ask, can they have anything but an adverse effect on the countryside, as they encroach more and more on the green areas of our land? In fact, never did such organisations show more concern for the farmers' problems, as their displays in the showground's Jubilee Area demonstrate.

The Jubilee Area gives exhibition space to a vast range of organisations whose interest in the county is not primarily agricultural. Here you may find represented the Council for the Protection of Rural England, the Camping Club of Great Britain, the York Archaeological Trust (exhibiting its famous Viking discoveries), the CoSIRA project for the conversion of disused farm buildings, the Yorkshire Farm Museum, the Farm Machinery Preservation Society and the National Trust, now surely recognised as one of the most stalwart defenders of our rural heritage. Here, too, might be found societies dedicated to the preservation of old and revived railways, like the Keighley and Worth Valley line, the North York Moors Railway and the Yorkshire Dales Railway. And to prove, if proof were needed, that farming is a truly modern industry, I saw a new special display to commemorate Information Technology Year.

acres, may enter, and the judges are themselves practical farmers who award their points for general management and the appearance of stock, machinery, land and crops. It always seems a pity that entire farms cannot be transferred by some kind of magic to the showground at Harrogate!

The scale of a show like the Great Yorkshire has to be seen to be believed. Despite its great success as a popular spectacle, however, its main aims remain as serious as they were when the show was born in 1837. On 10 October in that year a meeting was held at the Black Swan Hotel, Coney Street, York, to form a Yorkshire Agricultural Society whose aim was the promotion of agriculture 'by exhibition'.

An address issued to farmers and land-owners declared that the society hoped eventually to widen its scope to cover not only the breeding of livestock but 'the improvement of machinery in all its departments as applicable to agriculture . . . particularly . . . in a County so abounding in factories and food machinists as Yorkshire'. It was ahead of its time in that aim, just as it was in recognising the importance to Yorkshire of wool and of the small farmer.

The first show was held in 1838 on the barrack square at Fulford, York. The early years were a time of struggle – perhaps because Yorkshire farmers were even less conscious then than they are now that there was any room for improvement! For the first century of its life the show moved about Yorkshire, choosing a different site each year. Then in 1950, the society decided to buy an estate on the edge of Harrogate on which to develop a permanent showground.

The founders of the Show could have had no conception in 1837 of the growth which was to follow. It is a growth that will doubtless increase in the years ahead, as long, in fact, as the Show continues so successfully to introduce the town to the country and the country to the town.

What else can you see at the 'Great Yorkshire?' It might almost be easier to say what you *can't* see, for the Show as a whole seems to cover almost the entire range of human – and animal – interests.

Inevitably, the world of field sports is well represented with shows of fox hounds, beagles and terriers and a display on 'Hunting in Yorkshire'. A parade of hounds by some of the leading Yorkshire hunts invariably provides a lively finale. Altogether quieter and more contemplative are the fly-casting competitions and displays of the Salmon and Trout Association. (Quieter, yes, but if you think it's easy to land a fly within a given square yard of water, now is your chance to try.)

And if you have always yearned to tie your own flies, the Show provides an opportunity to see demonstrations by the experts.

Every aspect of forestry is on display at the Forestry Commission's stand; there are exhibitions of woodland wild-life and of children's play furniture, as well as demonstrations of wood-carving by skilled chain-saw operators.

The serious business of the Show will always be farming, and one of the most important competitions held here is one open to farmers in North, West and South Yorkshire, Cleveland and North Humberside for the best kept farm. All kinds of farms, ranging in size from 200 to 600

International Motor Cycling Race of Aces

Third week in July

Snetterton Circuit, Norwich.

Qualifying heats on Saturday followed by the race on Sunday. Pay to get into the circuit and again for the paddock or the stands. Free car parking.

Snetterton is between Thetford and Norwich on the A11. The circuit is by the roadside and easy to find.

Filey Open Sailing Regatta

Usually third Saturday and Sunday in July

Filey Harbour

Spectators welcome. There is a large pay and display car park on the cliff and limited parking on the seafront.

Lifeboat Day

Usually one Saturday in late July, 2.00 p.m.

Scarborough.

Run by the Yorkshire Coast Lifeboat Team. The Boat House is open all day and the lifeboat makes four trips out, one for the mayor and his party and the others for holiday-makers. The Boat House is in the harbour, on the seafront. This is also a flag day.

Parking restricted; nearest on the Marine Drive.

Leeds Dog Show

Saturday and Sunday, end of July

Harewood Park, on the Harrogate road out of Leeds.

Open to the public; there is an entrance fee. Ample parking space.

Clipping the Church Ceremony

Sunday, late July

Burbage Parish Church, near Buxton, Derbyshire.

A church service and interior procession in which the parishioners embrace the pillars of the church and thus enfold the building into the Christian body. Also held at Wirksworth on the Sunday after 8 September.

Burbage is a village south of Buxton on the A53. Park in the village.

Harrogate Festival

Usually lasts a fortnight in late July/early August

Chiefly a music festival but also features drama, exhibitions and lectures. Most events take place in the Conference Centre, Royal Hall and Lounge Hall, although Ripon Minster is used occasionally. Tickets and preliminary programmes are available from the Festival Office, Royal Baths, Harrogate HG1 2RR, tel. 65757.

There is adequate on-street parking in the evenings. Also a multi-storey car park in the town centre and an underground car park at the Conference Centre.

Fringe Festival also active throughout the fortnight.

Cultural centre of the universe

There are those, believe it or not, who maintain that Harrogate is too uppercrust for a Yorkshire town. Thus they reveal their ignorance of the all-embracing variety of the County of Broad Acres. For Harrogate is as much a part of Yorkshire in its many moods as the Dales, the moors, the mill chimneys (those that remain standing) and the seashore at Robin Hood's Bay. At times, Harrogate is Yorkshire wearing an opera hat instead of a cloth cap. For if you think that Yorkshire's cultural heritage is confined to brass bands and Handel's 'Messiah', you obviously know nothing about the Harrogate Festival.

THE CALENDAR YEAR

Every year – and that's an achievement in itself – Harrogate's hotels, halls and churches are the setting for a constellation of talent that shines for a full fortnight, leaving the town dazzled but revived.

The Harrogate International Festival is presented by a company called, rather surprisingly, Harrogate Festival of Arts and Sciences Ltd. That is because when it first began in 1965, its originators intended it to be unique in offering in its programme scientific lectures and exhibitions along with artistic events.

So Harrogate, which claims to have the best-known and longest-running of all Yorkshire Festivals, could surely also claim one of the most original in inspiration, even though the scientific aspect is no longer as much in evidence as was anticipated in the first flush of an enthusiasm which seems never to cool.

As Clive Wilson, artistic director from the start, explained in an interview with *Arts Yorkshire* (published by the Yorkshire Arts Association), 'We started as a Festival of Arts and Sciences, bringing people from both fields to Harrogate, but the scientists didn't see themselves as performers.' Today the sciences are introduced 'when something interesting crops up'. Explaining

the five 'flames' in the Festival logo, Wilson says they represent Science, Visual Arts, Literature, Drama and Music, though from the earliest days music has proved the most popular.

'If finances allowed,' he says, the Festival 'could be twice as long'. The total expenditure in 1982 was £150,000 and the income which covered this (no deficit!) included box office receipts as well as money from sponsors such as the Arts Council and other bodies, including local authorities which offer free use of concert halls. About 40 per cent of the costs should be paid from box-office receipts.

How much does Harrogate, or indeed Yorkshire, really value this highly original, ambitious and successful annual flowering of culture? According to Wilson, the North of England that gave it birth remains faithful in support, providing 75 per cent of the audience. Until two or three years ago, Harrogate was apparently acquiring an international following, too – 'We had quite a lot of visitors from the Continent . . . but because of the economic situation, we, in common with other organisations, have suffered a reduction in numbers of visitors from abroad.'

For six years Wilson voluntarily co-ordinated the Festival. In the very earliest days the event was an outgrowth from the Harrogate

Concert Society and the employment of professional staff was hardly contemplated. He is still at pains to stress that this is a home-grown product which has 'taken off', and that many people, both voluntary and paid, have contributed to its success – 'Obviously, no one could do it alone'.

In a sense, the success of the Festival echoes the success of Harrogate itself, the former spa which has adapted wonderfully to its new role as a conference, trade fair and exhibition centre. It could so easily have died when wealthy hypochondriacs ceased to flock here to take the waters and undergo the variety of remedial ordeals on offer.

Just as Harrogate's great hotels found a new life as conference and exhibition sites, so its many churches and halls lent themselves admirably to the purposes of the fledgeling Festival. Again aiming high, Clive Wilson followed the example of Aldeburgh by using many venues to create the Festival atmosphere; for instance, Christ Church ('marvellously acoustically'), the Old Swan Hotel ('an intimate setting') and Ripon Minster ('for big brass or choral works'). How he finds time not only to direct a Festival of such scope, but also to work as secretary to the Yorkshire Cancer Research Campaign, with all the organising and fund-raising that post entails, is something of a mystery. Perhaps it can only be explained by the fact that he has the utter dedication of a man who has no artistic pretensions of his own but loves the arts. Particularly pleasing to Yorkshire folk is the fact that this native of the county has seen fit to make Yorkshire the

scene of his successful enterprise.

Wilson attributes a large part of the Festival's success to Harrogate itself. 'It's such a pleasant place to visit,' he says. Other factors in the Festival's success he sees as an emphasis on the lighter side and the creation of a friendly atmosphere.

Examples of the lighter side in a recent Festival included such varied delights as the Late Night Shows 1 and 2 , which offered, respectively, satire in a 'Beyond the Footlights' Revue, and the wit and musical expertise of Richard Stilgoe; a Festival Fun Run – 'a 10-mile cross-country ramble/run (not a race) organised by the Harrogate Athletic Club'; and Cathie Berberian, the American soprano performing in her very individualistic style 'From Monteverdi to the Beatles – a panorama of revolutions in music'.

But as a festival, this is no lightweight event. The more 'serious' side of the same programme employed the talents of Julian Bream, Simon Rattle, Prunella Scales, Geraldine McEwan, Julian Lloyd Webber, Sir Charles Groves, the Medici String Quartet, Benjamin Luxon, Jon Silkin and Barry Tuckwell, to name but a few.

Here, too, is a Festival which has never overlooked the cultural needs of children. Hence the inclusion in that programme of the Northern Black Light Theatre presenting *Secrets of the Nile* and *Kimoon and the Paper Dragon*. Less sophisticated, though perenially popular, fare was provided by a Punch and Judy Show performed with glove puppets in the Crescent Gardens.

Harrogate is richly blessed in its Festival venues. Even Ripon's magnificent Minster, the setting for organ recitals and symphony concerts, is within easy reach, and offers the bonus of a visit to one of England's most historic cities.

Now the new Conference Centre, with its concert hall and all the most modern facilities of lighting and acoustic technology, has given the biggest possible boost to the Festival. In 1982, by a brilliant stroke which lifted

Harrogate from county to Continental status, the Eurovision Song Contest was held there before a television audience of 350 million in 30 countries. The music may not have been quite the sort a festival-goer would make his first choice, but – for good or ill – it pulled Harrogate smartly into the twentieth century. Just as important, by means of magnificent film inserts it not only showed those millions of viewers that Harrogate is indeed in Yorkshire, but that Yorkshire is a supremely beautiful part of England. And the Festival has directly benefited since, in anticipation of increased activity through the presence of the new Centre, the Arts Council increased its support.

Such progress deserves the adjective 'dazzling' – and yet the first object of the Harrogate Festival was to enhance life for the people of the town. 'There was a dearth of things like this in Harrogate,' Clive Wilson explains. 'Most of the festivals were in the south, so I thought, why shouldn't we have one in the north of England to plug the gap between King's Lynn and Edinburgh?' And he went ahead to prove that there was no earthly reason why not.

What of the future? 'I hope to make the Harrogate Festival number two to Edinburgh,' he says.

The Harrogate Fringe Festival, a comparatively recent development, is not quite so modest. Given a good response by the local community, its publicists say, 'the fringe can help to make Harrogate the cultural centre of the universe and leave the Edinburgh Fringe standing.'

Wakefield Festival

Usually in July/August and lasts a fortnight

Events take place in the cathedral precinct, the Elizabethan Gallery, Bishop Treacy Hall, Unity Hall, the new Wakefield Theatre and others. There is a charge for most events.

There are pay and display car parks in Drury Lane, Smyth Street and Northgate, all near the centre of town.

No official H.Q. at present but queries to the Wakefield Information Centre, Wakefield 370211.

In 1980, for the first time in over four hundred years, the complete Wakefield Cycle of Mystery Plays was performed. At three fixed stations in the neighbourhood of Wakefield Cathedral, the plays were enacted by about twenty-five local groups, who progressed with banners and music from place to place. In the cathedral grounds 'medieval' stall-holders offered their wares, and over a wide area of the city centre traditional entertainments were staged.

The plays now form part of the two-week-long Wakefield Festival revived as recently as the 1970s and comprising theatre, arts events and entertainments in various parts of the Wakefield district.

The 1984 festival is scheduled to coincide with the opening of the Wakefield Theatre in what was formerly the Opera House.

The Lavender Harvest

August

Caley Mill, Heacham, Norfork.

Heacham is a village near Hunstanton, north of King's Lynn on the Norfolk coast. It is famous for its lavender fields which are harvested in August and saleable goods such as soap are produced. There are tours around the mill in July and August, for which a small charge is made. Parking area near the mill.

Ilkley Annual Tennis Tournament

First week in August

Tennis Courts, Stourton Road, Ilkley.

The Tennis Courts are just outside Ilkley off the Skipton road – turn right past the Church. The Tennis Tournament is well signed. Tickets from the Tennis Club.

The event has grown considerably since Ilkley's first open tournament took place in 1885; it was won by one of the great characters of early Yorkshire tennis, Edward Fletcher.
The current tournament includes between 1,250 and 1,300 matches with around 450 competitors taking part in thirty-one events. The tournament changed character in the 1970s when tennis achieved professional status, and is now mainly a junior and family event with County players competing for major prizes.

Great Yorkshire Steam Fair

Usually first Saturday and Sunday in August

Castle Howard, York.

There is an entrance fee and a car park. Castle Howard is off the A64 south of Malton, North Yorkshire, and about 12 miles north-east of York.

And where better to show their paces than the hills which divide and yet unite the counties that have made and lived by machinery?

Since Manchester saw the birth of the Rolls-Royce, it is fitting that the Trans-Pennine Run should start in that city. At the Greater Manchester Driver Training Centre at Hyde Road, the grand reunion takes place between 7.45 a.m. and 9.30 a.m.; then the procession travels majestically by way of Rochdale, Todmorden, Hebden Bridge, Halifax, Shelf, Bradford, Shipley, Guiseley, Otley and Pool to Harrogate, there to bask in admiration from noon to 5 p.m. and to be judged in *Concours d'Elegance* and other contests, whose gleaming entrants win trophies for their dedicated drivers and slaves.

They were found – what was left of them – in scrapyards, or rusting on farms or forgotten behind hedgerows. And the stories they could tell might make two hundred books. A German goods lorry, built in 1921, had never left Munich until 1966 when it was taken to Ireland to star in the film *The Blue Max*. Restored in 1980-1, it once more wears the livery of the Löwenbräu Brewery, its first owner. There is a twelve-horsepower van, believed to be the only Rover van still in existence. Until 1962 it had been in daily use by a Derby wine merchant. Now, beautifully restored, it looks likely to continue a long life indefinitely. Some of these old stagers seem indeed to be blessed with more lives than one . . . like the Foden lorry built in 1933. Burnt out in 1935, it had to be completely rebuilt. Then, after the war, it travelled the road with a showman and was rather the worse for wear when its present owner bought it in the late 1970s and restored it immaculately to its 1935 condition.

An early 'thirties eight-wheeled steam wagon (Sentinel manufacture), one of only eight ever built, steams each year from Colchester to Manchester before completing the run to Harrogate (and then steaming back to Colchester). A 1928 Leyland Titan

Bridge, Halifax, Shelf, Bradford, Shipley, Guiseley, Otley and Pool and arrives at the Stray in Harrogate at about 12.00 noon. Vehicles remain there until 5.00 p.m. Free parking in nearby streets.

Ghosts cross the Pennines

From London and Scotland and the South Coast they come, enjoying their day of glory, with their brasswork glittering like the sun. Their days of useful toil are over. Now they are cossetted and fussed over as anxiously as any vintage Rolls pampered by a rich man's chauffeur.

Once a year in August the wheeled workers of a bygone world unite to span the Pennines: perhaps two hundred of them in a ghostly cavalcade – lorries, buses, fire-engines, military vehicles, both steam and petrol driven – all built in the half-century from 1912 to 1962. Many of them the last survivors of their kind, they are so well turned out they might have left the factory only yesterday.

Trans-Pennine Rally

First Sunday in August

Manchester to Harrogate.

The run begins at Greater Manchester Driver Training Centre at Hyde Road between 7.45 and 9.30 a.m. It travels through Rochdale, Todmorden, Hebden

TD1 bus is famous – it saw service in Glasgow, Keighley, Royston and Ilkley before being bought for preservation and restored in the livery of the defunct Keighley West Yorkshire Services Ltd! Besides being one of the oldest double-deckers in private preservation in Britain, it was one of the very first buses to be preserved, having been saved from the breaker's torch as long ago as 1962.

The mechanical work-horses of the past, they meet their relations – country cousins like vintage agricultural tractors and perhaps a fairground organ that will not need much persuading to play a few songs from the good old days! Then home they go to think fondly of the Historic Commercial Vehicle Society which organised their great day out, and of the *Yorkshire Evening Post* and Harrogate Borough Council, which sponsored it.

Blessing the Broads

First Sunday in August, 3.00 p.m.

Ruins of St Benet's Abbey, near Horning.

The Bishop proceeds by boat to St Benet's Abbey and holds a service there at 3.00 p.m. Possible to follow the Bishop down the river.

St Benet's Abbey is on the riverside very close to Ludham, off the A1062 to Potter Heigham from Norwich.

St Wilfrid's Feast and Procession, Ripon

First Saturday and Sunday after Lammas Day, which is 1 August

Procession begins in Blossomgate at 2.00 p.m. and proceeds through town to the Cathedral, where there is then a service. There is a car park in Ripon market-place and plenty of people watch the procession en route. Also five Sunday services for St Wilfrid in the Cathedral the next day.

Lord, keep the city

Every year in August, St Wilfrid, who founded Ripon Cathedral, returns to ride (by proxy of course) around the city on a white horse, presumably to make sure that everything is being done to his satisfaction. He may have been doing it for the best part of a thousand years now, ever since his Feast was founded by Royal Charter in 1108, and there can be little doubt that he enjoys his welcome – he was that sort of man.

Ripon certainly makes the most of its history and never more so than on this feast day, when representatives of the tiny city's daily life accompany the saint – recognisable by his mitre and crozier – in a long procession of floats and brass bands, watched by crowds thronging ancient streets with ancient names.

The saint himself is the epitome of dignity but on the whole this is a light-hearted occasion. I remember once seeing a pantomime cow, part of the Young Farmers' Club's contribution to the procession, trying to mount the cathedral steps and being energetically shooed away by the Dean.

St Wilfrid must have been a colourful and dominating personality or he could hardly have made such an enduring impression on Ripon. And the legends about him seem to support that theory: he once saved Christian converts from starvation by teaching them to catch fish. Being a Yorkshireman (at least by adoption) he liked to have his own way and if he didn't get it was inclined to quarrel with other bishops and even with kings.

Perhaps that's why Ripon is so fond of him! Ripon men warm to a good fighter, which is hardly surprising, for life here was not always as peaceable as it appears today. In 1319 Ripon was destroyed by the Scots. In 1536, many local men supported the Pilgrimage of Grace that protested against the closure of the religious houses. Some thirty years later, the ill-fated Rising of the North, another gesture in support of the Old Religion, failed, and three hundred of its supporters died rebels' deaths on Gallows Hill.

Ripon Cathedral (or Minster as it is more properly called) began as a Celtic monastery built of wood and founded in 657, by the Celtic monk Eata, Abbot of Melrose. When Wilfrid was appointed Abbot of the monastery in 661, he introduced Roman doctrine and, a few years later, when he rebuilt the monastery, he built in stone. That is why the crypt of Wilfrid's monastery survives to this day, while Eata's has vanished. Only eleven feet by eight and never quite reaching ten feet at the highest point of the barrel roof, this little room at the foot of twelve steps is considered to be one of the oldest Christian structures in England. Wilfrid surely recognises little else of 'his' minster when he pays his annual visit, for today it is a glorious mixture of styles soaring harmoniously to the top of the nave, which at more than ninety feet is one of the highest in England.

St Wilfrid is by no means the only colourful character you are likely to meet in Ripon. Every

week, when the Thursday Market is held, a man in a tricorn hat rings the corn bell to signal the fact that it is 11 a.m. and trading may now legitimately begin. (It has actually been going on for hours, but nobody seems to mind.) During the twelfth century, anyone caught trading before the ringing of the corn bell might well have ended up in the stocks. It all goes back to the time when King Stephen, William the Conqueror's grandson, granted the privilege of the fairs within the Liberty of Ripon to Archbishop Thurstan of York.

Archbishop he may have been, but Thurstan was not a man to forgo the perks of office. He imposed a corn tax and made sure that the man who was to enforce it had a good big pair of hands! Why? Because the tax was levied by the extraction of two handfuls of corn from each sack taken to the market. Farmers being farmers, they soon got the notion that it would pay them to make an early start and be away from the market before the Archbishop's minion had had time to levy the tax. 'I'll soon put a stop to that,' said Thurstan, in language appropriate to the period. 'Anyone who does business before my bell has sounded is for it!' And Ripon got another of its traditional observances.

Perhaps the best known of all the city's customs is the setting of the watch, which takes place every night at nine o'clock. Here again, a nicely old-fashioned note is set by the Horn Blower, who sports another tricorn hat (though when this custom was instituted no one had even seen such a headpiece). The watch has been set without a break for over a thousand years. It is linked with the days when, instead of a Mayor, the city appointed a Wakeman – hence Ripon's motto emblazoned beneath the pediment of the magnificent Georgian Town Hall: *Except the Lord keep the City the Wakeman waketh in vain.*

During the hours of darkness the city was indeed in the Wakeman's care and, should any robbery occur after the setting of the watch, the Wakeman was required not only to catch the thief but also to compensate the victim of the robbery. As a premium for this early form of insurance, the good folk of Ripon paid four pence per door per year.

Ripon no longer has a Wakeman, but still a great curved horn is blown every evening, once at each corner of the square and once in front of the Mayor's house. The Wakeman's House, however, does remain – a fourteenth-century, half-timbered building at the south-west corner of the square. Even after the office of Wakeman had been abolished, the house (now a museum and tourist information centre) was still used as a Mayor's official residence. Inevitably, it has undergone restoration, although a great deal of the original structure is intact.

Few cities in England take more pride in their past than Ripon, or have preserved it with so little change despite the ever-increasing pace of modern life. A note of dignity is struck in the very heart of the city, where one of the largest market places in the north of England – almost two acres in

area – stands in the shadow of a ninety-foot obelisk, surmounted by the city's badge, which William Aislabie erected in 1781. Aislabie, who lived at Studley Royal, a nearby mansion now burned down, raised his obelisk to celebrate the fact that he had been Ripon's M.P. for sixty years. Ripon, as we've seen, is a city not much given to change . . .

Another Aislabie, John, who was Mayor in 1702, presented the city with one of its treasures, a Queen Anne loving-cup. But this is a comparatively recent addition to a civic collection, some items of

which date back to the ninth century.

What a period they span! In Ripon Town Hall you may see the city's first 'charter', the horn of a wild ox presented to the city in 886, the twelfth year of the reign of Alfred the Great. Now encased in velvet and silver, the Charter Horn is mounted on a belt decorated with the badges of trade guilds of the Middle Ages and studded with the emblems of Wakemen and Mayors up to 1886. Another horn, similarly decorated and mounted, is known as the Millenary Horn, because it takes the history of the

118

Egton Bridge Gooseberry Show

Usually first Tuesday in August

St Hedda's Schoolroom, Egton Bridge, near Whitby.

Gooseberry weigh-in in the morning, open to the public in the afternoon. Small entrance fee, parking in the village.
Egton Bridge is about 8 miles inland, south-west of Whitby on the North York Moors.

Sanctity and stratagems

Egton Bridge, a few miles inland from Whitby on the North York Moors, reveres two things – the memory of its seventeenth-century martyr priest . . . and gooseberries. Nicholas Postgate, the Martyr of the Moors, hanged at York when

silver, such as a superb snuff box and a chalice; a Cromwellian whistling tankard; an inkstand presented by the Royal Engineers, who are Freemen of the City – all are items of a collection which may well be unique in England.

Proud though it may be of its past, Ripon is also very much alive to the present. Standing at the confluence of the rivers Ure and Skell and Laver, and well placed to benefit from the growing demands of tourism, it has a better claim than some to be called the 'gateway to the Dales'. Its shops and hotels are full of character – especially the Unicorn, an old posting house which some say is still haunted by a former member of staff. He first achieved fame as long ago as 1793, when the *Wonderful Magazine* wrote of him, 'By nature and habit he acquired the power of holding a piece of money between his nose and chin. His chief employment was waiting on the customers and from the circumstances of his cleaning their shoes and boots he went by the name of Old Boots.'

Even if you can't hope to see the remarkable countenance of Old Boots on your visit to Ripon, you can probably see a picture of him at the Unicorn. If you come in August you may make the acquaintance of St Wilfrid, too.

city into its second thousand years. Ripon's latest charter was granted by Queen Elizabeth II in April 1974, the year of local government reorganisation. Ripon and certain other 'old cities' received charters allowing them to retain traditional status and privileges.

In the Town Hall are the gilt spurs presented to James VI as he rode south to be crowned James I of England. Ripon 'rowels', or spurs, were already famous, hence the saying 'as true as Ripon rowels'. Maces, horns, chains of office; seventeenth-century York

he was 80, may well be canonised some day; a display in St Hedda's Roman Catholic Church tells you all about him. It is also at St Hedda's, in the schoolroom, that the village's Old Gooseberry Show, remarkable for its single-minded dedication to the humble goosegob, is held on the first Tuesday in August.

Every exhibitor must be a member of the Egton Bridge Old Gooseberry Society, founded in 1800. The Society strictly enforces a multiplicity of rules on the grounds that only the fair deserve the glory of winning – whether

their exhibited berry be a Prince Charles, a Princess Royal, a Lord Kitchener or a Thatcher (named not after a prime minister but because of its resemblance to a hank of thatch). Whatever the variety, unless the berry is as big as a plum or, better still, a golf ball, it has little chance of a prize. And in order to achieve the required prize-winning proportions, many secret stratagems are employed.

The 'trees', as they are called, are ruthlessly pruned and generously nourished with manure; nets protect them from the birds, while wasps, the grower's arch enemies, must be distracted by jam jars full of beer or other wasp lure. Nothing is too much trouble for the true devotee, who will even keep an umbrella handy to protect his berries from intemperate weather. In times of drought, tins of water are placed lovingly beneath a promising berry so that it may gain comfort from the evaporation. Never, some growers say, must the roots of their cherished trees be desecrated by the disturbing spade!

There are classes for the

heaviest single berry, for a pair of berries on one stem and for a group of twelve berries, to name but three. The entries are scrupulously weighed in drams and grains, and then the prizes – ranging from garden tools to kitchen-ware and tea sets – are presented. The day ends with tea accompanied by the lively music of a visiting village band. The revered Father Postgate would surely approve of such innocent fun!

Leeds Show

One weekend, early August

Soldiers Field, Roundhay Park, Leeds.

Formerly Leeds Flower Show. It is open to the public and there is an entrance fee. Normally a field is roped off for parking.

Soldiers Field is off Princes Avenue, Roundhay Road, which is to the north of Leeds.

The Leeds Show was run by the Roundhay Horticultural Society for sixty years until 1975, when the society ceased to exist. Offshoot members then founded the Leeds Horticultural Society and started the show again in 1977. 'Flower' was dropped from the title when the event expanded to encompass crafts, leisure activities, local societies, and so on, although eighty per cent of the show is still concerned with flowers. The Begonia Society, Fuschia Society, Geranium Society and Natural Vegetables Society have all participated.

Test Match, Headingley

Usually July or August

The Cricket Ground is off the A660 (Otley Road) out of Leeds, on St Michael's Lane.

Tickets are available beforehand, by application to the Test Match Office. A day out there can be quite an expensive affair, with a car park charge, ground admission, plus an extra charge if you want to reserve a good seat.

Reflections in the rain

The Battle of Waterloo may have been won on the playing-fields of Eton, but as any Yorkshireman of any maturity can tell you, that's *nowt* to what Len Hutton did at Headingley. Or Fred Trueman . . . or Wilfred Rhodes. But first let me introduce you to Headingley, Yorkshire's holy of holies, the Yorkshire County Cricket Club's ground in Leeds, and, to natives of the county, the only Test cricket ground that really matters.

There are those, of course, who say that Yorkshire's days of greatness as a cricketing county are over, or at least in eclipse. But every Yorkshireman knows that his team's remarkable self-restraint in refusing to win the county championship every year in recent times is born only of a generous desire not to discourage lesser sides.

But why Headingley? Well, where else, apart from Lord's and the Oval, would you want the world's top cricketers to stage their ritual battle? Headingley is in fact the only provincial cricket centre used as a regular Test Match venue. Until the mid-sixties, in a Test series of three or five matches, Headingley had to take its turn with Old Trafford, Trent Bridge and Edgbaston to stage a Test.

Then, to its imperishable credit, Essex saw the light and suggested that the Yorkshire ground should be raised to the status of a regular Test ground – one of the Big Three. The other counties agreed and so did the teams from abroad, who had long insisted 'We *must* play a game at Headingley.'

THE CALENDAR YEAR

There was only one condition for Headingley's elevation and that was that the Headingley pitch be maintained to Test Match standards. Perhaps it seemed easy enough to give that assurance, but the Headingley pitch at times has apparently had a mind of its own, if not a positive jinx on it. You get hints of this as you listen to Freddie Trueman's deceptively innocent comments during Test Match broadcasts from Headingley.

To ordinary mortals like you and me, Headingley may be no more than a cricket field but the game's high priests, such as Freddie, know it can do highly mysterious things with the bowling.

Furthermore, it cannot be entirely cleared of favouritism! The final day of the Fourth Test at Headingley in 1934 has passed into cricketing mythology. Noah's Flood may or may not have happened, depending on the inerrancy of scripture, but there can be no doubt about the effect of the deluge that descended on Headingley on the final day of that Test Match.

In their first innings, England scored 200. Australia replied with 584. England were 229 for six in their second innings when the Yorkshire sky flashed in fury and thunder growled. No doubt the Australians' hearts sank, and minutes later it seemed that everything in sight must also be submerged as the rain poured out of a leaden sky.

It was the end of play and the end of the match, which could only be a draw. Photographs of the Headingley pitch on that July day in 1934 are gloated over to this day by readers of books on cricket. The sensible Yorkshire crowd, apparently marooned on the stands, are clad in raincoats to a man; the seats around the edge of the field appear ready to float away, and the brave spirits who are actually walking about seem to leave a wake behind them in water apparently ankle-deep.

It wasn't the first time it had happened. In 1930 England were similarly rescued by the weather. Even the incomparable Don Bradman's incredible record score of 334 did not prevent England achieving a draw.

Headingley weather has been celebrated in innumerable cartoons. They show elderly spectators clapping, not in appreciation of the play, but simply to keep their circulation alive.

It hasn't always been the weather that has queered the enemy's pitch. Supporters of the 'Free George Davis' campaign, on behalf of a man who had been convicted of armed robbery, entered the ground during the night, inflicted holes on the wicket, and troubled the sacred turf by pouring oil on it. The groundsman, removing the covers at dawn, was doubtless struck dumb – at least temporarily – by such impiety. Grimly the two captains inspected the damage and decided that play was impossible. And so a great exciting match was aborted. They say the rain would have stopped the game anyway but rain, as we have seen, can be expected at Headingley. Sacrilege, as any Yorkshireman will tell you, is summat else!

But why, considering its tendency to alarums and excursions, should the Headingley ground be so universally approved as a Test Match venue?

It would be pleasant enough to think that something in the Yorkshire air produced this unanimous enthusiasm for the Leeds ground. The truth is even more flattering.

It was surely the Yorkshire crowd who won Test Match status for Headingley, and not only for the numbers in which they clicked through the turnstiles, but for the sheer joy that playing for them brought. In return, the players gave of their best at Headingley, enhancing its reputation for providing some of the finest cricket in the world.

The Yorkshire cricket spectator is a legend in himself, whether the enemy be Australian, West Indian, Pakistani, or from that other county across the Pennines. Since other than Yorkshire folk will read this book, I must tell you the most revealing, if one of the hoariest, of Yorkshire cricket stories.

Three men stood in a row at a Roses match at Headingley. Flanked by a supporter of Lancashire and a staunch Yorkist stood a visitor from the south whose recurrent outbursts of enthusiasm fell discordantly on the ears of Tyke and Lancastrian alike.

'Oh, well played sir, well played!' he applauded – once too often for the patience of the more taciturn northerners.

'Art thou from Yorkshire?' asked the Lancastrian.

The stranger denied it.

'Tha'rt 'appen from Lancashire then?' enquired the Yorkshireman.

And when a second denial was uttered, both Lancashire and Yorkshire spoke, for once, with one voice –

'Then mind thi own bloody business'.

But that is really a caricature of the Headingley spectators, one of whom doubtless invented the legend.

Indeed Headingley is alive with legend. It is a shrine for all who love cricket, but inevitably its appeal is strongest of all to the Yorkshireman. Why cricket should be so bred in the Yorkshire bone I cannot say. Nor can I say why, of all the cricketing counties, Yorkshire should be the one that still insists on its players having been born within the county's boundaries. Need I add that the requirement disdains latter-day bureaucracy by adhering to the pre-1974 Yorkshire territories. 'Off-comed' planners may sweep away the names of Yorkshire's ancient 'Ridings' and substitute colourless titles, but the Yorkshireman knows where his county begins and ends when it comes to things that matter.

Freddie Trueman, though his contribution now is from the commentary box, will remain one of those legends for years to come. When he first went to the Headingley nets as a lad of sixteen showing promise as a bowler, he was met by that giant of the game, George Herbert Hirst, who first asked Fred his name and then, more keenly, explored the

important matter of his place of birth.

'Is that in Yorkshire?' asked Hirst when the youngster said he was 'born in Stainton'. Could Fred have originated anywhere else but in Yorkshire? His father had taken the day off to accompany the lad on his momentous errand. And when Hirst approached Fred's Dad, that sport-loving miner, who had proved too heavy to be a jockey, instinctively stood and removed his cap before taking the great man's hand.

Harry East, my favourite cricket writer, recalls in his *Laughter at the Wicket** that he interviewed Hirst on his eightieth birthday in 1951. 'You'll have to make allowances,' he was warned by the family. 'He doesn't remember much.' Politely, the legend asked Harry, 'Did you ever see me play . . . Did I do owt?'

Harry admitted that he couldn't exactly recall, having been very young at the time. All he could remember was that men were going round the Headingley field with trays hawking 'George Hirst Toffee'. Hirst's faded old eyes lit up. 'By gum,' he smiled, 'it were good toffee!'

I was going to tell you what Hutton did at Headingley. By 'Hutton' I mean our Len (who became *Sir* Len) from Pudsey (where good cricketers are born). It produced, besides Sir Len, such cricketing folk heroes as 'Long John' Tunnicliffe, Major

Booth, Herbert Sutcliffe and Ray Illingworth. With such a cricketing history it should also be the heaven good cricketers go to when they die, and perhaps it is.

In Pudsey everyone, it seems, is an expert on the game. It was Sir Len's aunts who not only gave him his first lessons in cricket – or so they insisted – but bought him his first bat. And wasn't it Aunt Louise or Aunt Florence or Aunt Mary, or all three of them, who presented Len with *Playing for England* by Jack Hobbs?

But what did Len *do*? Far too much to recount in full here, but for one thing, in the fourth Test in 1948, opening with Cyril Washbrook against the Australians, he contributed 81 to an opening partnership of 168. Admittedly the Australians went on to win four out of five and draw one. But they'd been winning monotonously for far too long and the effect of this opening throw on the England supporters was electric. Inspired by such examples, Compton, Edrich, Evans and all gave of their best until stumps were drawn at 362 for eight with England leading by 400.

On the final day, England declared at 365 for eight and then, with everything apparently on their side, they gave the game away in the best British tradition, allowing the Kangaroo Brigade to score 404 for three, Bradman and Morris achieving a second wicket stand of 301. Another of those Funny Things which happen at Headingley, though they often seem less than humorous at the time.

Watching today's increasingly colourful Test Match scene, when taciturn Yorkshiremen and smiling, flag-waving Asians and West Indians find common ground on a cricket pitch, it is easy to think that of all England's gifts to the world, cricket is by no means to be the least esteemed. No more to be despised is Yorkshire's gift to cricket. Illimitable and immeasurable that gift may be in its entirety, but a part of it is Headingley.

*Whitethorn Press

Grouse Shooting

Season opens 12th August

Yorkshire Moors.

Private shooting.

All glorious on the twelfth

The so-called Glorious Twelfth of August can seem far from glorious on a chilly misty morning when, after gathering in some estate yard at an unearthly hour of the day, you are loaded into a Land Rover to begin a long drive to a grouse moor for the first shoot of the season.

It isn't the most comfortable of journeys and the travelling is by no means over when the vehicle comes to a juddering halt and you jump out and suddenly find yourself up to the knees in heather (if you're lucky – up to your neck in a hole if you're not), with a long walk ahead of you and no gumboots – because nobody told you to bring them.

The actual butts are often quite a long way from your point of disembarkation. You begin to trudge over the trackless heather . . . well, it's almost trackless, so the best and safest thing is to follow as closely as the page of Good King Wenceslas in the tracks of those who appear to know where they are going.

You can recognise them by their plus-fours and leggings and sensible boots. They wear hats or caps and waterproofs, too, or old sports coats with plenty of capacious pockets.

They carry guns, held under one arm and safely broken at the breech; shooting sticks and haversacks hanging over one shoulder complete their ensemble, while running alongside, with a business-like air and no wistful thoughts about gumboots, are dogs – black or golden retrievers.

On my moor, those in the shooting party have drawn lots for butts, philosophically accepting their luck – or lack of it.

There are eight butts, roofless, circular fortresses built of rough stone with heather and bilberry fringing their parapets. The party sort themselves out, with one to

shoot and one to load in each butt. Two shots are fired to tell the beaters to start the drive. And now begins the waiting . . . and waiting . . . and waiting.

As you watch the empty skyline, you realise just how cold an August morning on a North Yorkshire moor can be. And how silent, or nearly silent. The sigh of the wind in the heather, the occasional bleat of a sheep are the only sounds. There's an unexpected sense of drama in the air, a vague excitement that shouldn't really be aroused by mere birds. We would not be entirely astounded if a party of pillaging Highlanders, claymores at the ready, appeared over that empty skyline. The odd bird that we see now and then isn't a grouse.

Somebody says 'Look out!'

There's some coming.' But he has better eyes than mine, or knows better where to look. 'No . . . they've settled down again now', he says. So we, too, settle down, glad that someone has a flask with something more warming in it than coffee.

Again somebody warns us to 'look out'. We do, and discover that there really are some grouse on this moor after all. A small flock of them is approaching. Over our butt they fly and obliquely cross the whole line of bilberry-fringed forts.

'Behind!' comes the cry, and the guns train swiftly on the departing quarry. But of course they can't *hit* them – who could hit anything moving as fast as that?

There comes a little clatter of shots, like a bonfire-night jumping-jack, and two or three

birds drop like stones.

A distant shouting rapidly growing louder tells us the Highlanders really are approaching. But no, it's only the beaters. More grouse are coming, too, but they are flying too far to the left, so someone is sent out to 'flank a bit'. He sits about thirty yards to our left to wave a handkerchief in the hope of scaring the birds in the right direction – right for us, that is, not for them.

In a surprisingly orderly line the beaters bear down on us, waving, not claymores, but handkerchiefs tied to walking sticks. Twenty-five years ago they would have been paid about twenty-five bob a day. More recently, out-of-work youngsters got £7.50 a day plus a bottle of beer or lemonade for tramping over the moors all day in

any kind of weather. An eight-gun shooting party needs about twenty-five beaters. And as many as 1,500 might be hired for the season in North Yorkshire alone. It could give them forty days' work.

Grouse shooting has become big business in recent years. Rich sportsmen from the Middle East, America, Japan and Europe will pay hundreds of pounds a day to shoot on a moor where the shooting can be bought. But there are still moors where you have to be invited on the strength of your shooting and the agreeableness of your character.

Not all moors are owned either by belted earls or tycoons. The most famous moor in the world, at Ilkley, belongs to Bradford Council, which lets the shooting rights to a consortium, though it has been known to reserve places for industrialists who might be persuaded, after a shoot-it-yourself lunch at a moorland hotel, to bring new jobs to the city.

The tumult and the shooting dies and now everyone can relax for a while. The patient dogs are let go to retrieve the victims. Guns and loaders take their ease on the heather . . . until the next drive brings another flock of impossible targets whizzing overhead, to fall, some of them, as the guns crack yet again.

I still wonder how anybody ever manages to hit one. With a strong following wind a grouse can exceed a hundred miles an hour. Of all driven game it moves the fastest. And the reward for its speed is to be protected and coddled in infancy so that it may be shot and served at rich men's tables and expensive restaurants.

Veterans recall the days when shooting was shooting, when big estates had perhaps twenty keepers to look after maybe 12,000 acres. The Head Keeper in those days was a king in his realm, sometimes with gold braid on his hat to prove it. But those days will never return. For this is the age of science, not pageantry, when *Lagopus Scoticus*, the Red Grouse, is studied earnestly by researchers paid by the landowners to ensure a healthy and therefore profitable grouse population. And the findings of these experts would seem to suggest that – yes, being shot really does the birds good – at least as a species. It prevents them, for instance, from falling victim to *strongylosis*, a tape-worm-carried disease and *coccidiosis*, both of which result from over-population.

Life is no longer as simple as it used to be on the moorland. Once a free-flying, dashing chap, *Lagopus Scoticus* (Scotty to his friends) is just as much a victim of modern technology as the rest of us. Sometimes, believe it or not, he is equipped with a back-pack transmitter and tracked by radio wherever he or his family might choose to roam. But, like being shot at, it's all for his own good really: it enables researchers to discover where Scotty finds the

best vitamin-packed heather and bilberry for family picnics.

A great deal depends on the quality of these natural foods. Looking at them as they grow, an experienced eye can estimate the prospects for next year's sport. Will it produce a mere handful of birds or two, three, four hundred brace?

Whatever happens, only the grouse never grumble . . .

Veteran Motor Cycle Rally, Harrogate

Saturday of the third weekend in August, 9.30 a.m.

To and from the Royal Hall, Harrogate.

Biennially in Harrogate on odd years. See the motorcyclists drive off from Harrogate, or at mid day in Masham where they break for lunch. Masham is on the A6108 north of Ripon.

The Veteran Motor Cycle Rally makes its way through the countryside on an eight-mile round trip. The riders stop for lunch at Masham. This is an international rally with up to 180 participants. Entrants come from Germany, Sweden, Holland and Belgium. Motor cycles must be over twenty-five years old, and most average 20 m.p.h. on the run. The rally has taken place each year since 1973; every alternate year it is run from Cheltenham.

York Open Bowls Tournament

Late July/early August

Clarence Gardens, and other greens, York.

Public greens which are open from 1 May to 30 September, from 10.00 a.m. onwards. The tournament is open to the public and there is a small fee.

Clarence Gardens is a park between Wiggington Road and Haxby Road and there are two big pay and display car parks nearby. Wiggington Road is out beyond Bootham Bar, near the District Hospital.

As English as cricket

As English as cricket, bowls is the game for young and old, male and female, Armada scatterer or pensioner. Bowls is probably the gentlest of games – almost certainly nobody was ever killed on a bowling green; it is also one of the most idiosyncratic (and surely every English institution should be that).

Bowling is not so much a sport as a double act between a man and a black wooden sphere with a built-in bias. The object of the game, in the simplest terms, is to get your own 'wood' closer than any other player's to the jack (distinguishable by its smaller size). The skill is in the delivery, in the judgement which determines the degree of force required to send the wood the right distance in the required direction. It is necessary, of course, to bear in mind the effect of the bias and the fact that greens are either of the crown variety – that is, they rise from the sides to the middle – or they are flat (as in the case of the York greens used in the Open Tournament).

In their idiosyncrasies some bowlers recall the northern cricketing giants of bygone days – extroverts to a man, or, if *they're* not characters you might be forgiven, if you listen to the commentators, for thinking that the woods at least have a mind and a will of their own. They are described as 'tired' or 'brave' or 'lazy' or 'eager'.

'If they don't send 'em far enough they won't go', intoned one bowls pundit gravely on TV – almost as if the human player had something to do with it after all!

Like snooker, bowls has enormously enlarged its audience through television. The City of York Open Bowls Tournament,

first held in 1967, is now the biggest in Yorkshire – 'in the same range as the major seaside tournaments', its organisers tell you proudly. It is held usually in the last week in July during the York railway and chocolate factory holidays.

The HQ of the event is the bowling greens of Clarence Gardens, but most of the park greens in York have to be pressed into service to accommodate the hundreds of players who carry big canvas bowls bags to York from the North East, the Midlands and the South in ever-growing numbers. About 1,000 players can be attracted to the pairs events alone.

They certainly don't compete in the hope of winning rich prizes – the total prize money amounts to only £760 and the top prize is £50 awarded, along with the Whitbread Trophy, to the winner of the Men's Singles, which attracted 192 players in 1982. In the Ladies' Singles there were 128 players; the Men's Pairs attracted 128 pairs and the Ladies' Pairs 64. Most popular event of all is the Mixed Pairs ('Lady and Gentleman', explains the programme, to prevent any possible misunderstanding). In 1982 170 such duos competed for prizes of vouchers ranging from £6 to £30, the top scoring pair also receiving the Mackeson Rose Bowl.

Burnsall Fell Race

Saturday after the second Sunday in August

A 15-minute race from the green in Burnsall, up to the top of the Fell. Starts at 1.00 p.m.

Burnsall is a small village in the Dales, north of Skipton. There are pay and display car parks available.

Racin' ovver t'fell

A distant ribbon of figures, bright tints of red and white against the deep green of Burnsall Fell, winds up the hillside, ties itself into a knot while negotiating some vague obstacle, a stile or a wall, then unwinds and continues its tortuous progress – a centipede now – towards the nine-foot-high cairn that marks the half-way mark.

It's the annual Burnsall Fell Race, main event of Burnsall Feast Sports and since this is the centenary of the event, 'all living past Fell Race winners have been invited to attend,' says the programme, adding that the Committee hopes they have an enjoyable day.

How can they help it? Enjoyment is rampant today in this Dales village, whose spacious green beside the swift-flowing Wharfe is peopled with side-shows, barkers, a fortune-teller, a falconry specialist with some of his ever-watchful charges, Tombola, Roll-a-penny, Egg Throwing and 'Peggy', the skill in which consists of detaching and holding with one hand a greater number of clothes pegs than any other competitor.

Also on the green, the Lofthouse and Middlesmoor

Brass Band from neighbouring Nidderdale, glorious in maroon uniforms, play a sedate accompaniment. Their selection is punctuated at intervals by the cracks of the clay-pigeon shooters' guns and the tinkling bells and stick-banging of the morris dancers, performing with disciplined exuberance outside the Red Lion Hotel.

But the Fell Race is the event which has drawn the crowds – and the runners. There are 236 listed, some from athletic clubs as far away as Barrow, Blackheath, Blackpool and even Lochaber; some in teams – from the Parachute Regiment or Durham University; some 'unattached'; and a dozen with names like Carol, Val and Margaret, whose gentler contours belie the iron of their endurance.

At the start, avuncular police stop the occasional motorist, who would find progress impossible anyway, because the road beside the green is dense with lean and muscular figures trotting on the spot in anticipation of the starter's pistol.

They're away . . . In an incredibly short time they are scaling the steep fell side, ten yards of which would more than suffice for most of us. From Burnsall green, 473 feet above sea level, the runners have to reach the cairn of piled stones, which, at 1,345 feet, does not quite mark the summit of the fell, for at its highest it reaches 1,661 feet.

A good vantage point is the bridge over the Wharfe, whose parapet is lined with spectators. Here, those with binoculars provide a commentary for those without.

"E's *theear*! 'E's at t'top an' 'e's well in front. 'E's comin' down now . . . By gow, but 'e's shiftin' – 'e is that!'

It's difficult, anyway, to see how anyone could make such a descent slowly, especially with legs reduced to rubber by the rigours of the ascent.

What will his speed be? The first recorded professional time, 19 minutes 15 seconds, was achieved in 1903 by R. Spencer. With surprising consistency, the time

has been reduced almost every year. Until 1914 and the First World War, three runners in turn had almost a monopoly of success. In 1904, '5 and '6 it was one Kavanagh, who, on the occasion of his last success, achieved a time of 17 minutes 45 seconds. From 1907 to 1909 (inclusive) it was T. Metcalfe's turn and his fastest time was 14.23. Then from 1911 to 1913 R. Thomas had four successes, though his best speed was only 15.10. J. James, on the occasion of his fifth successive win in 1930, clocked 14.58, but since he could only manage a winning time of 17.7 the following year, he apparently hung up his plimsolls.

Apart from another war-time hiatus from 1940 to 1947, the event has been held without a break.

At the time of the centenary race the best recorded ascent time was 8.42 (M. Short, Horwich R.M.I.) and the best recorded descent time since 1948 was 3.58 (R. Wilde, Manchester H. and A.C.). Both these records, incidentally, were established in 1977. Wilde's 'amateur' time of 12.50 broke the controversial record of 12.59 established by E. Dalzell of Keswick in 1910, who, some said, did the descent in three leaps!

As the runners pant past the winning post, clicking the stop-watches on their wrists, two attendants struggle to record the numbers on the contestants' singlets, inevitably being frustrated as six runners arrive at once. The winner is J.R. Wild, Cumberland Fell Runners, who did it in 13.10.

Meanwhile, unruffled by the excitement, a fly-casting competitor makes his umpteenth attempt to land his cast in one of the hula hoops floating on the Wharfe, neither helped nor deterred by advice from the bank – 'Pull it back a bit, tha're goin' *too far!*'

For all its glamour, the race 'ovver t'fell' is still one event among many. Over 200 runners embark on the ten-mile road race with a flashing blue light escort front and rear and, for good measure, four policemen among the runners. The first three placed in this event all complete their tour of neighbouring villages like Grassington, Linton and Thorpe in less than 52 minutes.

Meanwhile, the leader of the morris men sonorously announces a special appearance by 'The dreaded Barguest of Troller's Ghyll'. The Barguest is Wharfedale's very own spectral hound and Troller's Ghyll a legend-haunted valley a short distance away. Even without the introduction you'd have known the dark-hued Barguest by his saucer eyes and fearsome great teeth. But he's no match for the morris men who sprinkle him with water, whereupon he dies, much mourned by the crowd.

How William Craven, who must have known all about the Barguest, would love it if he could return, for the happiness of Burnsall was dear to his heart. Even when he was Lord Mayor of London in 1598 he never forgot Burnsall or its neighbour,

Appletreewick, where he was born fifty years before.

William (Sir William) it was who built Burnsall's Tudor-style Grammar School, which now serves as a lovely village school next to St Wilfrid's Church, which Sir William 'butified', says an inscription inside the church. And he also rebuilt the bridge – no doubt altered since – which now serves as a graceful centre-point for this favourite among Wharfedale villages.

And the band plays on . . . The Teddy Bear's Picnic, The Twenty-third Psalm to the well-loved Crimond and the same happy, reassuring old favourites they've played and will play at Burnsall Feasts for years and years (with no more wartime intervals, let us hope).

Cactus and Succulent Show

Friday and Saturday of the third week in August

Bailgate Methodist Church Hall, Lincoln.

Bailgate is in Lincoln town centre. There is a small entry fee for members of the public. Plenty of car parking space – three car parks on Westgate and one on St Paul's Lane, both of which are off Bailgate.

Yorkshire Historic Car Club Rally

Nearest Sunday to 20 August, 12 noon to 5.00 p.m.

Halifax.

A static display of vintage cars to 1955. Usually around 100 entries. Held at the Piece Hall in former years. Contact the Automobilia Museum, Hebden Bridge (tel. Hebden Bridge 844775) for details of the current venue.

Louth Flower Show

Saturday, late August

Louth Town Hall, Eastgate, Louth, Lincolnshire.

10.00 a.m. to 6.00 p.m.; open to the public; small entrance charge. Pay and display car park to the right of the Town Hall.

The show began as a hospital carnival but thereafter was taken up by Toc H who have run it for the last thirty years. It is a local show attracting entrants from the Grimsby, Horncastle and Spilsby area. Besides the one-day flower show, the town runs a 'Lovely Louth' competition in which, for a period of two to three months, business premises and private gardens compete for an award for the best floral display.

Plague Memorial Service, Eyam

Last Sunday in August ('Wakes' Sunday)

Cucklet Dell, Eyam.

The Plague Hymn is sung to commemorate the village's fight against the plague in former years.

Eyam is a town in the Peak District, south of Hathersage and north of Bakewell.

The noble sacrifice of Eyam

At the village of Eyam, the word *plague* takes on a special and heroic meaning, and few villages have better reason to be proud of their forebears. There is a charm today about this Peak District village which would make the harrowing story of its sacrificial past seem almost incredible were it not for the relics that remain to remind us of those sad days. One day in August 1665 a box of cloth from London was delivered to the home of widow Mary Cooper, with whom lodged a journeyman tailor, George Viccars. Two days later, George was terribly ill, his body swollen and covered with a rosy rash – the 'ring o' roses' of the children's rhyme that dates from those days and describes the symptoms of the bubonic plague,

131

the Great Plague which raged in the capital:

> *Ring a ring o' roses*
> *A pocket full of posies*
> *Atishoo, atishoo*
> *We all fall down*

(The posies were nosegays carried in a pathetic attempt to fend off the disease, one sympton of which, like the final 'falling down', was sneezing.)

No doubt all the so-called remedies were tried – such as a mixture of olive oil, vinegar and garlic and other herbs – but without effect, and by 7 September George was dead.

In less than six weeks, two more of George's household had fallen victim to the dreadful disease carried probably by the fleas which had lurked in that harmless-looking bundle of cloth, waiting to make the fatal, germ-infected bite.

By now everyone in Eyam must have known the terrible truth that, perhaps as a punishment for sins they tried hard to remember – or perhaps to forget – the plague had been visited upon them. Maybe in an attempt to atone for those sins, the whole village made a sacrificial gesture that has transformed Eyam into a shrine to courage and a place of pilgrimage.

William Mompesson, Rector of Eyam at the time, is presented in his portrait as a long-faced, melancholy man, but there can be no doubt of his courage or of the spiritual power he exercised over his flock. With the former rector, Thomas Stanley, who had become a Nonconformist, he called a meeting of the 350 or so villagers

and made what must at first have seemed an incredible demand.

'We must all stay here,' said Mompesson to his people, many of whom must already have been planning with feverish haste to leave the village. 'Nobody must leave Eyam from this day forward.'

'But we shall all die,' they surely told him. 'And anyway, a few have left already.'

'If we spread the plague, many others will also die,' he no doubt replied. 'If we stay here, many will be spared.'

For the next fifteen months Eyam was a village that lived alone with death. Family after family fell victim to the plague. One woman, a Mrs Hancock, was seen to carry out seven of her family and bury them in her own field, for to prevent the spread of the disease the victims were interred close to their own homes. Those seven graves, encircled by a stone wall, can still be seen in the middle of a field at Riley Farm.

The Earl of Devonshire, whose descendants still live at the magnificent Chatsworth House not far away, helped Mompesson arrange for the stricken village to be supplied with food. It was left at the Eyam boundary stone or at

Mompesson's Well and paid for with coins left in vinegar or in running water.

Cut off from the rest of the world, the villagers also avoided contact with each other. No longer did they meet in church for worship but in the open air, where Rector Mompesson used a ledge of limestone rock for a pulpit. Neither Mompesson nor Stanley succumbed to the plague but Catherine, the rector's wife, fell victim. Her grave, beneath a table tomb, is the only plague grave in the churchyard.

In all, 260 villagers died. The fields around Eyam contain their memorials. Inside the church, St Lawrence's, the present-day visitor may see what the worshipper in plague times perhaps could not – a set of mural paintings, covered for fear of idolatry in Puritan times, then discovered about a hundred years ago, covered again, and rediscovered in recent times.

But today's visitors are more likely to look for the many objects recalling Eyam's heroic past, such as Mompesson's sturdy carved oak chair in the sanctuary. A former rector, Canon Hacking, who presented it to the church, found it in a junk shop last century and recognised it from carvings, including part of Mompesson's name and the name Eyam. It bears the date 1665 – the actual year of the plague. The Plague Cupboard, harmless now, is on the wall of the north aisle. Used today for storing hymn books, it is supposed to have been made from the box once containing the clothes which brought the plague to Eyam.

One of the most telling of all the exhibits is a list, contained in a glass case, of the people who perished during those fifteen terrible months. When the plague was at its height in the following year, 56 villagers died in July and 77 in August.

But by the end of that year the plague had run its course. The pestilence that had taken so many lives finally died itself, killed by a bitter Derbyshire winter. Its victims, in giving their lives, had won for Eyam an imperishable fame.

Lee Gap Fair

24 August and 17 September

Lee Fair Green, Baghill, Lee Gap, Woodkirk, West Yorkshire.

Woodkirk is off the A653 between Tingley and Dewsbury. It is usually possible to park by the roadside.

Thimble-riggers and garter-prickers

Lee Gap Fair, Woodkirk, one of the oldest horse fairs in Britain, is often said to have been founded in the reign of Henry I (1100-1135) though it may have existed earlier. Henry it was who granted (or confirmed) to the Black Canons of Woodkirk (a cell of Nostell Priory, Wakefield) a charter to hold yearly fairs on the Feast of the Assumption, 15 August, and the Feast of the Nativity of the Blessed Virgin Mary, 8 September. Over the centuries the fair dates have changed from the original feast days for which the charter was granted, and for many years the first fair was held on St Bartholomew's Day, 24 August, and continued, non-stop, say some authorities, to 17 September.

Since 1752 the fair has been held only on the first and last of these dates, which are known respectively as 't'first o' Lee' and 't'latter Lee'.

Lee Fair has generated its own legends, according to which, in medieval times, merchants from the Continent came to Lee Gap to buy stock as provisions for the winter ahead. Not only horses, but geese, goats, sheep and most other kinds of livestock apparently were sold, and the activities were equally diverse. At Woodkirk Church, it is said, a priest and clerk were available all day to perform marriages; and since there was a great deal of drinking, fighting and generally riotous behaviour, the Woodkirk monks would present the Townley Mystery Plays with the avowed object of edifying 'the idle multitudes' and diverting them, perhaps, from the snares of thimble-riggers, garter-prickers and other cheats.

Today Lee Gap Fair is only a shadow of its former self, but it

133

continues despite threats of building on the fairground. Horse-traders and gipsies still gather here to conjure up a flavour of bygone days. An escapologist or a fire-eater might be there to entertain the crowd, while children will probably find a few swings and rides to enjoy.

The fair is held on Lee Fair Green, Baghill, Lee Gap, Woodkirk, which can be reached via the A653 between Dewsbury and Tingley.

Burning of Bartle

First Saturday, Sunday and Monday after St Bartholomew's Day, 24 August

West Witton, North Yorkshire.

West Witton is a village off the A684 between Leyburn and Askrigg, some 3 miles west of Leyburn. The highlight of the weekend is when an effigy of 'Old Bartle' is burned on Saturday evening at Grass Gill End.

Free access for the public; parking in the village.

Once a year at West Witton in Wensleydale they burn Owd Bartle. On the Saturday following St Bartholomew's Day (24 August) at around ten o'clock in the evening there starts from the 'top' of the village a procession, the central point of which is Owd Bartle himself, or rather a straw effigy of him. This is carried in turn by three male volunteers and every few yards one of the men chants a piece of doggerel:

At Penhill Crags he tore his rags;
At Hunter's Thorn he blew his horn;
At Capplebank Stee he brake his knee;
At Grisgill Beck he brake his neck;
At Wadham's End he couldn't fend;
At Grisgill End he made his end.

Who was Owd Bartle? Although it may be significant that this custom takes place so near to St Bartholomew's Day and that Bartholomew is the patron saint of the parish church, local legend gives him a far from pious history Bartle was a rogue, they say, who preyed on the swine kept by the monks of Jervaulx Abbey. One night in August, nearly four centuries ago, his fellow dalesmen lay in wait for him on the 1800-foot summit of Penhill. They pursued him from 'Penhill Crags' to 'Grisgill [Grass Gill] End' where 'he made his end', being burned at the stake. This is the event which is re-enacted year after year.

In Victorian times, the custom was accompanied by a three-day

village feast with races for prizes of ribbons and copper kettles, as well as 'ribbon dances' at the village inn. Although it is not quite such a big event today, folk still travel many miles to West Witton in August to see Owd Bartle meet his fiery fate.

Bosun's Chair Descent of Gaping Gill

Saturday through to Friday of Spring Bank Holiday week and Saturday through to Friday of Late Summer Bank Holiday week

Gaping Gill, Ingleborough, Three Peaks.

Nearest car park – Clapham (pay and display). One hour's walk from there to Gaping Gill.

National Park Information Centre at Clapham will know whether or not the descent will be running, depending on the weather.

There is an entrance fee.

Caribbean Carnival, Leeds

August Bank Holiday

Headquarters are at the Community Centre, Chapeltown, Leeds and the Carnival takes place in the Potternewton Park/ Chapeltown area.

The Carnival Queen is chosen on Friday night and there is a procession on Monday. Anyone is welcome to watch the Parade and join in the Carnival. Parking may be restricted, but there is a regular bus service from the town centre.

Salt fish and fry domplin

It's August Bank Holiday Monday and Potternewton Park, Leeds, is blooming with an array of human exotica that might well astonish the worn grass and surrounding trees. Steel bands practise their rhythms; dancers cavort in fantastic costumes; alien odours spice the air from vans selling 'fried fish and johnny cake, curry goat and rice, salt fish and fry domplin', 'plantain and coconut tart' and mouth-scorching West Indian ginger beer.

Accents range from pure Caribbean to broad Yorkshire, as dispensed via the mike of a compère who, but for his colour, might be Les Dawson's brother: 'Will Mrs Brown coom to the stand 'cause 'er son Winston 'as lost 'er?'

No need to ask the way to Potternewton Park today. For hours along Chapeltown Road there has flowed a leisurely river of dark skins and bright clothing. Little groups of Caribbean immigrants, or their offspring, wander, on foot or in cars, towards the only destination that holds any appeal on this day of days in Leeds.

Their colours range from almost blue-black to pale coffee. On a park wall sits a group of elderly turbanned Sikhs whose grandchildren play around them, and a young Chinese father offers candy floss to the little son in his arms, who hides his face, unable to believe that such strange-looking stuff is eatable.

Soon there are more steel bands – Paradise Steel from Leeds, Contract from Leicester,

water-melon purveyors is a little green tent emblazoned with the message 'Salvation is of the Lord'.

But even pious West Indians and their progeny have their minds on lighter matters today. The processions of Carnival Queens and steel bands are what everyone has waited for, and now a chorus of ear-splitting rhythmic whistles from one queen's attendants announces that the main event is about to start.

As the glittering parade begins, the crowds lining the pathway to the park gates have to surge back to make way for the steel bands, their oil-drum tympany mounted on wheeled trolleys. Each lissome queen has her band, whose trolley is often towed by costumed attendants.

The queens and their troupes wear costumes designed with amazing ingenuity. Their creators have worked on them for months. One construction, its theme 'The Fountain of Love', is said to comprise 426 pairs of white tights, battery-driven car lights and welded metal piping. Into its construction went huge numbers of Christmas baubles, and the whole is mounted on wire frames which slot intricately together. The tights, dyed in rainbow hues, are stretched on wire frames in the shape of butterfly wings.

One queen's head-dress resembles an enormous bird. A stilt walker, made even taller by his red conical hat, towers above the rest of the procession. It's not always easy to know what the participants represent. One group look like elves in green and yellow, another can only be Robin Hood's merry band of outlaws – or something. The mysteriously-named Nager Busyness are all in black with towering black stovepipe hats. Carrying huge wooden tomahawks and wearing peacock-feather head-dresses, the Leeds West Indian Masquerade cavorts tirelessly in the wake of queens, steel bands and whistles. Dazzled hospital patients in wheelchairs sit at the front of the crowd with their attendant nurses.

Like a brilliant, half-mile snake, the procession winds along Chapeltown Road, Grafton Street

Bosco, again from Leeds, Royal Star and Star Quality, both from Manchester, and North Star Quality from Huddersfield. Their throbbing seems to leave an imprint on the air that persists even when the playing stops.

The Lord Mayor of Leeds is respectfully introduced and says a few words from the platform. Meanwhile the park has been gradually filling. Now it is so packed with brown skins that three white toddlers running about in the nude are as noticeable as snowmen in a coal-mine.

There's a deliberate eccentricity about the clothing. One youth wears jeans from which the middle part of each leg has been cut away, leaving his brown knees bare and his trouser bottoms held in place only by his shoes. It's all part of what West Indians understand by the word 'carnival'

– a deliberate up-ending of the accepted order of things. Anything to be different, boisterous, strange. To the music of one steel band, two highly decorated figures are dancing on stilts. The inventiveness of some of the costumes is mind-boggling – one group with fine head-dresses of peacock feathers seems to hint at memories of tribal costumes.

On a West Indian girl's T-shirt are the words 'A woman without a man is like a fish without a bicycle'. Satirical Caribbean feminists seem unlikely, but in this ideological free-for-all, the motives are as mixed as the colours. A man selling some Marxist sheet declares that it contains 'a spread on the Carnival'; it does, but on the Notting Hill Carnival, not the Leeds one. Someone else hands you a Baptist leaflet, and among the fried chicken, hotdog and

and North Street to Meanwood. It takes two hours to make its dancing, swaying, weaving, whistling, roller-skating way back to the park. Many among the crowds lining the roads are drawn irresistibly into the parade; and those content to watch compete for the best vantage points, some even climbing onto flat roofs.

The Leeds carnival is said to be second only to Notting Hill – 'but without the aggro'. Once again it lives up to its reputation: there have been no arrests and the police describe the event as 'totally peaceful'.

Tomorrow, Potternewton Park will be just another Leeds park and we shall wonder if any of it really happened . . .

Semer Water Service

Sunday of Late Summer Bank Holiday, 3.00 p.m.

An open-air service by the lakeside; the Hawes Silver Band or the Muker Band usually participate.

Free parking near the lake, although it's best to get there early.

Semer Water is about 2 miles south of Askrigg, off the A684. The lake is no more than a mile long and it is possible to walk to the service.

Galilean echoes

Semer Water in Wensleydale has as many faces as there are seasons. I have seen it on a winter's day, when swans, moving almost imperceptibly on its mirror surface, appeared as timeless as the surrounding hills.

From those hills, and from the little valleys of Raydale, Bardale and Cragdale flow streams to feed Semer Water ('the only true lake in Yorkshire', some say), which gently overflows to form the shortest river in England. I speak of the Bain, whose course runs a mere two miles before joining the river Ure, which gives Wensleydale its other name – Uredale.

At holidays and weekends in summer, crowds flock to Semer Water to rattle around in motor-boats, to skim along on water-skis, to laugh and frolic and shout, to sunbathe and picnic. Yet on the last Sunday in August, Semer Water wears a different face again, for then the motor boats fall silent, the water-skiers and the paddling children sit by the lakeside and listen as they gaze at a Yorkshire scene that has a Galilean touch. From a moored boat a few yards from the landing stage – provided the water is not too rough – the Vicar of Askrigg and Stalling Busk is preaching his annual lakeside sermon. (And just to prove that we are still in Yorkshire, a village band accompanies the hymns that are sung – sung with some surprise, perhaps, by a few folk who came out with no idea of joining in a service.)

Semer Water falls within Stalling Busk parish, whose church, St Matthew's, is said to be the smallest parish church in England. The custom of holding a lakeside service was begun in the 1950s by the Reverend Dale Chapman, a former vicar. His innovation has grown in popularity and now provides his successors with perhaps their biggest congregation of the year, augmented by holiday-makers, and with a bus specially run from nearby Hawes.

Certainly the present church at Stalling Busk would be hard-pressed to accommodate the many worshippers who might turn up for the occasion on a lovely summer's day. Its two forerunners, a church built in 1603 which was then rebuilt in 1722, may have been more commodious, but nothing remains of the first and little of the second, except for a few fragments of broken wall and the remains of a square bell turret crazily topping the ruin. A link with former days is the old font found in the ruined church and now installed in the present building, which dates from 1909.

Semer Water lies in a subsidiary valley of Wensleydale called Semerdale, which could well be named the Quaker Dale in honour of such gentle souls as that of John Fothergill. He was born in 1712 at Carr End Farm, two years after the Society of Friends had built their Meeting House beside the green at the northern end of the lake. John, who was described by Benjamin Franklin as 'a great doer of good', had left Semer Water and was practising as a doctor in London by the time he was twenty-six. His fame was such that he was invited to go to Russia to inoculate the Empress of Russia against smallpox; his indifference

to riches and honours, however, made him decline the offer and recommend another doctor for the task!

Fothergill was one of the great all-rounders who, from time to time, arose and flourished in the days before over-specialisation had taken hold. He was a naturalist as well as a physician and recorded thirty different species of birds on Semer Water's shores. His botanical gardens at Upton are said to have rivalled Kew in the variety and rarity of their specimens. He founded the Quaker School at Ackworth, near Pontefract, and was a tireless worker for good causes, including prison reform. Yet, if his housekeeper sister Anne had not kept a diary and written endless letters, we might never have heard of him, for John himself was far too busy for diaries.

Though Fothergill's is a ghost I would be glad to meet should he go haunting in Semerdale, there are other spectres, less reliably documented, that I would rather not encounter. Was the strangely shaped Carlow Stone on the edge of the lake (favourite of sunbathers) really thrown by a giant at the devil, and later used as a sacrificial altar by the Druids? And is there really a sunken city beneath the water, from which the faint sound of church bells can now and then be heard? That, at least, is the legend and it may have a foundation of sorts, for a lake settlement may once have stood here before being drowned by one of the sudden storms which occasionally blow up. There is an old story in these parts which tells of a beggar who passed this way when there was no lake here, but rather, a prosperous city. Nobody heeded the poor beggar's pleas for alms until, at a humble cottage, an old man and woman shared with him their roof and their meagre victuals. Next morning, from the door of the hillside cottage he looked down on the rich town, raised his arms – though not in benediction – and cried:

Semer Water rise; Semer Water sink;
And swallow all the town save

this lile [little] house
Where they gave me food and drink.
The thunder rolled, the lightning flashed and the rains began, never to cease until the valley was flooded and all the village drowned, except for the two generous villagers in their hillside cottage.

Hard luck, say I. But looking at Semer Water, floating in a hollow of the Wensleydale hills, I can't really say I'm sorry . . .

Whitby Regatta

Saturday to Monday, late August

Harbour and West Cliff, Whitby.

The Regatta begins at 10.00 a.m. each day and spectators are welcome. Parking difficult in season.

Kilnsey Show

August Bank Holiday

The Show is mainly agricultural and is held in the field opposite Kilnsey Crag. Kilnsey is on the Skipton to Kettlewell road.

There is an entrance fee, and fields are set aside specially for parking. Usually busy.

The homely show – that's Kilnsey

Yet once more the voice on the Tannoy reminded us that when we went home we should take our litter with us. 'We an't goin' yet, thank you very much an' we an't got no litter', said a woman in a slightly irritated tone. The owner of the disembodied voice had no chance of hearing her above the noise of animals and tractors and several thousand show-goers. Anyway, he was busy announcing that in the previous year there had been 16,000 visitors. So far nobody could say yet what the total would be this time at 'the famous Kilnsey Show'.

That description is fully justified: Kilnsey Show is as famous in its context as the Great Yorkshire Show is in its own larger sphere. This is the village show *par excellence* – tremendously successful yet still very much a family affair, which is why visitors are ready and willing to answer back to that disembodied voice if they feel like it.

It is the main event of the Upper Wharfedale Agricultural Society inaugurated in 1897. When the first show was held on 7 September of that year, there were those who said, 'It'll nivver catch on'; but it attracted entries of seventy-five sheep, fifty-one cattle, thirty-one horses as well as exhibitors of butter and cheese. Skipton Band played at a gala which followed the show.

It *did* catch on, and over the years it grew. In 1899 sheep-dog trials were introduced, and four years later horse jumping – but over only two hurdles. That same year, 1903, by the way, saw the first wet show in the seven that had so far been held. And the happy tradition holds, more often than not, which can hardly be disregarded as a factor in Kilnsey's success.

Classes for vegetables were added in 1922 and pig classes, only recently discontinued, were introduced in the late twenties.

It has not been all plain sailing. In 1924 the show made a loss and the president had to come to its rescue. Two years later, when it was still not out of debt, the Jeremiahs were doubtless saying 'I told you so', but the faith of the stalwarts was unshaken and by 1934 it was the only profitable show in the area.

Even during the war, token events were held to keep this proud Wharfedale tradition alive – sheep-dog trials provided a delightful relief from the depressing facts of wartime and there were also drystone-walling competitions. The proceeds of these wartime events were donated to St Dunstan's Home for Blind Soldiers and to the British Red Cross.

Surely the essential craft of the Yorkshire Dales, drystone-walling, has always been an important part of the Kilnsey tradition. It was in fact the subject in 1980 of a documentary film made by Thames Television. The title, 'One on two, two on one . . .', is itself a maxim of the drywaller's craft.

But it is the crag race which binds this show so firmly to its setting. Since 1899, souls possessed of bottomless stamina have raced up and down the famous crag. Trotting races, too, are an historic feature, but new classes – for walking stick making or for adult handicrafts – are constantly appearing in the catalogue.

For many, though, the best exhibit of all remains the setting. This is probably the most beautifully situated agricultural show in the region. Hills bearing the delicate Wharfedale tracery of limestone walls form a backcloth whichever way you look; and always the scene is most effectively 'made' by Kilnsey Crag rising dramatically to defy all those who see it for the first time to say precisely *what* it resembles – is it really like a clenched fist, or a

monkey's head? Anyway, on Kilnsey Show day who cares what it looks like? It's Kilnsey Crag and as long as the sky behind it is clear, all's right with the world!

Here, in the August holiday week, the flat floor of the Wharfe valley blossoms with marquees, trade stands, displays of produce, horticulture and handicraft classes; and with the wholesome and worthy products of the Women's Institutes.

At one end of the showfield are the sheep and sheep-dogs. At the other side of the great oval showring, men stand among the horse boxes, titivating the tails and manes of superb heavy horses.

A cattle class is entering the ring. Spotless animals are accompanied by stockmen and women in gleaming white coats. And the disembodied voice of the commentator confides that one of them is going to London as a Dairy Princess to compete for the title of Dairy Queen.

'She's a bonny lass,' says the voice, 'and just as nice as she's bonny.'

The *homely* show – that's Kilnsey . . .

THE CALENDAR YEAR

Scarborough Flower Festival

Thursday to Tuesday, late August

The Green Lounge, Spa, Scarborough.

The Spa is on the southern side of the South Bay. There is an entrance fee. Parking on the Spa itself and in the underground car park nearby; pay for both. Otherwise park on the Esplanade, where there are no charges, and go down in the lift.

Scarborough Flower Festival first took place in 1885; it is now organised by the Scarborough and District Horticultural Association. Entries cover floral art, flowers, vegetables and pot plants.
A centenary show, to take place in 1985 in the whole Spa complex, is planned.

Ebor Handicap and August meeting at York

Mid – late August

The Ebor is the oldest race of the August three-day event. The race course is signposted off the A64, Leeds to Scarborough road; there are plenty of AA signs. Free car park. Pay through the gate.

Tote and tic-tac

'Tomorrow we set out to see the new horse-course lately made at Knaresmire and to join in the great doings of the week in the like of which no city can compare for gaiety, sport and company.'
So wrote Simon Scrope in 1731, when York's first 'official' August Meeting was held (though racing at York first began in Roman times). That 1731 meeting marked the start of a Turf epoch; total prize money over five days totalled £155 against today's figure of more than £500,000.

Great races of the meeting now include the richest event, the £100,000 Benson and Hedges Gold Cup, and the Yorkshire Oaks, which sees the top fillies in action and which was first run in 1849. But York's longest established race is the Ebor Handicap, now known as the Tote-Ebor Handicap ('Ebor' being derived from

Eboracum, the old Roman name for York). This event, first run in 1843, remains the high spot of the second day. In 1982 the Tote-Ebor Handicap offered £30,000 in added prize money. It is the punters' favourite, with active ante-post betting up to one month beforehand. The most memorable winner in recent years was Sea Pigeon, an eleven-year-old champion hurdler, ridden by jump jockey Johnjo O'Neill, which took on and beat the cream of the flat horses in 1979 before a crowd of 35,000. The Great Voltigeur Stakes, named after a horse which ran – and lost! – in a famous race of 1851, is also run on the second day.

Founded in 1846, three years after the Ebor, the Gimcrack

Stakes for two-year-olds remains a great attraction on the third day of the meeting. It is named in honour of Gimcrack, a tiny horse foaled in 1760, which began its racing career at the age of four and won twenty-seven out of its thirty-five races. At a dinner held each December by the Gimcrack Club, the owner of the year's Gimcrack winner makes a speech which is traditionally expected to spark off controversy in the Turf world.

Southwell Show

August/September

A ploughing match and agricultural show. The venue is different each year on a 5-year rotation basis. Parking is always available. An entrance fee is charged.

Matlock Illuminations and Venetian Nights

Fourth week in August to fourth week in October

Matlock Bath.

Matlock Bath illuminations are down by the river, beside the pavilion. On Saturday nights there are also illuminated floats on the river and fireworks. There is an entrance fee.

Parking at Cromford Meadows is recommended; buses provide a shuttle service to Matlock Bath. It is difficult to park nearby at night.

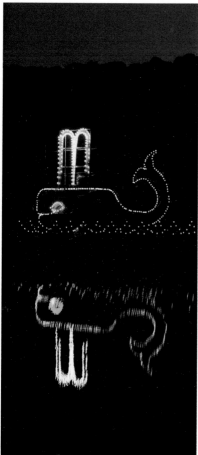

Autumn

Autumn Events

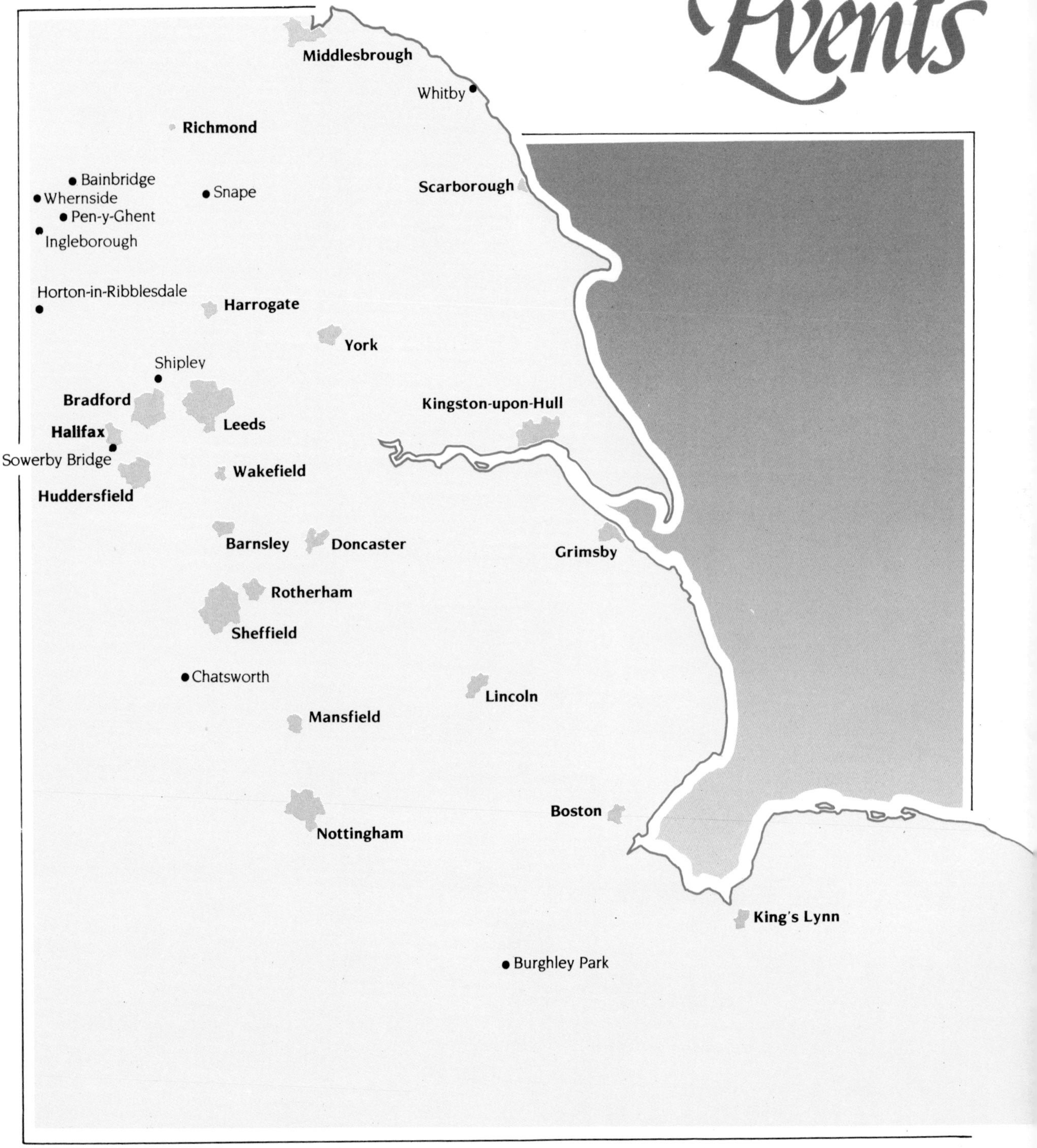

Middlesbrough
Whitby
Richmond
Bainbridge
Whernside
Snape
Pen-y-Ghent
Ingleborough
Scarborough
Horton-in-Ribblesdale
Harrogate
York
Shipley
Bradford
Leeds
Halifax
Sowerby Bridge
Kingston-upon-Hull
Wakefield
Huddersfield
Barnsley
Doncaster
Grimsby
Rotherham
Sheffield
Chatsworth
Lincoln
Mansfield
Boston
Nottingham
King's Lynn
Burghley Park

Sowerby Bridge Rushbearing

First Saturday and Sunday in September

A five-mile procession over two or three days starting from the Mason's Arms in Warley, just north of Sowerby Bridge, through Sowerby Bridge and on to Ripponden.

A full programme, with map showing stopping places en route, is usually available. A picturesque event featuring Morris Dancers, Craft Fairs, a Barn Dance etc.

Panama hats and clogs

Saturday morning at the Mason's Arms, Warley, near Sowerby Bridge, and the early September sun looks down in surprise on a scene of colour and activity that might have been enacted eighty or more years ago. Morris dancers limber up for their ancient, intricate performances, a brass band tunes its instruments, and the crowd lining the roadway waits expectantly and cheers every slight sign that 'summat's goin' to 'appen'.

Suddenly a bigger cheer rises as the centre-piece of the whole affair lumbers into view. What on earth is it, this antithesis of anything 'space-age'? It's like a haystack on two wheels, with a strangely mystical-looking triangle surmounting its front end. It is attended by about forty men of equally strange appearance. They wear panama hats, white shirts, black trousers and clogs. By means of wooden yokes ('stangs') these acolytes are preparing to draw their wheeled deity in procession. But it's not *really* the idol of some South

Pennine religion. It's a 'Slaithwaite cart' turned rush-cart, all of eighty years old, and it supports a thirteen-foot-high frame of rushes.

We are watching the start of the Sowerby Bridge Rush-bearing ceremony that is rapidly becoming one of the famous local customs of Yorkshire, and indeed of England.

From here the procession will make its boisterous way around the district – first stop the Maypole Inn where there will be morris dancing; then to St John's Church, where rushes will be presented; then to the Waiter's Arms; then to St Patrick's Church; and so on until the rush-cart reaches the Star Inn, from where the procession will begin again tomorrow, to dance, present rushes and refresh itself at the pubs on a different route until it fetches up at St Bartholomew's Church, Ripponden.

This must be the most popular anachronism in Yorkshire! Its traditional function, the provision of rushes to cover the floors of local churches, dates from the time when church floors were made of beaten earth or, at best, covered with stone flags. Once or twice a year the rushes were renewed and the necessity was made the occasion for processions, morris dancing and general jollification.

There can be very few churches, if any, with earth floors today, yet the custom, revived in 1977, goes from strength to strength and its scale would surely delight the people who trundled the old rush-bearing cart in 1906, when the festival was held for the last time in its pre-revival form. That occasion was the golden jubilee of the old Sowerby Bridge Urban District Council. Then, thirty men accompanied by morris dancers pulled the rush-cart through the town.

Over seventy years later, in Silver Jubilee year, celebration was again in the air and Garry Stringfellow, who lives in Hollins Lane, Sowerby Bridge, could think of no better way to celebrate than by reviving the old custom. He talked to friends about his idea and found them as enthusiastic as he was and just as confident that such a revival would put Sowerby Bridge on the tourist map.

He was determined to make it a 'Victorian' occasion, which in his view meant that the rush-bearers must wear panama hats and clogs. He searched the district but not a single panama could be found. Then, on holiday in Cornwall, he found a Mevagissey shop full of panama hats, so he bought sixteen of them and brought them back to Sowerby Bridge. But still he needed more clogs. He found the power-station had a supply of redundant industrial clogs ideal for the job and so close to the sort of clogs worn in 1906 that one of those old Edwardian rush-bearers would never have noticed the difference.

A plate to commemorate the revival of the custom was presented to the Mayor and Mayoress of Calderdale. Bearing a picture of the rush-bearing procession, it was one of a limited edition of 250, the rest of which were put on sale to help raise funds for the celebration.

The date for the revival of the great event was fixed for 3 September 1977. Four churches took part in the rush-bearing ceremonies and two teams of dancers, the Kirkburton Rapier Dancers and the Horwich Morris Dancers – a team which had also danced in 1906, though doubtless this time the personnel were different!

On 3 September the sun rose into a cloudless sky and, to the stirring rhythms of a drum and bugle band, the rush-bearers took up their stangs and the procession set out from Sowerby Bridge Wharf. At Christ Church, Sowerby Bridge, they delivered their rushes, downed stangs and invaded the Commercial Hotel – doubtless in search of a well-earned drink of water – while the morris men entertained the crowd. Then it was up stangs and off again to Tuel Lane Methodist Church. Next stop, St George's Church, Sowerby Lane, with pauses at suitable moments for refreshment and morris dancing.

Whatever else might be said about rush-bearing, it certainly offers a rich field for headline-writing punsters, who are able to use phrases like 'Rushing into next year's ceremony'. That certainly seemed an appropriate comment after the 1977 festival, which was such a success that

Garry Stringfellow and his friends could hardly wait for the next year, when, they promised themselves and Sowerby Bridge, the festival would be bigger and better than ever, lasting three days instead of two, with three groups of morris dancers and deliveries of rushes to five churches – comprising Anglican, Methodist and Roman Catholic, for the rush-bearers are admirably ecumenical! There were hopes, too, of a Victorian market and a barn dance. Speculation was that the event might eventually run into a whole week to incorporate the Halifax September Break.

Never did a small town event 'take off' with such rocket-like impetus. By June of the next year preparations were well under way. This time the procession would be led by a brass band and there was talk of a veritable army of rush-cart-pullers wearing white shirts, black trousers and – of course – clogs and panama hats.

Such a turnout, it was felt, cried out to be dignified by its very own banner. So Mrs Ann Schofield, of

Halifax, set about designing and making one. Five feet square, it depicted not only the rushes, but a castle, recalling the time when Sowerby was fortified, a chapel which once stood near the bridge commemorated in the town's name, and a check pattern from the arms of a local family. The procession alone was to last three and a half hours.

'Hoping for a rush' was the *Halifax Courier* headline, over a story announcing that a rush-bearing exhibition was to be held in the historic Halifax Piece Hall. No doubt the exhibition helped to make the 1978 Rush-bearing the success it was, and by the time it took place on Saturday and Sunday, 2 and 3 September, no one was apparently in any doubt that the custom must become an annual event. Not only had it raised money for charity, but sightseers had come from far and near.

After its triumphal progress, the rush-cart was taken to Ripponden Folk Museum, there to rest until the next year. Meanwhile the

THE CALENDAR YEAR

Sowerby Bridge Rush-bearing Association was formed, and before the end of January 1979 a concert to raise funds had been held in Sowerby Bridge.

It almost goes without saying that the 1979 Rush-bearing was bigger and better than ever, this time with the delightful additional feature of a local councillor voluntarily locked in the stocks to be a target for rotten tomatoes, and supervised by a nineteenth-century 'policeman'.

No sooner is one Rush-bearing over than plans are afoot for the next, with the *Courier* duly announcing, perhaps, 'A Sudden Rush of Culture' at Sowerby Bridge, where the proceedings will be enlivened by, say, the addition of a Medieval Fair, or a Flea Market, or whatever new accompaniment the Rush-bearing Association has dreamed up since the previous year.

By 1981 the event had extended itself to three days and attracted the attentions of the top stars of the morris dancing world, the Abingdon team from Berkshire, who trace their history at least as far back as 1554 and who in 1978 became the only English group or folk organisation to win the Europa Prize for folk art.

Nowadays the Rush-bearing custom seems to involve and embrace every aspect of Sowerby Bridge life. Shopkeepers decorate their windows with model rush-carts, models of morris dancers and Victorian markets and, of course, rushes. 'Rush boom!' comments the *Courier* – and no wonder.

After a recent Rush-bearing the inevitable promise of bigger and better future festivals was made at the Rush-bearing Association's annual meeting. More and more teams of mummers and morris dancers want to join the proceedings, more and more good causes benefit from the proceeds. Fortunately, having true Yorkshiremen as members, the Association acts with proper caution. Before giving away all the proceeds, they agreed to wait until the cost of replacing two tyres on the rush-cart was known . . . Long may it trundle!

St Leger

Saturday in early September, usually at 3.00 p.m.

Doncaster Race Course is on Leger Way, near Doncaster Common and the airport, in a residential area to the south of Doncaster.

The entrance fee varies according to which section of the stands you want to be in.

Race course car park is free to racegoers.

A day at the races

Charles Dickens was enough of a Victorian to moralise about the evils of horse racing when he found himself in Doncaster during Leger Week. It was 1857, and Dickens and his friend Wilkie Collins were working on a series of articles for the magazine *Household Words*, a series which finally developed into the *Lazy Tour of Two Idle Apprentices*. In the course of their tour, on Monday, 14 September, they booked in at the Angel Hotel, a hostelry very much to the novelist's taste.

'We are living in very good, clean and quiet apartments on the second floor,' he wrote in a letter home, 'looking down into the main street, which is full of horse jockeys, bettors, drunkards and other blackguards from morning to night – and all night.'

Despite this apparent disapproval, one can't help sensing a certain relish in the company of such ruffians. But his enjoyment, if any, was short-lived. Dickens was in Doncaster to work, and the town seemed to be conspiring to prevent that. So when the Mayor discovered the great man's presence in the town and called at the Angel to invite him to a public dinner in his honour, Dickens, to use his own words, 'graciously rejected' the invitation. As his life-long friend Forster later remarked, 'the impressions of race week on the novelist were not favourable. It was noise and turmoil all day long, and a gathering of vagabonds from all parts of the

racing earth. Every bad face that had ever caught wickedness from an innocent horse had its representative in the street.'

Notwithstanding these distractions, Dickens and his collaborator stayed the whole week. On the Friday, Leger Day, perhaps with a sense of relief that he would soon be moving on to more peaceful scenes, he ordered the driver of his hired open carriage and pair to take him to the race course.

On arrival he at once bought a race card and declared he would pick the winners of the three main races. And although he didn't know the first thing about racing, each of his choices came in first! Dickens was delighted: he called it 'a wonderful, paralysing coincidence'.

Alas, his pleasure did not last. He was appalled by the enormous losses on every hand and the apparent absence of winners. A man, having lost £2,000, sought solace in drink and, as the landlord explained, 'took terrors' and lay in the doorway of Dickens's bedroom most of the night like 'a groaning phantom'.

The fact that Dickens chose to visit Doncaster rather than York gives some idea of its growing eminence in the racing world of the time. For York might well claim to be Yorkshire's premier racecourse: there was racing near the city even in Roman times in the open spaces of the Forest of Galtres, but the St Leger, last of the annual classics, is run at Doncaster, as well as the William Hill Yorkshire Chase, known as 'the Yorkshire Grand National'.

There was racing at Doncaster before 1600. Until 1766 it was a purely local affair, but in that year a gold cup event was added to the programme and since these trophies were much coveted at the time, the Doncaster course immediately grew in importance. Ten years later the St Leger was instituted, but for some years the Gold Cup remained the great event at Doncaster.

It was in 1776, too, that the decision was made to leave Cantley Common and set up a new course on Doncaster Common with 'a commodious stand . . . The expenses to be paid by the Corporation'. From then on the popularity of the Doncaster course increased by leaps and bounds.

The St Leger, which today draws crowds of thousands to the town, began life quietly enough on 24 September, 1776 as 'sweepstakes of 25 guineas each, for three-year-olds; colts 8st, fillies 7st 12lb'.

It did not appear in *The Racing Calendar* under its present name until 1778. And it was given that name in honour of a renowned sportsman, Colonel Anthony St Leger. An Irishman and a former M.P., the colonel had married an heiress at Wombwell and bought an estate. He never won the race that bore his name, though in the first and fourth years his own horses came in second.

By 1800 your chances of finding a bed in Doncaster during Race Week were virtually nil. Every inn, every house was overflowing and an air of excitement and carnival pervaded the town.

Racing was only a part – if the main part – of the jollifications. You could ride to hounds with the Badsworth or the Sandbeck, wager on a cockfight, or a prize-fight, watch sales of livestock outside the Salutation Inn; there were

'balls, assemblies and routs', plays at the theatre and, for VIPs, no end of hospitality provided by the Corporation. What had been a small local race meeting had become a great northern sporting and social event patronised by the aristocracy.

In 1803, Doncaster Corporation, clearly prepared to go to any lengths to ensure the success of municipal hospitality, 'ordered that the Mayor shall hire that fat cook at the Angel called Winterbotham to be cook at the Mansion House upon the same terms as the other two women kept there and paid by the corporation.' Seven years later a council minute authorised the payment to the fat cook of a rise to 10s 6d a week.

There were times, perhaps, when the city fathers wondered if they had created a monster.

The chief cause of alarm was the gambling frenzy which seized the town during Race Week, both on and off the track. Gaming tables were erected in the market place and high rents were charged for rooms hired for roulette games.

It wasn't so much the gambling as the attendant evils which worried the authorities. Most of the games of chance (so-called) were almost certainly rigged. The cock-fighting too, was attended with unseemly practices – a welsher could find himself suspended in a basket above the pits as a visible discouragement to others similarly tempted.

In 1808 there was a great scandal. A number of horses were poisoned with arsenic placed in the water troughs on Town Moor. Presumably the culprit got away with his crime – if so, he was lucky to do so: a man found guilty of a

155

touch luggage . . . Guards whispered behind their hands to station-masters of horses and John Scott. Men in cut-away coats and speckled cravats fastened with peculiar pins, and with the large bones of their legs developed under tight trousers so that they look as much as possible like horses' legs, paced up and down at junction stations, speaking low and moody of horses and John Scott.'

The ghost of John Scott surely attended the 200th anniversary celebration of the St Leger in 1976, an occasion worthy of the old city fathers who originally launched and promoted the event with such panache. Scott's spectre would doubtless be as recognisable as he himself was in life, with his drab knee breeches, gaiters, black coat, broad-brimmed hat and dazzling white handkerchief. For many years that had been what your true horsey man wore to the St Leger and Scott was the last of his generation to be seen thus attired.

On that 200th anniversary occasion in 1976, the names of 199 St Leger winners of the past lived once more as Boy Scouts and Girl Guides carried them around the course inscribed on wooden signs.

Allabaculia, Ambidexter, Ambrosio . . . Scott would have known the names, if some in that crowd of 1976 could hardly pronounce them. Such legendary winners included Antonio, the horse which in 1819 won, lost and won again! In the first race Antonio was away so quickly ahead of the rest of the field that a false start was declared and his victory was overruled. The race was re-run but this time Antonio himself failed to start and the prize was awarded to a horse called Sir Walter. However, an appeal was made to the Jockey Club, who declared that the first decision was the right one; Antonio was the winner, they said, and the race should never have been re-run.

In 1821, another Scott famous in the annals of the Leger, William Scott, won the race on a formidable mount called Jack Spigot, despite the fact that the

similar offence a few years later at Newmarket was hanged from the top of Cambridge Castle before a crowd of 12,000.

Still the abuses attendant upon wild gambling continued, but when the authorities tried to suppress it in 1825 the result was little short of open rebellion and the 3rd Light Dragoons and 3rd West Yorks Militia were called out.

Obviously nothing was going to be allowed to rob Doncaster of its Race Week fun. At the Mayor's ball of 1830, one of the most interesting guests was the beautiful Countess Sarwitzzi, widow of a Polish nobleman, who had written to the Mayor, from her lodging at the unfailingly fashionable Angel, inviting herself – provided the mayor considered it would be proper for her to go 'unattended except by servants'.

Every attention was lavished on the glamorous countess until some redcoats from a local barracks greeted her with great back-slapping familiarity as 'Rose'. I hope the bigwigs who had been the victims of Rose's joke took it all with the same good humour!

At the time of Dickens's visit, the hero of Doncaster and the St Leger was John Scott, the 'Wizard of the North', who won the race that year with his own horse Imperieuse and trained 14 other Leger winners.

Dickens claimed that he arrived at Doncaster Station to find the entire staff gripped by St Leger fever. Forty extra porters were on duty, but he found 'all of them making up their betting books in the lamp room or somewhere else and none of them to come in and

animal could not stand the sight of him! The horse was said to fly into a tantrum at the mere sound of the jockey's name and he would never allow him to enter the box.

The following year the race was won by a lame horse, Theodore, though at first his jockey, John Jackson, refused to ride 'such a cripple'. In view of the colt's condition, one of the eccentric bets laid against him was £1,000 to a walking stick.

Memnon, Elis (for whom the first horse-van was made), Voltigeur . . . the names of these winners still resound in the chronicles of the Turf and many were the treasured relics of them. John Scott, the legendary trainer, used a carving knife made from

the shankbone of Rowton, the winner of the 1829 event, and ink-stands were made from the feet of the 1835 winner, Queen of Trumps.

Today the Doncaster course is regarded as possibly the best in England. For the statistically inclined, the flat-race course is 1 mile 7½ furlongs, with a minimum width of 90 feet. The St Leger is run over a distance of 1 mile, 6 furlongs, 127 yards so, like all other races of more than one mile, it takes place on the round course. Just over half a mile (4½ furlongs) from the winning post, at the run-in, the round course is joined by a straight mile. The course is completely flat except for a short rise between the 1½ mile and the finish. National

Hunt racing, over steeplechases and hurdles, is run on a left-handed course of approximately two miles.

The St Leger continues to draw the finest bloodstock and the best riders to Doncaster. Held in early September, it is a truly international event, frequently attended by Royalty. As Yorkshire's only classic race, the Leger sheds lustre on both the town and the county that gave it birth. It is, in fact, the world's oldest classic, being the first of its type. Of the other classics, the Oaks (Epsom) was first run in 1779, the Derby (Epsom) in 1780, the 2,000 Guineas (Newmarket) in 1809 and the 1,000 Guineas (Newmarket) in 1814.

Chatsworth Country Fair

Saturday and Sunday, early September

Chatsworth Park, Edensor, Derbyshire.

Car park charge also lets you into the grounds, where the fair is held. There is an additional fee for the house, but reduced rate for Country Fair visitors.

Scarborough Cricket Festival

Ten days in early September

Cricket Ground, North Marine Road, Scarborough.

North Marine Road is on the north side of Scarborough, on the cliff. Parking is limited, so it's best to get there early. Tickets are available from Scarborough Cricket Club or on the gate.

'Nowt else to touch it'

Freddie Trueman – and who should know better? – has gone on record as saying of the Scarborough Cricket Festival, 'Believe me, sunshine, it's the greatest in England – there's nowt else to touch it.'

It is surely fitting that the uniquely Yorkshire resort of Scarborough should be the setting for this festival of the Yorkshire game and that Frederick Sewards Trueman's opinion on the subject should be respectfully recorded. For Freddie is in the grand tradition of Yorkshire cricket characters such as graced the game a century and more ago and helped to establish the Festival as an event of classic stature.

The reason for the existence of the Scarborough Cricket Festival can best be sought in the pride and ambition of the Scarborough Club and the men who made it. It was founded in 1849 and reconstituted in 1863 when it acquired a new ground in North Marine Road. In 1871 the new ground was the scene of a forerunner of the Festivals when Lord Londesborough's XI played Scarborough Visitors. So proud was the club of its new ground and the pavilion, which in 1874 cost £234 to build, that Yorkshire were urged to stage a fixture there.

One name in particular is revered in the Scarborough club's annals – that of Robert Baker, the one-time secretary who with Lord Londesborough in 1875 brought about a match at Scarborough between Yorkshire and MCC. It ended in a draw, as many good matches do, but proved decisive enough in its purpose, for the following year saw the launching of the Scarborough Festival with a full nine days of cricket. The MCC became regular participants, as did the touring sides and the holders of all the greatest names that have adorned the most English of games.

For the best part of a century now – excluding only the war years – Scarborough has provided cricket with an historic showpiece.

For a sample of the superb quality it offers, look at the programme of the 1982 festival – an Under-Nineteen Test Match between England and the West Indies; D.B. Close's XI v Pakistan; the ASDA Challenge, played out between Yorkshire, Lancashire, Nottinghamshire and Derbyshire; Yorkshire v Derbyshire in the Schweppes Championship; and a Battle of the Brewers between a Courage XI and a John Smith XI.

Anyone watching a Scarborough Festival match today is participating in a ritual which might well induce a 'timeslip' experience, especially if he has recently been poring over his old copies of *Wisden* . . . Under the Scarborough spell he might, for instance, fall into a happy daydream in which the players defending their wickets against a visiting MCC bear the names *Bates* and *Emmett*!

Emmett . . . *Emmett*? Can it be possible that this is the one and only Clown Prince of Yorkshire cricket? Of course it's not possible – and yet . . . look harder at the player at the crease, noting the moustache that might have been borrowed from a dashing young walrus, the white-spotted tie which looks as though some joker

has taken the scissors to it, the quizzical eyebrows, and the cap that only just covers the top of the bullet head, the nose, as bright and red as the ball itself. It must be – it can only be – *the* Tom Emmett.

Then doubtless Tom was one of those to blame for the fact that play hadn't started until 12.45? 'It 'ud be Tom all reight', says the spectator on the observer's left, having presumably read his thoughts. ''E nivver was famous for turnin' up early wasn't Tom.

But he can laik cricket though, can our Tom. He can that!' 'It's a good job 'e can – they've been throwin' t' match away up to now', says the spectator on the right in tones more appropriate to a national disaster of unprecendented proportions.

Certainly the Yorkshiremen have lost their first five wickets pretty cheaply. When Emmett took his stance at the crease opposite Billy Bates the scoreboard showed no more than 59 and one of the casualties had

been the autocratic, aristocratic captain, the future Lord Hawke himself, who was caught for 25. It had been the best of a poor lot, but as the spectator on the right of our observer pontificates, 'By rights, 'Awke shouldn't be laikin' at all – nivver mind bein' captain!'

'Why not?' asks our observer in reckless innocence.

''Cause he was born somewhere near *Gainsborough*, that's why not. An' Gainsborough,' added the spectator on the right, with the

patience of one imparting difficult propositions to a half-wit, 'is in *Lincolnshire*. So he's nobbut a *yellow-belly*.'

Clearly our observer fails to see the point. Consequently the combined effect of glacial looks both from left and right freeze him to silence for the rest of the afternoon. More eloquently than any words could have put it, those glances say, 'If this idiot doesn't know that you have to be born in Yorkshire to play for the county, we neither accept responsibility for him, nor even acknowledge his existence on this planet'.

Thereafter they talk round, past and over him. And their talk is all of Tom Emmett and his erratic, joking ways; his cheeky manner in dealing with his blue-blooded captain. And all the time, as if in contradiction, Tom is batting with a steadiness that Wisden will applaud, while Billy Bates at the other end is bringing the Yorkshire crowd to its feet as he piles run upon run.

Halifax-born, Tom Emmett had himself been professional captain of Yorkshire for five seasons before handing over his wayward collection of players to that ambitious amateur and gentleman, Martin Hawke. 'Louis Hall and ten ale cans', his lordship was to call them in later years, Louis Hall being the sober-sided, chapel-going exception whose gloomy, dark-whiskered visage sticks out in team photographs as cheerful as an alcoholic at a temperance picnic.

Tom Emmett was one of the best bowlers of his time, but like other of the 'ale cans', such as 'Happy Jack' Ullyett and Bobby Peel, he did not always take his cricket too seriously. Even when reporting on the failings of a temporarily butter-fingered Yorkshire side he had been unable to do it with proper solemnity – 'You'll find there's an epidemic in this team,' he told Lord Hawke one day, 'but don't fret yerself, sir, it isn't catching'.

'Hey up!' says the spectator on the left, "E's out! Bates is out!'

'Caught Wright,' says the spectator on the right.

'And bowled Billy Barnes,' says the spectator on the left. 'For seventy-five.'

'Nine fours, five threes, five twos an' fourteen singles,' says his statistical companion. 'Hurray, hurray,' he cries, joining in the chorus of acclamation that greets Bates as he strolls back to the pavilion. 'Well done the Duke . . . they call 'im that,' he adds confidentially to anyone who cares to listen, "cos he dresses like a toff.'

"E's a good singer though,' opines the spectator on the left

inconsequentially. 'When he went to Australia an' t' ship called at Sandwich Islands, cannibal king came on board every day to hear Billy Bates sing "The Bonny Yorkshire Lass" for 'im.'

'Who's goin' in now?' enquires the spectator on the right.

'Mary Ann,' is the somewhat confusing reply. 'Go on, Ephraim lad.'

The new batsman's official name is Ephraim Lockwood, but to his team-mates he is invariably Mary Ann, a cognomen he accepts without demur, having no illusions either about the quickness of his wits or his undoubted abilities as a cricketer.

But this isn't Ephraim's day. Top of the batting averages he may have been when Richard Daft took a team from Yorkshire and Notts to America in 1879, but today he manages only a miserable two before being caught out. Even so, he does better than E.T. Hirst, who achieves only a duck despite the gentlemanly 'Esquire' that follows his name.

Being a mere professional, Tom Emmett, whose 'sound and steady', if low-scoring, batting is also to win Wisden's praise, has no esquire to his name but he manages a score of nineteen before he becomes the fifth victim of the relentless Barnes. It is off a Barnes ball that H.E. Rhodes (Esq.) is caught by Schultz – and his wicket goes for nothing.

Then begins a partnership which raises the Yorkshire crowd's hats, hearts and voices as Ted Peate and Bobby Peel defend their wickets against the best and worst the enemy can throw at them. Together they contribute eighty-one to Yorkshire's first innings score of 228. MCC and Ground, as the visiting team are cumbersomely named, then score 222, which seems to promise that the second day will produce a keen contest.

Perhaps it is the sheer nerve of the visiting team in almost equalling the Yorkshire score that makes 'Happy Jack' Ullyett open his mighty shoulders and knock spots off the visitors' bowling. Before his wicket is skittled, he has

knocked two sixes out of the ground, ten fours, eight twos and sixteen singles, a total of eighty-four.

During that second Yorkshire innings the Hon. M.B. Hawke scores twenty-two and 'Mary Ann' Lockwood makes amends for his meagre two in the first innings by scoring a 'very fine' seventy-nine. Thereafter, the highest Yorkshire score is twenty-four by E.T. Hirst, and of the six players that follow, three score ducks.

Now MCC need 269 to win, but they have only fifty minutes left to play and the sum total of their efforts is sixty-three for three. And so, according to the peculiar logic of cricket, the game is declared a draw.

Then, and only then, does our observer notice the date on the Leeds Mercury carried by the spectator on the right. It is 1 September 1883 . . .

Emmett and the rest of the 'Ten Ale Cans' had their being in what has been called the Golden Age of Yorkshire Cricket; but here at Scarborough the golden age seems as permanent as the golden sands. A selection of golden moments might include 'Buns' Thornton, the Botham of his day, making 107 in seventy minutes in 1886 and landing one of his eight sixes in Trafalgar Square outside the ground . . . the immortal George Hirst saying farewell to cricket from the pavilion balcony in 1921 . . . Hobbs's and Sutcliffe's partnerships in 1931 of 243 against New Zealand and 227 against the Gentlemen.

But the great names and heroic feats must not eclipse the dedicated efficiency and enthusiasm behind the scenes; it wins all too little recognition, though without it the golden moments would have no setting. As Freddie himself would doubtless tell you, 'There's nothing like it, sunshine.' And as the Festival moves on towards the start of its own second century, we can be confident that the unsung heroes, as well as the stars, will ensure that 'Scarborough' remains a jewel in the crown of cricket.

Burghley Horse Trials

Wednesday – Sunday,
second week in September.

Burghley Park, near Stamford.

The trials consist of dressage,
cross country and show jumping
(Sunday) and attract spectators
from miles around. Buy tickets at
the event; entrance is usually
charged by the car and there is a
large car park. Tickets are dearer
on Saturday.

Burghley is off the A1 near
Stamford and the event is well
signed by the AA.

Old Masters, young riders

Just a mile to the south-east of
Stamford is Burghley House, built
by Sir William Cecil, Lord Burghley
(1520-1598) Secretary of State and
Lord High Treasurer to Queen
Elizabeth I. Now the home of the
Marquess of Exeter, it is one of the
most important surviving
examples of Elizabethan
architecture, with three
completely different façades and a
roof fantastic with spires and
cupolas. The fifth and ninth Earls
of Exeter are chiefly to thank for
the splendour of the interior, hung
with many Old Masters collected
by the ninth Earl. He was also
responsible for the layout of the
grounds and park, which come
alive with activity during the great
international Burghley Horse
Trials.

Burghley always attracts a large
entry of experienced riders. It has
been the venue for World
Championships and European
Championships, as well as
European Junior Championships,
but takes pride in the fact that on
only a few occasions during its
history of over twenty years has
the winner been a rider from
overseas.

On arrival, the riders are briefed
and introduced to the roads and
tracks and courses they are to use,
and the horses are given a
veterinary examination. The first
two days are taken up with
dressage, well described as 'ballet
for horses', during which the
Ground Jury award marks to
horses whose performances of
drill movements indicate
suppleness, obedience and
calmness. The most popular
section is the cross-country phase
on the following day, with maybe
twenty-seven fences. The last day
sees the show-jumping phase,
during which the horses'
suppleness and obedience
(despite the exertions of the
previous day) are tested over a
course of ten to twelve obstacles.

Besides the Three-Day Event,
there are classes for Ridden and
Working Hunters, Pony Club
Jumping and parades of horses
and hounds, all of which help to
make Burghley one of the great
equestrian events of the region
and, indeed, of the country.

THE CALENDAR YEAR

Harrogate Autumn Flower Show

Thursday – Saturday,
mid-September

New Exhibition Hall, Harrogate.

Open to the public. There is an
entrance fee.

The car park may be in use, but
there is a reasonable amount of
parking space in the roads nearby.
Town centre parking usually
restricted to 2 hours.

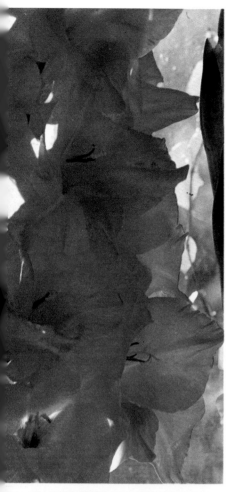

Northern Antique Dealers' Fair

One week's duration in late September

Royal Baths Assembly Rooms, Crescent Road, Harrogate.

Open to the public. There is an entrance fee.

There is a pay and display car park to the rear of the Royal Baths, in Montpellier Gardens, off Royal Parade.

To stand the test of time

'High quality', said the man at the press preview for the Northern Antique Dealers' Fair, 'is the only thing that stands the test of time.' A truism on the face of it, but a comforting one, nevertheless, and one that we are learning to appreciate more and more. Belief in personal immortality may have faded, but the thought that beauty will resurface and assert its claim to our attention after years of neglect seems to tell us that some things, at least, are lasting, no matter how fashions may fluctuate.

There never was a time, indeed, when we were told so frequently that there's 'a future for the past' – a headline-writer's cliché, of course, but clichés are never without an element of truth and usually a large one at that. Nor was there ever a time when experts on past craftsmanship, such as Arthur Negus, could be surer of an admiring following.

'While major fairs in London are jockeying for positions of priority and prestige,' says the Fair's publicity, stoutly, 'the Northern Antique Dealers' Fair still claims its prime position as Britain's leading antiques' fair.' Furthermore, 'while some fairs are adjusting their date-lines nearer our own times – some even to the immediate pre-war period – the NADF adheres strictly to its 1840 furniture date-line . . . We are an ANTIQUES' fair, and that is what we intend to remain.'

Such phrases carry the ring of pride and confidence that throughout the fair pervaded the Royal Baths Assembly Rooms, a

building which might well be claimed as an antique in its own right – as indeed might Harrogate itself – and a highly successful one. Yet when it was opened in the 1890s, the purpose of the Royal Baths was anything but antiquated. It was indeed the height of fashion to come to Harrogate for hydro-therapeutic treatment – and to Harrogate they came in their thousands, from far beyond Yorkshire, for this was an international healing centre.

Would it be whimsical to claim that its effect is therapeutic still? That the 10,000 visitors the organisers were hoping for would receive a balm to their spirits whether or not they made a purchase to enrich their homes or as a hedge against inflation?

You can, of course, see lovely things in museums, but even the best of museums, with or without stuffed animals, is in a sense a graveyard. At Harrogate, on the other hand, we have a *fair*, and though there are no roundabouts or coconut shies, it is the fair atmosphere that prevails. There is, too, a calm and scholarly *busyness*, a controlled delight in beauty, and the somehow reassuring knowledge that the pictures and furniture and silver and glassware

TABLES SEEN
GROWN BY:
NNELL? OF
DEN } LEEDS
R CONSUMATE

THESE PLANTS WERE
ALL FED WITH
CHEMDAK LIQUID
FERTILIZERS

that we saw could be bought by those with money enough, and handled and examined even by those who could afford no more than the entrance fee.

The variety of articles displayed on more than fifty stands, by almost the same number of exhibitors, seemed limitless. Pride of place, perhaps, was held by the Kniphausen Hawk, on loan from Chatsworth House. Dated 1697, it had once belonged to 'George William Kniphausen, Count of the Holy Roman Empire', who, according to its Latin inscription, 'dedicated the eagle bespangled with gems to eternal remembrance'. As magnificent as its inscription suggested, the eagle was intended to 'remain for ever in the possession of the illustrious lords of the castle of Nienort' in Germany. In fact, it vanished from the castle in the eighteenth century. It was exhibited at the Great Exhibition

of 1851, on loan from the Sixth Duke of Devonshire, though how it came into the Chatsworth collection remains something of a mystery.

Vignettes of the fair linger vividly in the mind: a wall full of marine paintings, one of them a whaling scene and therefore a rarity in itself, explained the exhibitor; oriental carpets; an eighteenth-century bronze sundial; a morrocco-bound Breeches Bible of 1597; a seventeenth-century carved oak cradle believed to have come from the Bishop's Palace in Carmarthen; a magical candlelit market scene by Peter Van Schendel (1806-1870) and – a homely touch – a hand-coloured lithograph by J. Stubbs, captioned 'Spa Well, Low Harrowgate, 1829'.

But every visitor takes away a different set of images – of a lovely George I walnut bureau, perhaps, or an Anglo-Dutch chest of

drawers, circa 1690, decorated with marquetry of a barely believable intricacy, or Sarah Millington's sampler of Solomon's Temple, finished in 1849 (surely Solomon in all his glory could not have commanded more dedication than went into Sarah's stitches depicting his temple, with its pillars and turrets and rows of many windows).

Perhaps this is partly why the exhibits had an appeal quite unrelated to their estimated £3 million value. Here were no plastic products of a mindless machine: *somebody* poured into each of these artefacts all the skill and talent that gave him purpose and status in a life that ended long ago. Who was Sarah Millington?

What sort of lives were led by 'JO' and 'OM' whose initials, with the date 1590, are carved on the headboard of an oak poster bed? We wonder, and by wondering, we somehow bring them back to life.

Snape Castle Chapel Harvest Festival

Sunday, last weekend in September

Snape Castle, near Bedale, North Yorkshire

Snape is about 2 miles south of Bedale and 9 miles north of Ripon on a minor road west of the A1. The service is open to the public and there is parking in the village.

Diocesan Harvest Thanksgiving

Second Sunday in October, 3.00 p.m.

Lincoln Cathedral.

Church service, open to the public. A number of public car parks in Lincoln Town Centre.

Harvest Home

Each autumn, the air of churches ranging from the fifteenth-century Snape Castle chapel to magnificent Lincoln Cathedral is tinged with the ravishing 'incense' of fresh fruit and vegetables. If there were a league for delightful harvest festivals, these two might well be near the top. At Snape the village church is the erstwhile castle chapel, and here the home-grown produce that delights the senses (even before it is eaten) has rich wood carving and medieval glass for a background, while the ceiling bears faint traces of an ancient fresco. At the other end of the scale is Lincoln Cathedral (once the centre of a diocese stretching from the Humber to the Thames), with its two large circular windows, the 'Bishop's Eye' and the 'Dean's Eye', and the splendid 'Geometrical' Angel Choir dating from 1255.

For all its popularity and well-loved hymns, the harvest festival church service is of comparatively recent origin. After the harvest, farm labourers, who were paid in gold sovereigns (called hossmen because of the image of St George), saw more money than they had seen in the whole of the year, and the temptation to booze

THE CALENDAR YEAR

away a raging thirst was usually all too strong. Late on the night of the Harvest Home, the supposed breadwinner might stagger home with a skinful of ale but little money to ensure full bellies for his family during the coming winter.

We probably have a Cornish vicar, R.S. Hawker of Morwenstow, to thank for our harvest festival services. In 1843 he reintroduced to his parish the ancient thanksgiving festival of Lammas, switching it from 1 August to 1 October, and throughout the country other conscientious clerics were quick to follow his lead with the aim of bringing a 'respectable' element to the harvest celebrations and pointing out the waste of hard-earned money.

For all our nostalgic imaginings harvest was in days gone by a tight-lipped, anxious, no-nonsense sort of time, when success or failure depended largely on the moods of the Corn Mother or earth goddess: the Greeks called her Demeter, the Romans, Ceres, and the British, rather surprisingly, and pessimistically perhaps, the 'White Lady of Death', for the continuance of life itself was in her hands.

If she had been happy through the year, then *everyone* was happy, for the harvest would be a good one: men and women and their children could hope to eat and live through the dark, bitter months.

Early harvesters had little to learn from today's time and motion experts: those early methods were undoubtedly primitive but the full human resources of the group, family or farm were marshalled. In command of casual labourers hired for the season was the man whose title Lord of the Harvest, reflected the importance of his task. He led the men who formed a dogged, tireless line the width of the field, each of their sickles cutting an armful of corn with every step which the old men, women and children who followed would gather and bind into sheaves for other workers to set up in stooks to dry.

The Lord of the Harvest was often assisted by his Lady, who led the female workers. Both were elected by the labour force and represented them, like early shop-stewards, in negotiations with the farmer.

In the old hand-reaping days, the work had to be done with the utmost speed, and anxious glances were raised to the sky whenever a cloud obscured the sun. Even when the whole field stood to attention, a parade-ground of stooks, there was anxiety lest the white Lady of Death should frown and the drying of the corn should be delayed. Once it was dry, the corn must be stored in barns until threshing time in the winter.

Wagon after wagon was loaded and sent trundling away, and as each wagon was filled the hearts of the workers became a little lighter, for the chances were visibly growing that the field would be cleared that night.

No wonder, then, that the loading of the last wagon of all was a joy in itself, in spite of aching backs and limbs. This wagon even had a name of its own – the Hock or Horkey cart; its horses were gaily decked with ribbons and flowers and the last sheaf that was gathered was twisted and formed into the shape of a woman and set on the very top of the load – it represented the Corn Mother riding in triumph as her progeny was carried home.

Now the grateful poor would trickle hopefully into the field to glean, as was their right, whatever was left. And since gleaning could last for three weeks, there must have been plenty. Fights, alas, were apt to break out over these leavings.

From the very last sheaf of corn were also made the corn dollies, which again represented the Corn Mother, though different areas had their different shapes. Thus, in Suffolk we find the horseshoe and in Cambridgeshire the bell; there was the harvest cross of Devonshire, the fan of the Welsh

borders, and the lantern of Hereford and Norfolk. Whatever shape it took, the 'idol' (which is the real meaning of dolly) was believed to contain the spirit of the corn. It had to be preserved so that it might be born to fresh life the following spring. In return, it protected the household from the perils of the winter ahead.

There was no time like the harvest for fun and frolic! Indeed, it was possibly the only time our hard-working ancestors really let off steam. Without a good harvest, folk would be lucky to have a Christmas dinner, or even, perhaps, to avoid starvation.

The Harvest, Mell or Horkey Supper is still held on many farms even today, but it is rarely the occasion it used to be when working hours were long and pleasures were simple and came but rarely. Flowers adorned the barn or shed cleared out for the occasion; there was abundant food and drink of every kind – a traditional dish was huge pies made from rabbits shot in the cornfields. Toasts were drunk, games and jokes were played, and for those still able to stand, the evening ended with dancing.

The Lord of the Harvest had many duties, which varied from

one part of the country to another. In parts of East Anglia he would go begging contributions for the supper from tradesmen who dealt with the farm, or indeed from anyone who might pass the harvest field. And he would initiate newcomers to the field by tapping their shoe soles with a stone and exacting a shilling for beer as payment. At the supper itself he might don a mummer's robe and become a master of ceremonies for the jollifications which followed.

Often these were inseparable from the main business of the evening – drinking! In some parts of the country, tall hats were handed out to the men and full mugs of beer or cider placed on top of the hats. Now, balancing the mug on the hat, the men had to drink the contents of the mug without handling it, jerk the mug in the air and catch it, as it fell, in the upturned hat. If they failed, they had to do it all over again – and naturally it didn't get any easier. However, since the chairman usually had to have a drink whenever a competitor did, the supervision was possibly not over-strict!

In another game a lighted candle placed in a glass of beer had to be held in place by the drinker's nose and the glass emptied while the onlookers sang a song. There must have been a few burnt noses after harvest suppers.

The object of many of the games seems to have been to make the main activity – drinking as much as possible – as difficult as possible. In Norfolk, the specially potent Horkey (harvest) beer would be sent by one man to 'chase the old fox down the red lane' (the tongue, down the throat), while his neighbour did all he could to prevent the operation. And the song that accompanied this game ran 'Lift up your elbow and hold up your chin and let your neighbour joggle it in'. It is hardly surprising that in some areas the harvest supper was followed by a day's holiday called the Drinking Day – presumably a euphemism for Hangover Day!

Three Peaks Cycle Race

Last Sunday in September,
10.00 a.m.

Starts at the Café, Horton-in-
Ribblesdale and covers
Pen-y-Ghent, Whernside and
Ingleborough.

Horton-in-Ribblesdale is about 5
miles north of Settle and
accessible by road. Open to
observers; parking nearby.

Fellow mortals,
only thinner

From Skipton onwards the signs
were unmistakable – little knots of
pedalling pilgrims all heading
towards Horton-in-Ribblesdale.
And at Horton itself, yellow No
Parking cones lining the roadside,
police at junctions, a mountain
rescue Land Rover, and
everywhere the crowds who were
there to see the impossible –
at least for most of us – the ascent
of the Three Peaks by men on
bicycles.

Besides the six men comprising the Swiss and British teams, there were 139 other entrants, including three women, from clubs as far afield as Bournemouth, Cardiff, Dundee, and Sussex and Kent. Due to land erosion ('caused by bad weather and walkers', as a press release put it), the original route had had to be changed, making it longer by three kilometres, a total of fifty kilometres in all.

Whernside, Ingleborough and Pen-y-Ghent may be mere midgets by Himalayan standards, but they present a unique challenge to the British cycling fraternity. And not just to them, for more recently the Swiss, too, have succumbed to the lure of Yorkshire's family of mini-mountains. But if 'the world's toughest cyclo-cross race', organised by Bradford Racing Cycling Club, is now an international event, it remains as truly Yorkshire as the Scarborough Cricket Festival; and it was a Keighley rider, Eric Stone, leader of the British team (all from Yorkshire) who pedalled home first, for the fifth time (that was a record in itself), with Swiss riders taking second and third places.

Two-wheeled conquest of the Three Peaks is a comparatively recent development. The first 'Three Peakers', as members of this élite fellowship are called, made the circuit of summits on foot. Why did they do it? Because the Peaks 'were there', of course, but more especially because they were close enough together to make the journey feasible within about twelve hours.

The present-day wheeled flyers are the heirs and successors to the very first Three Peaks Walkers – or at least, the first on record – who were two masters from Giggleswick School, Canon J.R. Wynne-Edwards and D.R. Smith. One day in 1887 they set out to walk by way of Ingleborough (790 metres) to the Hill Inn, Chapel-le-Dale, where they had tea. Then, obviously well fortified, they embarked on the conquest of Whernside's 806 metres. After that, they just had to get the better, that same day, of

Pen-y-Ghent (758 metres).

They little knew what they had started. In time, the walkers gave way to runners and last, and most spectacularly, came the cyclists; though even they have to resort to their feet for at least eight kilometres, during which they push or carry their machines. Hardly surprising, is it, that during those fifty kilometres a cyclist might lose three or four kilograms in weight?

From a sports field at Horton-in-Ribblesdale the contestants ride to Selside, then on to Ribblehead where the twenty-four arches of the Ribblehead Viaduct on the famed Settle-Carlisle line challenge the vast bulk of Whernside.

If they allowed themselves to notice it, they would surely lose time by admiring the view. Beyond Ribblehead the road passes between Whernside and Ingleborough, the smooth flanks of the former perhaps dappled in sunlight, while Ingleborough's jutting, challenging profile sulks blackly beneath lowering clouds.

In elevation, the course resembles a giant switchback. From the summit of Whernside it swoops down to Chapel-le-Dale, whose little church contains a monument to navvies who died in their hundreds in a smallpox epidemic during the building of the 'Settle-Carlisle'. Their rumbustious ghosts must surely utter silent cheers as the flying wheels go by, climbing again, now, by way of Skirwith, to the crown of Ingleborough, so named because beacons once blazed there at times of national ferment.

From Ingleborough, it's down again to Horton and then up to Pen-y-Ghent, whose Celtic name conjures visions of the Brigantes, then back down to Horton, where a shivering crowd receives a laconic broadcast commentary on the progress of the two leading riders as relayed to the commentator by radio: 'Stone is still leading . . . but it's like my front room – there's not much in it!' There were in fact only twenty seconds between them at one point.

And here at last the conquering hero comes . . . Eric Stone, the

North of England cyclo-cross champion from Keighley, bowls into the field and straight for the finish line, with time now to grin through the mud on his face and to acknowledge the cheers of his fans. He had led virtually from the start and he finished 1 minute 29 seconds ahead of Arthur Manz, the Swiss who won the previous year, while Eric was apparently taking a rest (just like the year before, when John North took the prize with a lead time of 3 hours 16 seconds).

Stone's time today is 3 hours 12 minutes 10 seconds, by no means his best – eleven years ago, when the distance was forty kilometres, he did it in 2.37.33, which has remained a record since the event began in 1961. Well might he look happy as he crosses the line – he's done it again, at thirty-seven, five years older than 'Turi' Manz and *seventeen* years older than Philip Webster, the youngest member of the British team. And he's done it in gruelling conditions of wind and rain, bounding up mountainsides like a chamois – if chamois were ever known to carry bicycles on their shoulders.

Well done, Eric lad! And well done John Rawnsley, who not only organised the race but also competed, and finished it for the twenty-second consecutive year, bringing his total of Three Peaks conquests, by bike and on foot, to ninety. Well done, in fact, all the 118 who finished the course . . . or who simply did the best they could.

Leeds International Pianoforte Competition

Triennial event held in late September

Main events take place in the Town Hall, Headrow, although some are held at the University. Tickets usually available from the Tourist Information Office in Calverley Street, which is the main box office for the Town Hall.

Free parking in the evening in the streets around the Town Hall. There is also a large car park behind the International Pool, Westgate, some 10 minutes walk away.

Blessing the Boats, Whitby

End September/early October 2.30 p.m.

Harbour Front and Fish Pier.

Open air service taken by the Rector of Whitby and one other. Open to the public.

A garland on the sea

It happens in autumn at Whitby. Holidaymakers, in a few moments of solemnity, join the quayside crowd for the blessing of the fishing fleet. Their mood is more than merely curious, for we are an island people and the sea flows strong enough in our veins for us to understand the prayer of the Breton fisherman –

Protect me, O Lord;
My boat is so small
And your sea is so large
Even the names of the Whitby boats – names like *Pilot Me* – are sometimes a prayer in themselves.

Seashore folk the world over have always feared the power of that same mysterious ocean from which they drew their life. Upon its moods their very existence depended, and so the sea – or the spirits that stirred beneath it – had to be soothed and gratified; its rage, once aroused, was terrible.

Long ago, the favour of the sea-gods was sought by the offering of sacrifices . . . human sometimes, though in gentler ages a less

ferocious deity might accept garlands cast upon the sea's surface. In England, the Church converted such ceremonies, just as it christianised so much else of life, but the roots remain the same. And so there may well be a surprising kinship between the noisy, colourful Dragon Boat Festival in China and the homely festival on the quayside at Whitby, when God's blessing is sought for the fishing fleet and the men who man each boat.

Whitby bears upon its very stones the imprint of England's Christian history. Overlooking the harbour and the red-roofed old houses, on a hill to the east of the River Esk, stand the ruins of Whitby Abbey. The Abbey was founded over 1300 years ago. Then, in 867, the same Vikings who first brought the design of the present-day fishing coble to these shores, set its walls of wattle and daub ablaze against the eastern sky. The Normans refounded it but, following the Dissolution of the Monasteries, it fell into ruins. During the First World War, other enemies added their quota of destruction with high explosive shells hurled from the sea.

Ruin though it is, it seems almost designed for its cliff-top situation. Its great north transept and other ragged fragments survive as memorials to the glory of the Early English style. Here, in the Saxon abbey, ruled one of the great figures who have made the name of Whitby secure in history – the lady Hild (St Hilda), the formidable and legendary abbess who had power over even the animals. She turned serpents into stone, it was said, though in sober fact, the 'snakes' are really ammonites, fossilised molluscs.

Hilda it was who encouraged Caedmon, the poetic cowherd, to sing the songs of creation which first came to him in a dream. And so Caedmon became 'the father of English sacred poetry'. Close to the ruins there stands today a twenty-foot cross to his memory, unveiled in 1893 by Alfred Austin, then Poet Laureate, and inscribed with the first nine lines of Caedmon's wonderful hymn. Next to Caedmon's Cross is St

Mary's parish church at the top of Yorkshire's best known steps – 199 of them, as many Yorkshire children have laboriously discovered by counting them as they climbed. The church is a treasure house of Whitby history. Here in the Sanctuary is the Scoresby Chair made from timbers salvaged from the wreck of the *Royal Charter*, in which William Scoresby had earlier sailed to Australia to test a compass of his own invention. The chair, carved with the Scoresby Arms, was presented to the widow of Whitby's whaler-turned-priest.

That Scoresby was the son of an equally remarkable father, also named William who, in the port's great whaling days, caught more than five hundred 'fish' during his thirty trips. The better to see his giant quarry from a distance, Scoresby invented the first crow's nest, which he introduced in his own ship in 1807. With such a father it is hardly surprising that the younger William Scoresby stowed away when he was no more than ten to make his first voyage in one of Dad's ships.

But even Scoresby would doff his cap to the greatest seaman ever to sail out of Whitby harbour, James Cook, who once lived in the town and whose first great voyage was made in a converted Whitby-built collier of only 300 tons in 1768. She bore a new name, *Endeavour* (today, in Cook's honour, the name of a busy Whitby wharf), and it was from her deck that Cook first sighted Australia.

Cook's statue now looks out to sea from a plinth which depicts another Whitby-built ship, *Resolution*, on which, along with *Discovery*, Cook made his fateful voyage to Hawaii, where he died when relations with the natives suddenly soured.

Everyone, it seems, goes to Whitby, even Count Dracula, the most famous of vampires! The actor-manager Bram Stoker got the idea for his best-selling, purely fictitious shocker in Whitby when he was staying at a house in East Crescent in 1896.

Stoker's descriptions of the

Whitby is part of our maritime heritage. Historic, picturesque, its story is inextricably entwined with the story of England. No longer does the whaling skipper Scoresby make his record catches, but a whalebone arch on the West Cliff stands as an unforgettable memorial to those days. The whale, whose jawbones form that arch, was eighty-two feet long and weighed 111 tons – truly one of the wonders of the deep seen by men who go down to the sea in ships.

Forest Horn Blowing Bainbridge

From late September to the end of March each year

The horn is blown each night at 9.00 p.m. in the main street. Bainbridge is a small village just south of Askrigg in North Yorkshire. Parking in the village.

From Monks to Metcalfes

In the quiet of a Wensleydale evening, three sonorous notes sound a melancholy blast that has been variously compared with a cow and a banshee. It is in fact neither: it is 'young Alistair Mecca' blowing the Forest Horn and thus carrying out a custom that has been the prerogative of his family – the Metcalfes, to give them their official name – for untold generations. The horn is blown nightly at 9 p.m. from Holyrood in late September until Shrovetide.

How long the Metcalfes have been doing it – or even quite why – is a matter of some dispute. Raise the question in the Rose and Crown at Alistair's home village, Bainbridge, where the custom is carried on, and you may be offered one of several explanations.

'It was t'Romans started it,' says one authority (and indeed the Romans came to Bainbridge and built a fort called Virosidum, traces of which may be seen on a mound to the east of the village).

'Nay, nowt o' t'sort,' snorts another bar-parlour historian. 'Ivverybody knows it was William the Conqueror.'

town have been praised, but perhaps the man who most successfully captured Whitby's atmosphere was Frank Sutcliffe, whose photographs must now be among the best known pictures of rural and sea-coast life ever taken in England. Sutcliffe's salty seamen, his sturdy ploughboys and fisherwives, recall a vanished world with amazing accuracy. Quite apart from their historical interest, they are works of art in their own right. Leeds-born Sutcliffe never thought very highly of his craft – he considered it a lazy way of making pictures. But he has more than once been called a genius and second only to Cook himself among Whitby's adopted sons.

'They tell me it were t'monks 'at started it – to guide folk over t'fells when t'dark weather began . . .' And so it goes on . . . Alistair was eleven in 1983 when he took over the duties of hornblower from his great-uncle Jack Metcalfe, whose death at 83 ended his own 36 years of hornblowing. Jack had taken over the task from his father, Jamie (hence his full Dales title of 'Jamie's Jack' – with so many 'Meccas' in the dale, such studbook nomenclature helps to prevent confusion). Jamie had taken over from his own father. Only a Metcalfe, apparently, is up to this task: they say it takes a son of the clan to make the note carry a full three miles or to hit a top C.

Alistair bears a name that has been as illustrious in Wensleydale as it is ubiquitous there today. James Metcalfe, who founded a dynasty which used to rule the dale, returned rich from the French campaign of 1415 and was made Chief Forester of Wensleydale. When Sir Christopher Metcalfe was made High Sheriff of York in 1555, he rode to his appointment at the head of 300 Metcalfes, each riding a white horse.

When 'off duty', the horn used to hang in the Rose and Crown along with another said to date from the fourteenth century. But in view of his youth, Alistair is allowed to keep the operational horn at his home during the blowing season. Perhaps if that older horn could talk it could tell us the true history of the custom, which probably dates from the time a kinsman of William the Conqueror built foresters' villages to make possible the patrolling of land in the Forest of Wensleydale, set aside as hunting grounds by the Norman lords of Richmond and Middleham.

One of these villages was Bainbridge. It takes its name from the shortest river in England, the Bain, which makes a two-mile journey from one of Yorkshire's few lakes, Semerwater, to join the Ure, principal river of Wensleydale, whose alternative name is Uredale. The 'bridge' which forms part of the village's name affords a view of Bain Fall, where the waters cascade over a great crescent of Yoredale (Uredale) limestone.

The story that the forest horn was first blown in past days to guide benighted travellers over the lonely and hazardous fells is well-established and respected. But it may indeed be true that the custom originated in Roman times, or that the horn used to be sounded as a signal to warn the monks who once pastured their herds here that it was time to make them safe for the night. Or it may have been a curfew horn.

One thing seems certain. As long as there's a Metcalfe in Bainbridge, the Forest Horn will continue to awaken echoes of Wensleydale's past.

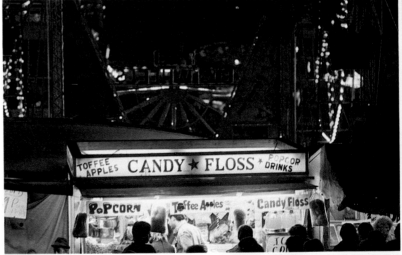

Goose Fair

First Thursday, Friday and
Saturday in October

Goose Fair Site, Forest Recreation
Ground, Nottingham.

The Goose Fair Site is only a ten-
minute walk from the city centre,
on Gregory Boulevard. The Goose
Fair is a large fun fair and there are
free parking facilities.

Aw Dad, give us a goose!

You're hardly likely to see many
geese nowadays at Nottingham
Goose Fair. But time was when
geese in their thousands were
driven from the surrounding
countryside to be sold on
Nottingham fairground.
According to some authorities,
the fair has been held since at
least as early as 1155; others say it
started in 1542. Whenever it
began, in its earlier forms it lasted
for three weeks and it was
undoubtedly the event of the year
in the Midlands. Only the direst
circumstances could prevent it —
the plague in the seventeenth
century, for instance, and the two
world wars.

It was held when geese were at
their best. They had been allowed
to 'go a-stubbling', or gleaning
what was left in the fields after the
harvest, and were therefore in
prime condition for the
Michaelmas feasts at which roast
goose was traditional fare.

In times when country folk came
to the city from remote parts of the
forest and the Fens, the Goose Fair
was a dazzling magnet for rustics
who saw little during the rest of
the year but the fields and farms of
their own villages. And this fact
gives rise to a story offering a *less*
obvious explanation of how the
Goose Fair got its name. A farmer
whose three grown-up sons had
led extremely sheltered lives in
their forest home decided to
widen their horizons by taking
them to the Fair. Hardly surprising
that everything they saw was
a source of wonderment,
particularly the girls with their
ribbons and bows and roguish
glances.

The young men had never seen
anything like this! 'What be they

179

Father?' they asked in delighted astonishment.

'Silly geese! That's all *they* be,' snapped the father.

And when, feeling generous after a good day's trading, he asked his sons to choose a gift to take home, with one voice they replied, 'Aw Dad, give us a goose!'

Over the centuries the fair has changed its setting as well as its form. At one time it was held in the city's fine market-place, and now it takes place on the Forest Recreation Ground, Gregory Boulevard. Like so many other ancient fairs, its purpose today is solely to give pleasure to the million or so who revel each year in the delights of its eighteen acres of Ferris wheels, roundabouts, stands, stalls and side-shows.

Chatsworth Horse Trials

Saturday and Sunday, early October

Chatsworth Park, Edensor, Derbyshire.

Car park charge also lets you into the grounds, where the horse trials are held. There is an additional fee for the house, but reduced rate for Horse Trials visitors.

The Chatsworth Horse Trials, held on a weekend in October in Chatsworth Park, Derbyshire, fall into place behind Badminton and Burghley as the third most popular in the country and attract between 15,000 and 20,000 people over two days. There are usually around fifty trade stands.

Hull Fair

Saturday to the following Sunday of the week including 11 October, 12.00 noon onwards each day

Walton Street, Hull.

This is the largest funfair in Great Britain. Walton Street is down Anlaby Road on the west side of Hull, about ½ mile beyond the Infirmary. It may be difficult to park nearby. 20 minutes walk from the railway station.

A moveable feast

Irene Thompson's family have visited Hull Fair for far longer than she can remember, and if she has her way they'll be visiting it for many a year yet at its Walton Street site, with their round stall, side stall, shooting gallery and Swinging Jims.

Hull Fair has been held in Walton Street since 1888. It was banished there by those who saw it as a blot on the city's respectability. Before that, it had spent an existence as nomadic as that of the gypsies who attended it to tell fortunes or work the roundabouts: first in one area, then another. At one time it was held in the streets of the old town and on the Railway Dock site; it has held sway, too, on the Town Fields and Park Street, but its home in recent years has been Walton Street.

No matter how much criticism has been heaped upon it, there can be little doubt that the city loves its wandering child which returns for about one week every year, unwaveringly confident of its welcome. And the fair has been made what it is by people like Irene, a sturdy, happy, sensible breed, whose blood seems to pulse with the jolly beat of fairground music. Irene's grandfather had a shooter wagon – the clients fired with a ·22 rifle at bottles balanced on water jets. But the fairground which had given him his living also cost him his life when an accidentally caused gunshot wound turned gangrenous. Irene's grandfather had a horse called Old Tom that nobody could persuade to work on a Sunday! Her step-grandfather,

too, was a traveller, whose contribution to the fair was a Cake Walk – until it had to be sold when times were bad.

Time was when Irene would have found it hard to settle down to life in a house – life as the 'Flatties' (non-travellers) know it. But she feels that perhaps she could anchor herself now. Not that her life lacks comforts: her caravan is far from spartan: 'I've got plenty of room – a six-foot bedroom at one end and another bedroom at the other. I've a folding kitchen, too. When we travel, we put all the things like the fridge and the cookers and the washing machine in the living-room. Then, when we stop, the kitchen unfolds from the side of the van and all the things are put back'.

Like all women travellers, Irene has as full a round of domestic duties as any 'Flattie' wife and

mother, but she works in the fairground, too, helping the men to put up the Swinging Jims whilst accepting philosophically that men are 'no good at helping in the van.' So it's housework in the morning and working on the shows from two in the afternoon. No easy life, but would she change it? Irene has never even given that a thought.

Hull's 700-year-old fair (probably founded in 1278) had its charter renewed in 1299 by Edward I, just as it was he who bestowed on this maritime city its full title – Kingston (King's Town) upon Hull. He had a soft spot for the Humberside town and although the fair was then more in the nature of a market than the present glittering, rumbustious monument to enjoyment, it nevertheless had its less respectable side – or so some of the disapproving citizens thought.

The King himself seems to have been less easily outraged. He entered so heartily into the spirit of the fair that he ate a plate of peas there one day on his return from hunting and the royal stomach was somewhat disturbed! A divine judgement, snorted the more strait-laced among his subjects.

Despite its present fame and success, Hull Fair has had a chequered history and there have been times when its future seemed highly uncertain. In 1874 a rather toffee-nosed reporter of a weekly Hull paper commented, 'The age of fairs is fast passing away, and ere long the Hull festival will be numbered among the things that were. We will not regret the loss, as these fairs are chiefly frequented by the least respectable portion of the community.'

Despite his gloomy forecast, the fair eventually achieved respectability and acceptance by the city, though its disreputable image was not shed without a struggle. Instead of the space-age rides of today that vie with older favourites like the ghost train, the big wheel and helter-skelter, the old-time fairgoer could indulge in such doubtful diversions as cock-fighting, riding at the ring, pricking

at the belt and 'tappy towsy'. And as he did so he could stuff his gaping mouth with – not candy floss – but Labbergob and Whoa Emma (whatever they were).

By the nineteenth century, the brutal aspects were moderating: there were even elements of 'culture' – of a sort – in the form of the 'penny gaff', an incredibly concentrated show which squeezed two or three tragedies and always one farce into a mere twenty minutes. There were waxworks, a wild beast show, and a ghost show which promised such satisfactory horrors as 'skeletons gliding out of chests, goblins carousing in churchyards, spectres terrifying travellers, bogies bursting their cerements and coffins cracking their sides'. There was no pretence at edification, unless a retired hangman's demonstration of his craft, using a wax 'murderer' could be considered uplifting to public morals.

Time passed; the age of mechanisation affected the fair rides just as it did every other aspect of life. The crowds flocked to the new centrifugal railway and the steam roundabouts. Edison's Electric Animated Pictures replaced the penny gaffs. And all the time the fair was growing, living up to its reputation as the biggest in Britain and the biggest movable fair in Europe.

Hull Fair even inspired a Victorian best seller. Over a hundred years ago, Catherine Deck, the daughter of the vicar of St. Stephen's (whose church was to be destroyed in the blitz), would accompany her father when he visited the fair folks' caravans parked, each October, near his dockland vicarage. Catherine grew up to become Mrs. O.F. Walton, whose children's book *Christy's Old Organ* was translated into two hundred languages and sold by the million. She followed that success with another, based on her memories of visits to Hull Fair with her father. It was called A *Peep Behind the Scenes* and its grotesque characters, such as the dwarf Mother Mannikin, might be said to have stepped straight from the fair into the pages of her story.

THE CALENDAR YEAR

The book was an immediate success when it was first published in 1877. Even today, children who get the chance will read it with enjoyment – though they no doubt skip the 'improving' passages which Mrs Walton, as a parson's wife, felt she must include. The swing-boats, the coconut shies, the 'houses on wheels' that she knew as a child are still there, larger no doubt, gaudier and noisier. And just as exciting to a child of today as little Catherine Deck found them a century and more ago.

THE CALENDAR YEAR

Yorkshire Canary Show

Usually held on the last weekend in October

Victoria Hall, Saltaire, on the Baildon road out of Bradford.

The show is open to the public and there is a small entrance fee. The free car park is about 50 yards away from the hall.

Gentleman Of The Fancy

Every year, on the last Saturday and Sunday of October, the Victoria Hall, Saltaire, Shipley, rings with the song of hundreds of canaries. Tiered rows of cages fill the floor. Knowledgeable men brood on their occupants or admire the trophies piled high on a table at the end of the hall. For this is the Annual Open Show of All Yorkshire Canaries.

You feel that Sir Titus Salt, the millionaire philanthropist who built Victoria Hall, along with the rest of Saltaire, for his mill-workers (but declined to equip his model village with a pub), would give all this innocent activity his solemn approbation.

It is difficult nowadays to realise quite what a cult the Yorkshire Canary attracted before the First World War. You get the impression that every street in Yorkshire rang with bird-song. Sid Alderson, one of the judges, and Yorkshire Canary Club chairman for twenty years, told me that in Baildon alone there must have been at least twenty breeders and exhibitors, whilst 'every other street' in Bradford had its back bedroom expert devoted to the propagation of the 'Gentleman of the Fancy', as the 'Yorkshire' is still reverently called.

Aficionados used to say it must be small enough to 'go through a wedding ring'. They call it the 'Gentleman' because it displays an 'arrogance' in its 'position', that is, the angle at which it perches: 'the head should be at five-past and the tail at five-and-twenty to'. But it would be a very large wedding ring that a modern Yorkshire Canary could pass through, because it is a much bigger bird than it was when it first emerged as a breed about 1880.

An admixture of blood from the Norwich Canary and – dare I say it – a variety called the 'Lancashire Coppy' has bulked out the native Yorkshire breed, which is in fact by no means the simple and unmistakable bird the uninitiated might suppose.

Sid Alderson, who has been breeding Yorkshires for forty-seven years, is a big, gentle-looking man in his seventies who can talk bewilderingly about cinnamons and greens, chromosomes and genes.

The 'fancy', they say, is growing. Sid attributes this, partly at least, to football hooliganism. 'It's turning people back to the fancy'.

Reverently, Sid showed me the ideal to which they are all aspiring today. For the canary world it is almost an icon – a drawing signed by S.R. Golding, now in his nineties, depicting the acme of Yorkshire Canary perfection. To the uninitiated it may look a top-heavy, rather portly bird, but to the Yorkshire Canary breeder it represents an impossible ideal that he is prepared to spend a lifetime merely approaching. He must be prepared for lots of failures on the way – 'The big fault is a dropping tail,' said Sid. 'You can only sell any which turn out like that for singing birds.' So that yellow prima donna trilling away in someone's parlour window may be a failed Miss Canary World.

Nearly seven inches long, the Yorkshire should ideally present 'a long-legged look' and 'a fearless carriage'. In judging, points are awarded for a 'full, round and clearly defined backskull'. The eyes should be as nearly as possible in the centre of the head. The breast should be full and deep, the beak neat and fine. There are six 'Technical Marks' – one on each eye, one on each wing and two on the tail feathers. And then the classification becomes more and more technical, with clear, ticked, lightly variegated and cinnamon marked birds.

To anyone but an enthusiast, the thought must occur that the degree of scientific study devoted

to the breeding of this little bird is rather akin to using a pile driver to crack a nut. Handbooks are written, such as *Cinnamon Inheritance in Canaries*. A slim volume, even for the 1s. 6d. it cost when first published, it supplied a two-page glossary in which terms like Autosome, Gamete, Heterozygote and Homozygote are explained.

Sid, a long-time devotee, is full of such eugenic wisdom – 'If you get two yellows together, you get a finer feather . . . if you pair two marked birds together, you get a "self" . . . you get size by double buffing' (the main colours are buff and yellow, but green is not uncommon). Intensive and incestuous line breeding can have horrific effects, called 'Grecks', unfortunate little monsters that come into the world with two heads or only one leg. Or a bird may 'go light' (succumb to TB) or, too often in these days of toxic chemical sprays, it can easily be poisoned by a bit of innocent-looking green stuff picked up in the fields.

Nor is canary breeding the cheapest of hobbies. 'During the war,' said Sid, 'seed cost £1 a pound.' Yet somehow the 'fancy' was kept alive by men like Billy Johnson, revered almost as a patron saint of 'Yorkshire' breeders. Billy, who was in charge of the docks at Barrow-in-Furness, made it his business to set up 'Yorkshire' fanciers returning from the Forces with stock so that they could resume their hobby – though 'hobby' is hardly the word to describe the passion that culminates in Saltaire every year in October.

In classes for Clear, Ticked or Lightly Variegated, Green Marked, Cinnamon Marked and Any Other Variety Yorkshire, they compete for prize money ranging from 45p to £1 and for more than twenty trophies, each of which confers a canary world immortality on donors such as Arthur Burton, Fred Thompson, Stanley C. Hodgson . . .

The little bird from the Canary Islands has become an international figure. The Yorkshire Canary Club has 450 members all

over the world – Belgium, Australia, New York, South Africa. 'I've exported birds to China myself,' says Sid. As for Italy, 'you wouldn't *believe* their birds could have improved the way they have!'

Sid feels 'the fancy' is in good heart and on the right lines. The Golding model is canary perfection in his eyes. But breeders face problems unknown in earlier years. 'We get 700 entries at our October show. When we could send birds by rail we used to get 850. But it's so expensive now. You used to be able to send a box for 1s. 6d. Now it costs about £10 - £15.

How does the breeder view the little yellow birds on which he expends such care and thought? Does he love his feathered aristocrats half as much as their less successful relations are loved by the little old ladies into whose

lives they bring companionship and music?

Sid's attitude towards his fourteen hens and ten cocks might best be described as one of knowledgeable respect, which shows itself in the oddments of information he chooses to illustrate his conversation: 'Every colliery still keeps two pairs of canaries to supplement scientific methods which they use to test for methane gas underground – one whiff of that and the birds die . . . The Yorkshire is a very nice singer, but the Roller Canary is the one for singing – that one will sing till it drops dead. But the Yorkshire is nicer to look at than all the other birds – the Norwich is the ugliest bird.'

In terms of character, too, the Yorkshire wins Sid's vote. Its ideal pose may be 'arrogant', but its nature is friendliness itself. As for

the domestic virtues, the canary hen is an excellent mother and the cock so conscientious as her helpmate that he has to be barred from the parental cage: while the hen is sitting he feeds her so assiduously that he's apt to make her overweight and then she can easily crush the eggs.

But what about the ethics of canary breeding, you may ask? Is it fair to play eugenic games with any species? Should man employ selective breeding to change the natural forms of the creatures with which he shares the earth? Sid's answer could only be yes. And while it's difficult to get an opinion from the canaries themselves, seven hundred of them at the Victoria Hall, Saltaire, look – and sound – happy enough.

Watch Out At Hallowe'en!

For those unfamiliar with American customs, let me explain that at Hallowe'en small Americans, thinly disguised as witches, warlocks and what-have-you, arrive at your door demanding, with the cry 'Trick or treat!', to be bribed not to put your cat in the washer or Granny in the deep freeze. Americans, in their folly, shower the small gangsters with goodies . . . Now this *may* date back only to Al Capone, or it may in some form have been taken over there by the Pilgrim Fathers. If so, may Heaven forgive them.

Hallowe'en customs – fortunately, perhaps – have not survived all that well in England! Not many of us, in fact, have a very clear idea of what precisely the observances mean, though we do have a vague idea that they are concerned with things that go bump in the night (in addition to those kids, that is).

Just to remind you: 31 October offered a last chance to the agents of evil to make nuisances of themselves before the suffocating odour of sanctity brought on by All Saints' Day, 1 November, made the place too hot even for them.

It all goes back to the Celts and the Druids, to Samhuinn or 'summer's end', when the oncoming season of death was softened by the belief that life would return, and not only to nature but to the human dead, who might well be expected to drop in at this most haunted of seasons.

They wanted, poor souls, a good warm by the fire before winter set in, and a bite or sup to sustain them through the cold hard months. And in their simple kindliness, folk would leave food on the table and the door unlocked when they retired to bed.

Bonfire Night is generally accepted as being inseparable from Guy Fawkes and the Gunpowder Plot, but it seems almost certain that the fires which blaze on 5 November are the successors to the great Hallow Fires which once marked this season. The fires were accompanied by games in which

young men would leap through the flames.

Derbyshire used to be rich in Hallowe'en customs. Sometimes a farmer would light a small fire in one of his fields. His family would kneel around it remembering the family dead. When it was blazing brightly the farmer would take a forkful of burning straw and — from the highest part of his land — hurl it as far as he could, thus purifying the ground and making it fruitful.

In Derbyshire, too, as well as in other Midland counties and in Yorkshire and on the Welsh border, 'Soul Cakes' were made and eaten and children would travel the neighbourhood collecting them. Hallowe'en was the season for magic — girls in Derbyshire would put a sprig of rosemary and a crooked sixpence under their pillows in the confident belief that their future husbands would appear in their dreams.

Above all, Hallowe'en is the time for witches, of which Yorkshire, at least, has had its fair share, from Mother Shipton the Knaresborough prophetess, to the High Priestess of the Sheffield Coven, Patricia Crowther, still very much alive and the author of a

'handbook for witches' entitled *Lid Off The Cauldron*. Witchcraft, she says, is the craft of the Wise; it is the old pre-Christian religion, essentially good though rarely understood and, as we all know, mercilessly persecuted in past ages.

Be that as it may, the stories still told of witches seem to concern mostly bad ones, like this tale of a witch named Aud Nanny who was active in North Yorkshire about two hundred years ago.

One day Martha Sokeld fell ill and sent for her cousin, Mary Langstaff, to come and care for her. The two women were very attached to each other, so Mary wasted no time in setting off to walk the considerable distance to Martha's home.

On the way, Mary noticed an old woman hobbling along the road and for some reason she immediately felt certain that the woman was 't'auld witch' she had heard about. Not wishing to speak to her, she stooped to gather some hedge flowers to take to her cousin.

This enraged the old woman, who swore she would 'pay Mary oot' for not having the courtesy to pass the time of day with her. She banged her stick on the ground

three times, then disappeared! No doubt Mary was a little disturbed by this, but not too much, because she was wearing a corsage of rowan berries and everyone knew in those days that rowan berries or rowan wood were a sure protection against witchcraft.

When Mary reached her cousin's house she found that Martha had almost recovered. Nevertheless, having made the journey, she stayed a few days and then returned home. Two days later, who should walk into the house but Martha herself, who said she had been 'takken bad again'. 'Ahs'll not live long,' she told Mary, 'but before Ah go, Ah want to see mi sister Hannah.' However, since she was very tired she asked Mary to take a message to Hannah's house while she, Martha, snatched a little sleep on the settle.

Obediently Mary set off on her errand, but so uneasy did she feel that she was soon hurrying back to her own home. There, anxious not to disturb her cousin, Mary peeped through a crack in the shutters and saw a sight which astonished and horrified her. Far from being asleep, Martha was sitting before a blazing fire while she dropped things into a pan and mumbled the following chant:

> Fire cum,
> Fire gan,
> Curling smoke
> Keep oot o' t' pan.
> Here's a toad, theer's a frog,
> An' t' heart from a crimson ask [newt];
> Here's a tooth fra' the head
> Of one that's dead,
> An' niver got through his task [a suicide];
> Here's writ in blood a maiden's prayer
> The eye of man mayn't see;
> It's writ reet through a still warm mask
> Wrapped aboot a bright green ask,
> An' it's all for him an' thee,
> It boils, thoo'll drink,
> He'll speak, thoo'll think,
> It boils, thoo'll see,
> He'll speak, thoo'll dee.

As Mary listened, it dawned upon her that this was not her cousin but the witch in disguise, and that the spell was meant to cause mischief between her sweetheart and herself.

There was no time to waste! Marching boldly into the house Mary seized her Bible and challenged the witch to do her worst.

With a shriek of fury the witch upturned the pan on the fire. 'Thoo's escaped me this time, but Ah'll get thi yet,' she spat, and vanished.

Next morning Martha was reported missing. Three days later her body was found on the moor and everybody knew — simply knew — that the witch had lured the ailing girl on to the moor and taken away her soul by enchantment so that she could occupy Martha's body herself and work her evil will on Mary. Fortunately she had not succeeded; nor did she ever, for Mary lived to be eighty-five and brought up a large family. So this was one case, at least, of a witch being outsmarted.

A frightening tale but nothing for us to worry about you'll agree. We know things like that just don't happen . . . except, perhaps, at Hallowe'en.

Guy Fawkes Night

All over England on 5 November bonfires bring a lurid glare to a night sky bejewelled from time to time with rockets. Dogs and cats often cower in terror as squibs and jumping crackers explode all too close for comfort. And, usually when the blaze is at its height, the effigy of a human figure is hurled into the flames.

It happens, as I say, all over England. And yet at St Peter's School in York, one of the oldest, public schools in Europe, it does *not* happen, the reason simply being that 'you don't burn an old boy', no matter what he's done — not even in effigy, not even if his name was Guy Fawkes.

Guy may well be the most famous Yorkshireman of all — and justly so, some might claim of a man who tried to blow up Parliament! After all, how many of us have not had a sneaking desire to do precisely that?

What sort of man plans such an undertaking — daunting even for a Yorkshireman? Guy was born in York and baptised an Anglican on April 16, 1570 at the Church of St Michael-le-Belfrey, in Petergate, next to York Minster. He had had a good start in life and, but for his father's death, might well have grown up to follow a comfortable if uneventful career. Guy's father, a notary in York's Ecclesiastical Courts, died when the boy was only nine; his mother married again and Guy found himself with a stepfather, a Catholic named Baynbridge who lived at Scotton near Knaresborough.

Presumably it was his stepfather's influence that made young Guy renounce the faith instilled into him at St Peter's School and embrace all things Roman Catholic. He joined the Spanish Army and fought in the Netherlands, becoming an expert in mining and the use of explosives. He was brave and efficient and was entrusted with hazardous and demanding missions. Influenced, no doubt, by the hardships of Catholics in England, he became less and less 'English' and even changed his name to the Spanish 'Guido'. He must have seemed a truly heaven-sent choice for enrolment into the audacious plot to blow King James I and Parliament sky-high before placing one of the royal children on the throne and introducing a new Catholic order.

Enlisted at Ostend by Thomas Winter, one of the inner circle of conspirators, Guy took ship for England, where he was virtually unknown after a ten-year absence. The plotters rented premises near Parliament House and Fawkes assumed the guise of one John Johnson, servant of Thomas Percy, another of the conspirators. Gunpowder was secretly conveyed down the Thames and stored in the plotters' house. Now Guy and his friends began to tunnel through the wall of the cellar in order to reach the cellars of the House of Lords. But when it was discovered that they could lease a vault actually under the House of Lords itself, the plotters abandoned their original plan and arranged for the powder to be transferred to this new hiding-place. Faggots and iron bars were placed over the barrels . . . all seemed ready for Guy to light the fuse the plotters hoped would set all England ablaze with rebellion.

All might have gone according to plan had the plot not been delayed by the postponement, twice, of the opening of Parliament. As nerves became stretched, one of the plotters (just which is still uncertain) wrote to the Catholic Peer Lord Monteagle warning him to stay away from the House on the day of re-assembly. The result, as surely all must know, was that the cellars were searched and Guy was arrested and on November 5, 1605, taken for questioning.

Guy admitted his identity and his intention to destroy King and Parliament, but courageously refused to name his fellow conspirators. When told that his silence served no purpose, for their names were known already, Guy simply replied that if that were the case, then he need not name them. He was warned, though he must have known it, that continued silence could only

result in his being tortured. With simple dignity, but surely with a sinking heart, he answered that he was sworn to silence and must try to keep his vow.

So, tortured he was . . . but though he was first hung up by the thumbs, then stretched naked on a hot stone, he told his examiners nothing. Next he was subjected to the most fiendish device of all, the rack. On November 9, four days after his arrest he signed, in agony, the confession his torturers thrust before him, then swooned into insensibility. No doubt he hoped that by this time his fellow plotters had escaped; but one by one they were all killed or captured. Parliament, having met in safety, made the most of their deliverance by appointing a special day of celebration.

Guy and his seven fellow plotters, on the other hand, had no reason to rejoice. On January 30 four of them were executed — inadequate term — in St Paul's churchyard. According to sentence, they were hanged, cut down while still alive, castrated, drawn and quartered and had their entrails burned before their eyes. On the following day, the remaining four faced their deaths, Guy being the last to ascend the scaffold. Though his tormented body would hardly bear his weight, he insisted on climbing to the topmost rung of the ladder and there he prayed for forgiveness. Perhaps he realised that, far from easing the lot of his fellow Catholics, his actions would result in a worsening of their plight. Maybe he saw, at last, that murder is murder, whatever the motive — that courage and conviction are not enough.

As he hung by his neck, a kindly fate decreed that he had suffered enough. When the executioners cut him down, his neck was broken and no further outrage could cause him pain.

Winter

Aldbrough St. John ●

Middlesbrough

Richmond ●

Goathland ●
Staintondale ●

● Bedale

Kirkbymoorside ●

Scarborough

● Ripon

Brompton ●

● Aldwark

● Malton

Harrogate ●

York

● Easingwold

● Driffield

Bradford

● Beverley

Halifax
Pudsey

Leeds

Kingston-upon-Hull

Todmorden ●

● Dewsbury

Huddersfield

Wakefield ● Wentbridge

Barnsley

Doncaster

Grimsby

● Haxey

Sheffield

Rotherham

● Handsworth

● Louth

● Retford

Lincoln

● Winster

Mansfield

● Blidworth

● Newark

Ashbourne ●

● Kedleston

Nottingham

Boston

● Grantham

Hunstanton ●

Cawston ●

● Loughborough

King's Lynn

● Ely

Thorpe Abbotts ●

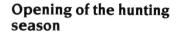

Opening of the hunting season

November

Hunts over winter in most parts of the region.

Boxing Day Hunts at the following:

Badsworth – Wentbridge, West
  Yorkshire. 11.00 a.m.
Bedale – Village Green, Bedale,
  North Yorkshire. 10.45 a.m.
Derwent – Green Farm, Brompton,
  North Yorkshire. 11.00 a.m.
Holderness – Beverley
  Grandstand, Humberside.
  11.00 a.m.
Middleton – Driffield,
               Humberside.
               11.00 a.m.
            – Market Place,
               Malton,
               North Yorkshire.
               11.00 a.m.
Staintondale – Shepherd's Arms,
  Staintondale, North Yorkshire.
  11.00 a.m.
Sinnington – Market Square,
  Kirkbymoorside, North
  Yorkshire. 11.00 a.m.
York and Ainsty North – Aldwark,
  North Yorkshire. 11.00 a.m.
York and Ainsty South – Market
  Place, Easingwold, North
  Yorkshire. 10.45 a.m.
Zetland – Aldborough St. John,
  North Yorkshire. 11.00 a.m.
Belvoir – St. Peter's Hill,
  Grantham, Lincs. 11.00 a.m.
Grove and Rufford – Market Place,
  Retford, Notts. 11.00 a.m.

THE CALENDAR YEAR

Maynell and South Staffordshire –
   Kedleston Hall, Kedleston,
   Derby. 11.00 a.m.
South Notts – Car Colston, near
   Newark, Notts. 11.00 a.m.
Quorn – Loughborough Town
   Hall, Leics. 11.00 a.m.
South Wold – Cattle Market,
   Louth, Lincs. 11.00 a.m.

Christingles Play

Mid-December

Fulneck Boys' School, near Pudsey, Leeds.

A service followed by the Christingles. Mostly attended by parents, but some locals also go along. Outsiders may apply to the school to attend – entrance is limited. There is parking space for a small number of cars.

The school is on a Moravian settlement just outside Pudsey.

Handel's Messiah

Third week in December
Town Hall, Huddersfield.

There is usually a day on which tickets are available to the public and people queue at the Town Hall to obtain them.

There is a multi-storey car park alongside the market, and the civic centre car park is free in the evening. Also street parking around the Town Hall.

"Damn your eyes, Praise the Lord"

Messiah is as much a part of our national heritage as *Land of Hope and Glory* or the National Anthem. And nowhere is it more revered than in Huddersfield, where the Huddersfield Choral Society's annual performance of the work in the Town Hall expresses more than any other event the corporate soul of the town.

   Less than a century after John Wesley had visited the town – and, incidentally, said of its folk,

'A wilder people I never saw in England' – the society was born, on 7 June 1836.

The 'Preamble' drawn up at that first meeting raises a smile today. At monthly meetings each member was allowed 'three gills of ale and bread and cheese', but 'any member being intoxicated or using obscene or abusive language or calling any other members *bye-names* . . . shall forfeit *sixpence* for each offence'.

When, in 1842, Huddersfield's old Philosophical Hall became available for meetings it was decided that no one who lived more than six miles from the new meeting place should be allowed to join the society and if he removed beyond that distance he must forfeit membership.

It would probably be fair to say that in those early days the members had no inkling of their future fame. Their sole object, in the earnest manner of the time, was their own education and enjoyment, with a practice once a month and quarterly performances for friends and subscribers.

Concern was expressed by the society's officers when a sinister place known as the 'Hall of Science' was opened. Not only did it compete with the Philosophical Hall as a place of entertainment but it was let to dangerous characters like secularists and socialists. The officials of the Choral Society knew that firm action was called for! 'No person', they resolved, 'shall be a member of this Society, who *frequents* the "Hall of Science" or *any* of the "Socialist Meetings", nor shall the Librarian be allowed to lend any copies of music (knowingly) belonging to this Society to any Socialist, upon pain of expulsion.

Sixteen years later, in 1858, the horrified words were surely heard – 'a chap fra' *Leeds* for t'conductor?' But the chap fra' Leeds, Robert Senior Burton, organist of Leeds Parish Church, was appointed, and under his influence, the society began to emerge from its earlier narrowness. He even persuaded them to pay small fees to principals! In 1862, when Burton was able to take the society to an important concert at the Crystal Palace, the advance to greatness had really begun.

When Huddersfield became a borough the Choral Society's committee was influential in persuading the civic authorities to include in the design of the new Town Hall a large concert hall and organ for the performance of choral works on a grand scale. At the three-day festival to mark the opening of the Town Hall in October 1881 Charles Hallé came to conduct his famous orchestra. At the end Hallé said he had conducted many choruses but never had found a better – or indeed one so good – for refinement, perfect truth of intonation and expression and especially for power.

The choir has been fortunate indeed to have a concert hall with such excellent acoustics, where generations of singers have been able to develop their skills. Thus the Town Hall has contributed to the success of the Choral Society and the Society's performances to the fame of the town.

The first overseas tour took place in 1928, since when the 'Huddersfield Choral' has won acclaim in Vienna, Berlin, Munich, Brussels and Boston. Visits to London are now almost routine. In 1951 the society was the first to give a choral concert in the newly opened Royal Festival Hall. In 1982 alone there were three visits to the capital during the first of which the society promoted their own concert – an enormously successful *Dream of Gerontius* – in the Festival Hall. Mahler's Second Symphony was performed later in the year in the Albert Hall with the Young Musicians Symphony Orchestra and the newly opened Barbican Centre rang to the concert version of Puccini's *Turandot*.

You can hardly write about the Huddersfield Choral Society without mentioning one of their brightest stars, Susan Sykes, who was to become Mrs Sunderland – the Mrs Sunderland whose name is annually recalled at Huddersfield and very much farther afield by the musical competitions which bear her name. It was to her that Queen

THE CALENDAR YEAR

Victoria said: 'I am Queen of England, but you are Queen of Song'.

Other great names from past and present days recall renowned chorus masters such as Herbert Bardgett, Douglas Robinson and, most recently, Nina Walker (deputy chorus master at the Royal Opera House, Covent Garden). Owain Arwel Hughes, who became principal conductor in 1980, continues the distinguished line which includes Sir Henry Coward and Sir Malcolm Sargent.

These Huddersfield choristers, despite their society's humble origins, have proved a nursery of song, providing choristers for the Chapels Royal and for almost every cathedral in England. They have been conducted by Elgar, Parry, Walford Davies, Coleridge Taylor, Vaughan Williams, Sir Henry Wood, William Walton and Victor de Sabata, of La Scala, Milan. And if they are proud of their attainments, who can blame them?

Sir William Walton, who wrote *Gloria* for the Society's 125th anniversary in 1961, had begun to write a new work, *Stabat Mater*, for the 150th anniversary in 1986, but died before it was completed.

Many legends linger from the early days. One concerns the double bass player whose enthusiasm prompted him to exclaim, 'Pass me yon' resin an' Ah'll show you who t' King o' Glory is!' And there was the bandsman who could play any Handel music on any instrument. He specialised in the trombone, but when there was no trombone part blared forth the cello part instead. Even a certain conductor sometimes succumbed to the general fervour and in the massive choruses of the *Hymn of Praise* had been known to lash the choir to even more thunderous efforts by the exhortation 'Damn your eyes, PRAISE THE LORD!'

But if Messiah is a joy to sing, there are those who have found it less than a joy to play. It's said that in a corner of the Gents in the basement of a hall in Liverpool there reposes the wreckage of a double bass. It has been there

since its player flung it to the floor mid-Messiah. 'I'm fed up with this bloody job', he told his fellow musicians, the conductor, the audience and no doubt Handel himself. And he strode from the hall, never to be seen again.

Handel's great work has entwined itself with Yorkshire folklore: a visitor from Mars might be forgiven for concluding that Handel was himself a musical Super-Tyke. Thus we have stories like that of David Turton, an eccentric and self-taught composer and bass viol player, born at Horbury in 1868. David made a great local reputation, but no fortune from his music. Some of his psalms and chants were published and sung in his day, but in the view of the Rev. Sabine Baring-Gould, who wrote *Onward Christian Soldiers* and was once a curate at Horbury, he did not win the recognition they deserved.

David, a handloom weaver by trade, was especially well-versed in Handel's works and once performed the surely unique feat of using George Frederick's music to rout an angry bull. The bull, bellowing furiously, confronted David as he was taking a short cut through a field recklessly carrying his bass viol in a *red* bag! David listened appreciatively – 'Just as Ah thowt', he said, 'double B natural', whereupon he embarked upon a Handelian rendition in harmony with the bull. Unable, perhaps, to participate on equally musical terms, the bull turned and fled.

But the most characteristic example of Yorkshire's conviction that it owns a controlling interest in *Messiah* is provided by a Yorkshire composer who, having decided that it was time for a change, submitted to Novello and Co. what he entitled A *New Messiah*. That was in 1895, but even in Yorkshire they're still performing Handel's version.

Ringing the Devil's Knell

Christmas Eve

Dewsbury Parish Church.

The tenor bell is rung from 11.00 p.m. onwards; one stroke for every year since the birth of Christ. The bell is known as Black Tom of Soothill and is called after Sir Thomas de Soothill who is said to have begun the custom to atone for a murder he committed.

As tolled by Black Tom

At Dewsbury each Christmas Eve they toll the 'Devil's Knell', or, as the locals sometimes call it, 't' Owd Lad's Passin' Bell'. The thinking behind this custom is that 'the devil died when Christ was born' and so, to mark his passing, the tenor bell in the parish church bell tower is tolled once for every year since the Nativity. The tolling is exactly timed to end at midnight, thus neatly disposing of Satan the moment before the dawning of Christmas Day.

The custom is said to date back to the fourteenth or fifteenth century and to have originated in neighbouring Batley where, in the hilltop village of Soothill, the local squire, Thomas de Soothill, 'Black Tom', murdered a servant boy in a fit of rage and flung the body into the dam of a forge. Nobody seems to know whether the law exacted a penalty for the crime, but it must have weighed on the squire's conscience for, in expiation, he instituted the custom by presenting the tenor bell to the church. On the face of it, he seems to have got off very lightly. (Indeed, would-be sleepers who have gone early to bed on Christmas Eve within earshot of Dewsbury's parish church bells may feel that they, and not 'Black Tom of Soothill', are really doing penance for that crime of long ago.)

Although this Dewsbury custom fell into disuse for a time during the eighteenth century, it was revived by the Reverend John Buckworth in 1828 since when the bells have remained silent on Christmas Eve only for two short periods — during their recasting over a hundred years ago and, of course, during the Second World War when the ringing of church bells was forbidden unless to signal an invasion. The original tenor bell, called 'Black Tom' after its repentant donor, no longer exists as such; in the recasting, all the bells were melted down to make the new ones. But the metal of Black Tom is mixed into the present ring of bells.

Climb the spiral staircase to the ringing chamber in the church tower sometime before eleven o'clock on Christmas Eve and you will find a team of ringers 'ringing up the bells', in other words raising them from the normal resting position to the ringing position with the mouth upwards. One member of the team will probably already be sitting in a corner with a pad on his knee ruled into squares; if this were the year 2000, there would be 20 squares, each divided into a hundred smaller squares. At a precisely calculated moment, one of the ringers starts to toll the knell and at each sonorous stroke of the tenor bell a diagonal pencil stroke is made on the pad, marking off one of the 'years' on the squared chart. The tolling of the Devil's Knell for yet another year has begun.

At intervals of ten or fifteen minutes a new ringer will take over the tolling of the tenor bell. The change must be made carefully with the two ringers pulling together for a while. Naturally, the more ringers that can be assembled, the easier the task of tolling will be, although on more than one occasion it has been known for the whole knell to be tolled by a single ringer.

But whether there is one ringer or a team, the long-drawn tolling of the Devil's Knell at the rate of one stroke every two seconds or so eventually nears its end. Soon there are only a few squares left to mark, only a few remaining strokes for the great tenor bell to sound . . . three, two, one — and at the last stroke, the church clock begins to chime midnight. The ringers, feeling that they, at least, have earned their Christmas

peace, put their signatures on the pad and it is dated. For another year, the parish is safe from the attentions of Old Nick . . . at least we hope so.

As the clock stops striking, the ringers slip into the pews at the back of the church where the congregation is assembled for the first Christmas service of Holy Communion. Now human voices singing a Christmas hymn take over from where the Knell has left off. The ringers will reassemble to ring the bells announcing to the parish and the town that Christmas Day is here and inviting the people to join them in celebrating the birth of Christ.

A carol published in 1853 might well owe its inspiration to Black Tom of Soothill and the custom that was instituted as a result of his infamous behaviour. It begins:

Toll! Toll! because there ends tonight
An empire old and vast,
An empire of unquestioned right
O'er present and o'er past. Toll!

And it ends:

Joy! Joy! because a Babe is born
Who after a many a toil
The scorner's pride shall laugh to scorn
And work the toiler's foil. Joy!

Sponsored Swim

Christmas Day, 11.00 a.m.

Hunstanton, Norfolk.

Between 70 and 80 people swim in the sea, in front of the green, whether the tide is high or low. One can either join in or fill in a sponsor form beforehand. The event is organised by the local Round Table and the money raised goes to charity. There is also a fancy dress parade.

Car parks are free in winter months.

Sword Dance

Boxing Day

Handsworth, near Sheffield.

The sword dance takes place at 12.00 noon outside the Parish Church, Handsworth, which is on the main Worksop road. Parking on the roadside. A collection is made afterwards.

Handsworth is just east of Sheffield on the A57. The dance is also performed at Woodhouse at 11.15 a.m.

Sword Dance Play

Boxing Day

Ripon.

Traditional mummers' play performed throughout the day in the streets of Ripon. Parking in the city centre.

Things to do ~ Places to go

Middlesbrough

Richmond Georgian Theatre
Richmond
● Bolton Castle
Thorp Perrow Arboretum

Rievaulx Abbey
Shandy Hall
Gilling Castle
Nunnington Hall
N.Y.Moors Railway
Scarborough
Ebberston Hall

Norton Conyers
Fountains Abbey
Ripley Castle ● Newby Hall
Skipton Castle
Broughton Hall
Bolton Abbey **Harrogate**
White Wells
East Riddlesden Hall ● Ilkley Manor
Worth Valley Railway ● House
Brontë Parsonage ● **Bradford**
Cartwright Hall
Halifax
Bankfield Museum
Shibden Hall

Hovingham Hall
Castle Howard
Sutton Park
Beningbrough Hall
Harlow Car Gardens
Stockeld Park
Harewood House
Bramham Park
Lotherton Hall
Temple Newsam

Sledmere
House
Sewerby Hall
Burton Agnes Hall

Treasurer's House, York
National Railway Museum
York
Burnby Hall Gardens

Wilberforce House
Maister House
Burton Constable Hall

Bolling Hall ● **Leeds**
Red House ● Oakwell Hall

Wakefield
Nostell Priory
Huddersfield
Ackworth School
Denby Dale Yorkshire Sculpture Park
Cannon Hall
Barnsley **Doncaster**
Epworth Old Rectory

Kingston-upon-Hull

Normanby Hall

Elsham Hall
Grimsby

Rotherham

Sheffield

Clumber Chapel
The Old
House Museum ● Chatsworth House Doddington Hall
Hardwick Hall
Haddon Hall
Mansfield
Lea Rhododendron Gardens
Newstead Abbey

Lincoln
Harrington Hall
Gunby Hall
Auborn Hall
Tattershall Castle

Nottingham
Wollaton Hall
Holme
● Pierrepont
Hall
Elvaston Castle Thrumpton Hall

Fulbeck Hall
Boston
Marston Hall
Belvoir Castle

Holkham Hall
Felbrigg Hall
Walsingham Abbey
Mannington Hall
Sandringham
Houghton Hall Blickling Hall

Springfields Gardens
**King's
Lynn**
Medieval Merchant's House
Peckover House

Burghley House ●

Elton Hall ●

Ackworth School

Ackworth, about four miles from Pontefract, West Yorkshire

The buildings are open to the public by appointment during the school vacations, 10.00 a.m.-4.00 p.m.

Car and coach parking facilities; free admission; no refreshments available.

Ackworth School was founded in 1779 by Dr John Fothergill for the education of Quaker children. The original Georgian building, dating from 1758, is now the main school block.

Auborn Hall and Gardens

Auborn, Lincoln

This late sixteenth-century house is open to the public on Wednesday afternoons during July and August from 2.00-6.00 p.m.

Access to house is unsuitable for wheelchairs; dogs not allowed; no refreshments.

Bankfield Museum

Half a mile north-east of Halifax, West Yorkshire, on the A647 Halifax to Queensbury road

Opening times: Monday to Saturday, 10.00 a.m.-5.00 p.m.; Sunday, 2.30-5.00 p.m.

Free admission.

This early nineteenth-century stone mansion contains collections of costumes and fabrics. There is also a military display.

Belvoir Castle

About seven miles west of Grantham, Lincolnshire, off the A607

Belvoir is open to the public from Easter to the end of September (October — Sundays only, 2.00-6.00 p.m.): Wednesdays, Thursdays, Saturdays, (12 noon-6.00 p.m.), Sundays (12 noon-7.00 p.m.) and Bank Holiday Mondays (11.00 a.m.-7.00 p.m.)

Dogs not allowed; the Castle can sometimes be hired for large banquets, conferences, etc.;

special Sunday events take place during the summer, such as medieval jousting tournaments, mock battles and car rallies.

Belvoir Castle was originally a fortress. It was completely rebuilt during the seventeenth century, and further reconstructed in the early nineteenth century by James Wyatt. It is now the home of the Duke and Duchess of Rutland.

Beningbrough Hall

Eight miles north-west of York, two miles west of Shipton off the A19

Season runs from April to the end of October: every day, except Mondays and Fridays, 12 noon-6.00 p.m.; Bank Holiday Mondays 11.00 a.m.-6.00 p.m. The garden is open from 11.00 a.m., last admissions 5.30 p.m.

Refreshments available; toilet facilities and access to the ground floor of the house for the disabled; no dogs allowed; picnic area; adventure playground for children under 12.

Beningbrough Hall is an early eighteenth-century country house. It was re-opened in 1979 by the National Trust and now contains a series of exhibitions — the domestic life of the house at all levels is illustrated through audiovisual displays.

Blickling Hall

Off the B1354, one mile
north-west of Aylsham, Norwich

Hall and gardens are open daily
(except Mondays and Fridays)
during April, May and October,
2.00-6.00 p.m.; on Tuesdays,
Wednesdays, Fridays and
Saturdays, 11.00 a.m.- 6.00 p.m.,
Sundays, 2.00-6.00 p.m., from the
end of May to the beginning of
October; and on all Bank Holiday
Mondays (except Easter Monday),
from 2.00-6.00 p.m.

Car park and picnic area;
refreshments available at
lunchtime; fishing (permits from
the Park Warden); two wheelchairs
available at gatehouse; toilets for
disabled, also access to ground
floor rooms; dogs on leads
allowed in park and walled picnic
area.

Blickling Hall dates from the time
of James I and was built by Sir
Henry Hobart, his Chief Justice.
The late eighteenth-century
Orangery was probably designed
by Humphry Repton.

Bolling Hall Museum

Bowling Hall Road, Bradford, West
Yorkshire

Opening times: April to
September, Tuesday to Sunday,
10.00 a.m.- 6.00 p.m.; October to
March, Tuesday to Sunday, 10.00
a.m.-5.00 p.m.; closed Mondays
except Bank Holidays.

Admission free.

The first known reference to the
manor of Bolling is found in the
Domesday Book of 1086. Since
then it has passed through several
families, including the Bollings,
Tempests and Woods. It is now
run by Bradford Corporation as a
museum.

Bolton Abbey and the Strid

The Abbey is about five miles east
of Skipton on the B6160; the Strid
is two miles further along the river
Wharfe

The public can visit at any time of
the year.

Car park at Bolton Abbey and also at the entrance to the Strid Wood nature trail; café; dogs allowed.

Bolton Abbey was built around 1150 for Augustinian canons, who remained there until the dissolution of the monasteries. Although much of the building is now in ruins, the nave is still used for church services.

'The Strid' is the name given to a small section of the river where water flows rapidly through a very deep, narrow gully, creating dangerous whirlpools as it does so.

Bolton Castle

Castle Bolton, five miles west of Leyburn, North Yorkshire

Open daily, except Mondays, 10.00 a.m.-6.00 p.m.

The Great Hall is used as a restaurant.

Bolton Castle was first built for the Scrope family as a manor house in the last quarter of the fourteenth century. It was later extended and made into a fortress, then virtually demolished during the Cromwellian period. Mary Queen of Scots was imprisoned at Bolton from June of 1568 until the following January.

Bramham Park

Five miles south of Wetherby, West Yorkshire, off the A1 (main approach signposted)

Except for the week of the Bramham horse trials, the house is open to the public from Good Friday until the last Sunday in September: Sundays, Tuesdays, Wednesdays and Thursdays, Easter Saturday and all Bank Holidays, 1.15-5.30 p.m. (last admission 5.00 p.m.)

Tea room; gift shop; gallery; children's playground; free car parking.

Bramham Park was constructed between 1698 and 1710 by Robert Benson. It contains collections of furniture, porcelain and paintings by Reynolds, Kneller, Agasse and other sporting artists, and there is also a set of House of Commons Journals which has records of the Members' reaction to the Gun Powder Plot and the indictment of Charles I.

The garden and wooded areas, laid out in the French style after Le Nôtre, have been described as miniature versions of the gardens at Versailles and Vaux le Vicomte.

a.m.-5.00 p.m., Sundays and Good Friday 2.00-5.00 p.m.

Self-service catering facilities in the Orangery; parties of between twenty and fifty people may book set meals in advance (except on Sundays and Bank Holidays).

The house was built between 1546 and 1587 on the site of a twelfth-century monastery. Special features at Burghley include wood carvings by Grinling Gibbons, silver fireplaces, painted ceilings and private collections of Baroque art.

Bronte Parsonage

Above the parish church off the top of Main Street, Haworth, West Yorkshire, eight miles west of Bradford and three miles south of Keighley

Open every day of the year, except for three weeks in December: 11.00 a.m.-5.30 p.m. (April to September), 11.00 a.m.-4.30 p.m. (October to March).

Ample car parking space; limited access for wheelchairs; no dogs allowed.

The Georgian parsonage, which used to be the Brontës' home, is now a museum that allows visitors to see where and how the family lived.

Broughton Hall

Three and a half miles west of Skipton, North Yorkshire, on the A59 Skipton to Clitheroe road

Open Tuesdays and Thursdays during May, June and July for parties of between 15 and 30

people (individuals may be able to join an existing party booking). Times should be arranged with the booking, though casual visitors may call between 2.00-5.00 p.m. on weekdays during May, June, and Spring and Summer Bank Holidays.

Refreshments are not normally included with the tour of the house; however, tea or coffee and biscuits can be provided by special arrangement for those travelling long distances.

Broughton Hall was built in 1597 by Henry Tempest and still remains the Tempest family's home. It was substantially altered in the eighteenth and nineteenth centuries, which accounts for its present Georgian appearance.

Burghley House

One mile south-east of Stamford, Lincolnshire, off the A1

Burghley House is open from April to the beginning of October, weekdays and Saturdays 11.00

Burnby Hall Gardens

Pocklington, Humberside

Gardens open: Easter Saturday, Sunday and Monday, 2.00-7.00 p.m., then every Saturday, Sunday and Bank Holiday to the end of May; from May to mid-September, Monday to Friday, 10.00 a.m.-7.00 p.m., Sundays 2.00-7.00 p.m. Museum and café 2.00-5.00 p.m. on all days when gardens are open.

Burnby Hall Gardens were created by the late P.M. Stewart prior to, and just after, World War II. The two lakes have probably the finest collection of water lilies in Europe whose display lasts from late June to late September. The museum houses a unique collection of trophies from Major Stewart's many overseas expeditions.

Burton Agnes Hall

Six miles south-west of Bridlington, North Yorkshire, off the A166

Hall and gardens open daily (Saturdays excepted) from 1 April to 31 October, 1.45-5.00 p.m.

(Sundays 1.45-6.00 p.m.) Also open to the public Easter Sunday and Monday.

Free car park; teas available; wheelchair access to the Hall's ground floor rooms; toilet facilities for the disabled; dogs on leads allowed in the grounds.

Burton Agnes Hall was begun in 1598 and completed in 1610. It has been altered little since, and is still the home of descendants of the family who built it.

Burton Constable Hall

About four miles north-east of Hull, off the B1238

Open each weekend from Easter Saturday until the end of September, 12.00 noon-5.00 p.m. During August the Hall is open Tuesdays, Wednesdays and Fridays.

Caravan and tent site half a mile from the Hall.

Built in 1570 and remodelled during the eighteenth century, Burton Constable Hall is situated in the Plain of Holderness. As well

as the house and its grounds there are agricultural machinery and vintage motor cycle museums, and a collection of Georgian scientific equipment and natural history specimens.

Cannon Hall

Cawthorne, about four miles east of Denby Dale, near Barnsley, West Yorkshire

Open weekdays 10.30 a.m.-5.00 p.m., Sundays 2.30-5.00 p.m.; closed Good Friday and 25, 26 and 27 December.

Admission free; wheelchair access to all ground floor rooms; no cafeteria; garden centre; dogs allowed in the park.

Cannon Hall, a late seventeenth-century house remodelled by John Carr of York during the mid-eighteenth century, is surrounded by seventy acres of parkland. It was opened as a country house museum in 1957 and has collections of furniture, glassware and paintings.

Cartwright Hall

Lister Park, about one mile from the centre of Bradford, West Yorkshire, on the A650 Keighley road

Closed Mondays, except Bank Holidays. Daily opening times are 10.00 a.m.-6.00 p.m. (10.00 a.m.-5.00 p.m. from October to March).

Parking on adjacent streets; admission free; dogs not allowed; café.

Cartwright Hall was built in 1904 as an art gallery in the Baroque style. Collections include nineteenth- and twentieth-century British art, contemporary prints, Old Master paintings by English and Continental artists and, for those interested in natural history, a display of mounted birds.

Castle Howard

Fifteen miles north-east of York, three miles off the A64

Castle Howard is open every day from 25 March to 31 October: grounds — 10.30 a.m.-5.00 p.m.; house and costume galleries — 11.30 a.m.-5.00 p.m. (last admission 4.45 p.m.)

Cafeteria serves hot meals and snacks; licensed restaurant available for parties booked in advance; facilities for the disabled; only guide dogs allowed into the house and costume galleries.

From the York road the approach to Castle Howard is a delightful drive along a straight, undulating avenue that passes through a stone arch (Carrmire Gate) and, a little further on, an impressively constructed Gate House; these are just appetisers for what lies ahead. At the top of the hill a large obelisk with inscriptions (one dating from 1731, another even earlier) straddles crossroads from which it is a matter of minutes to the stables. These now form the public entrance to the property and they also contain the Costume Galleries. The Galleries have the largest private collection of period costume in Britain and selections are displayed in

tableaux which change every year. To view the House a short, free ride on the colourfully designed Kelly Car (an elaborate tractor-drawn vehicle) will soon take you to Castle Howard's west wing tourist entrance.

Castle Howard's history began when the third Earl of Carlisle, Charles Howard (1669-1738), asked the playwright John Vanbrugh to design an elegant residence for him. This was to be on the site of an old castle among some hills to the west of Malton, about fifteen miles from the centre of York. Vanbrugh's response, with the help of the renowned architect Nicholas Hawksmoor, eventually resulted by 1714 in a domed centre block, an east wing and a south front. (The rather sombre-looking Mausoleum which stands in isolation within Castle Howard's grounds is another building, though on a different scale, which reflects the greatness of Hawksmoor's talent.)

The two men's inspiration was not entirely conventional, for the House faces north and south instead of the traditional east and west. Nor were the two fronts built in the same style; the south front, with its Grecian pediment above the entrance hall, is characterised by Corinthian architectural features, whereas the north is recognisably Doric. The dome, which rises high above other rooftop ornaments, was the first of its kind to be incorporated into a private residence. This was probably due to Hawksmoor's involvement with the design for one at Greenwich Hospital. Although there was a serious fire in 1940 that burned part of Castle Howard's dome, restoration work was carried out in 1960 to return it, as near as possible, to its former splendour. It spans the magnificent Great Hall where high walls with gently coloured frescoes and white, stone pillars lead the eye upwards to the large and impressive painting of sun horses on the cupola.

A further addition to the House was made by Sir Thomas Robinson, son-in-law to Charles Howard. After the Earl's death, his

son, Henry, gave Robinson permission to add a west wing. When it was finished, however, it did not really blend with Vanbrugh's style. This wing contains the Long Gallery where today there is a varied assembly of paintings, including two by Hans Holbein — one of Henry VIII, and the other a portrait of Thomas Howard (1474-1554), third Duke of Norfolk. Throughout the House, the selection of paintings by numerous Masters is tantalising for the connoisseur — Rubens, Tintoretto, Gainsborough, Sir Joshua Reynolds...

There is also much ancient art to see, for which the fourth Earl of Carlisle, Henry Howard (1694-1758), may be thanked. He sent a great deal of material to England from Italy, including Roman busts and fragments from Egyptian artefacts. One of Castle Howard's characteristically light and airy corridors, the so-called Antique Passage, houses some early eighteenth-century tables whose tops have been made from Roman mosaics.

Castle Howard has always remained in the same family. George Howard, the present head of the household, continues in the tradition of his forbears to welcome visitors to this historic spot where the rustle of pheasants in long grass around corn-cut fields, the honking of geese over the lakes to the north and south of the House and the squawking of tame peacocks have all become familiar sounds. (Additional interest has been provided recently, too, with the interment of a 'time-capsule' whose twentieth-century artefacts will fascinate future generations in hundreds of years' time when they come to decipher its strange contents.)

Open House
by
the Duchess of Devonshire

Among the deluge of paper which arrives on my table every morning there is the inevitable quota of forms to be filled up for every conceivable eventuality. Most of them have a heading called OCCUPATION. Like many other women I could with truth put Company Director, Farmer, or even Author now, but I consider that Housewife is my occupation as it has been for forty years, so that is what I write on the dotted line.

The house I am wife of is Chatsworth. It is very big. The roof covers 1⅓ acres, there are 175 rooms, some of them bigger than squash courts, 3,426 feet of passages, 17 staircases, 359 doors, 24 bathrooms, 52 wash hand basins, 29 sinks and 53 lavatories, all lit by 2,084 electric light bulbs.

Chatsworth has been open for people to see round ever since the original house was built in the 1550s. I believe the route you follow is the longest of any house which is open: over a third of a mile on the flat plus 101 steps up and 60 down (you emerge on a higher level).

I have lived in this house for 23 years, but I still have to think which is the quickest way before I set forth to visit some distant room, and I am still apt to open a wrong door. I have put down my bag in a rare part of the house and not seen it again for months. The joys and problems of living in a huge house are all magnified. Everything is bigger than life size. The indoor distances, the faraway meals, the long passages and stairs for luggage all add to the complications of life. It is a terrible place to house-train a puppy. But children can roller-skate for miles and on a wet day you can walk for hours, be entertained by what you see and keep dry.

You lose things, but you never know what you may find. Once, on a winter afternoon when it was getting dark, I journeyed to the last room of the East Attics to look for something. It is quite a trek to get there – down the Book

Passage, through the nurseries, along the Bachelor Passage, up the stone stairs, past the lamp cupboards, turn right and it is the third room on the right. I opened the door and stopped dead, amazed to see an old man sitting among piles of books, reading under a strong lamp. I was so surprised I said something like, 'I'm so sorry to disturb you', and fled back the way I had come. I have no idea who he was and what he was doing and for all I know he may still be there.

This may give you an idea of the size of the place. The contents are another matter. The house is full of works of art of all descriptions: pictures, sculptures, drawings, prints, books, silver, furniture, china, textiles and many curiosities besides, collected by fourteen generations of Cavendishes.

The majority of these are what museum people describe as 'important'. A great number are out on view, but many (like the Old Master Drawings) are too fragile to stand the light and are put away. Besides which there is no room for more to be on show. Perhaps the rooms are already too crowded.

The reason for this huge quantity of 'things' is that the contents of several other houses (notably 2 Carlton Gardens and Chiswick House in London) have devolved upon Chatsworth.

I have used a lot of furniture and pictures in two hotels (the Devonshire Arms at Bolton Abbey in Yorkshire and the Cavendish at Baslow in Derbyshire) but the attics at Chatsworth are still crowded with objects of every kind.

All these things have to be looked after, both those on show and those which are stored, and ultimately that is the responsibility of the housewife.

I used to think you could *arrange* one of the big rooms, that it could be frozen like a photograph and nothing need be changed as long as it was kept clean. I was wrong. Curtains, bed hangings, coverings on furniture and silk on walls fade and perish with alarming speed. Furniture and leather bindings (like the beasts from which they are made) must be fed. Paintings on walls and ceilings grow dim and must be restored; carpets must be mended if old and beautiful, or replaced if new and much walked on. To keep rooms and their contents in good order for people to see is a constant work which does not show except that it halts deterioration. It is like running on the spot.

The same applies in the garden. Like the house, it is outsize. 105 acres of land are enclosed, and as well as the obvious work of planting and weeding, mowing and sweeping, there are miles of paths, with their attendant drains, stone steps, balustrades, wrought ironwork, lead and stone statues to be looked after, and to cap it all the fountains and cascade which are world-famous. The water which supplies them is held in two eight-acre lakes on the plateau five hundred feet above the house. These in turn are fed from conduits dug for two miles on the moor, higher still.

Luckily for Chatsworth the people who look after it all are experts in their own fields, from drainer to silver steward, engineer to librarian, joiner to needlewoman, gardener to electrician, housekeeper to gamekeeper, book-keeper to telephone operator. There is a permanent staff of over forty, augmented by about ninety extra when the house is open. Sometimes it feels like running a mixture of a museum and an hotel, as well as my family home.

The house and garden seem to have some compelling power or charm which holds people and keeps them interested in the place and its well-being. It is this which makes the work of the housewife so intensely interesting, the human side of the place which is inextricably mixed up with the building and what is in it and the garden, farms and woods by which it is surrounded. Most of the people who work at Chatsworth live in estate houses. This spreads the interest even wider as these buildings are also the responsibility of Chatsworth and there is an endless programme of maintenance and improvement in the surrounding villages as well as on the house itself.

Chatsworth is a traditional place for a day out for people from the industrial towns of the East Midlands. It has been ever since 1849, when the railway opened to Rowsley three miles away. 80,000 people came to see the house and garden in that year, and the number was exceeded when the railway reached Manchester in 1863. No charge was made and all the rooms were open except the Duke's private apartments on the west front.

The first year in which a charge was made was 1908 and from then till 1939 the money taken, after paying the guides who were estate pensioners, was given to local hospitals.

A girls' public school, Penrhos College, occupied the house from 1939–46 and it was reopened to the public in 1949. Since then the entrance fees have gone towards the upkeep of the house and garden.

In spite of the huge contribution this makes to the expenses there is still a sizeable deficit. In an attempt to make the place self-supporting my husband and son decided to lease the house, garden and park to a charitable trust and to fund the trust with money from the sale of some books and a painting by Nicolas Poussin. This was done in 1981. The income from this fund is now available to help with the upkeep.

Sometimes people ask us if we mind the crowds of visitors who arrive every day during the season. The answer is very definitely NO. The scale of the place is so enormous it needs people to bring it to life and to my mind it greatly enhances it. Far from being in any way annoying it is extremely cheering to see people enjoying themselves and looking with interest at any new work which has been done, a rearrangement of rooms or a new planting in the garden. A lot of people come so often we have introduced season tickets.

Why do they come? What is it about Chatsworth that attracts people year after year? Is it the history of the place, the sheer size of it, the things in it, the quality of the landscape and the beauty of the exterior of the house? Is it the garden with its famed waterworks, the fountains and the cascade, the huge space of the park, hard grazed by sheep so it's like walking on 1,000 acres of lawn?

It is certain you cannot relate any of it to real life. It is impossible to imagine knitting in front of a fire in the state rooms, or cooking with the giant pots and pans of heaviest copper. Only in a dream can you imagine eating in the dining room with its vast table laden with silver, china and pink Bohemian glass set out for a ghostly dinner party which never takes place. (I once heard this room properly cut down to size by a Yorkshireman whose wife was dallying next door, shouting to her over his shoulder, 'By, tea's laid, Mabel'.)

Perhaps people like it because of a certain freedom. You are not hustled into an 'area' if you wish to have a picnic but you can settle down on the lawn or wherever else you like. Children can run till they have to cool off in the cascade and dogs are welcome in the garden.

There are no guides in the house so you can spend as long or as short a time as you choose, and even on the most crowded days you only have to walk a little further to find peace and solitude in the garden, in the open expanse of the park or in the woods on the steep hill above the house.

Perhaps people just feel the magic of the place. I have travelled in many parts of the world and seen much beautiful scenery and many beautiful buildings, but I have never come home without being struck anew by how lucky I am to be the housewife at Chatsworth.

Chatsworth House

Eight miles north of Matlock, Derbyshire, off the B6012

Open every day from 1 April until 30 October: House 11.30 a.m.-4.30 p.m.; farmyard and adventure playground 10.30 a.m.-4.30 p.m.; garden 11.30 a.m.-5.00 p.m.

Parking; toilets for the disabled (though wheelchairs cannot go into the house because of the stairs); shops; tea rooms; dogs on leads allowed in the grounds.

Chatsworth, near Bakewell and Buxton in Derbyshire, can be enjoyed long before arriving at the magnificent building; its surrounding parkland attracts many visitors to walk beside the river Derwent or just picnic lazily in some quiet corner. The House is the home of the Duke and Duchess of Devonshire — ever since Bess of Hardwick and her second husband, Sir William Cavendish, began building it in 1552, this grand residence has remained a living part of the Cavendish family. Each successive generation has added to, altered, or generally improved Bess's original Tudor construction. The very first Duke of Devonshire, William Cavendish (1640-1707), created the west and south fronts and erected new outbuildings. The sixth Duke, William Spencer Cavendish (1790-1858), took a great interest in the garden and brought exotic plants from abroad; he had a large glass house built to accommodate them all. He was also responsible for the addition of the north wing, including the Sculpture Gallery in which to display his beloved collection of stone and marble masterpieces, and the Orangery where special plants could be nurtured. Today a few precious inanimate objects, like the stage coach, share the Orangery with a gift shop.

Owing to the penchant of other Dukes besides William Spencer for accumulating artefacts, Chatsworth is the proud possessor of several fine collections. The library has a rich collection of books, such as Henry Cavendish's on science. Henry was the grandson of William, the second Duke; he studied the make-up of water and discovered that hydrogen formed an essential part of it. Another set of books came from the fourth Duke's

211

marriage to the daughter of the third Earl of Burlington who, being an architect, had a large quantity of volumes on the subject.

From a distance Chatsworth's mullioned windows, well-proportioned wings and classical features are all set against a scenic backcloth of lawns and thick woodland. Inside, as you tread reverently from one room to another, you are besieged by the splendour and richness of its art. One of the first rooms to be entered is a perfect example — in the Painted Hall everything reflects attention to detail, from the geometrically patterned black and white marble floor, up the red-carpeted staircase with an intricate gilt ironwork banister either side, to the gallery facing Laguerre's busy scenes of Julius Caesar's life. These paintings date from the latter part of the seventeenth century; as figures are caught by light, groups on the walls and ceiling reverberate with movement and vitality.

Together with carved woodwork around door frames and windows, above fireplaces and along the tops of the walls on cornices, ceiling paintings are a marked feature of the State Rooms in the Dining Room one of Verrio's works from 1691-2 incorporates the figure of a rather dully-clad woman with what looks like a large pair of scissors in her right hand. She apparently represents a fury cutting the thread of life from a nearby victim. It has been said that, because of his dislike for the woman, Verrio based the lunging figure's face on that of the first Duke's housekeeper.

The State Music Room contains an element of fun as well. Behind the bright green of a Siberian malachite table is a door which, when opened, leads to another. On this second door hang a violin and its bow . . . or do they? If you were to touch the instrument you would run your fingers over a flat surface, for the door is made up of two sections — a painted upper, and a carved lower. The *trompe l'oeil* is an ingenious curiosity which draws the eyes back time and time again in disbelief. It was painted by Jan van der Vaart (c.1653-1727)

and was only brought to Chatsworth during the 1830s. The State Rooms were originally intended for display purposes and did not actually host royalty until Victoria became Queen.

Throughout the house furniture, carpets, decorations and tapestries are in keeping with Chatsworth's luxuriousness. Even wallpaper deserves some attention before passing by — in some bedrooms Chinese paper, in varying shades of green, is ornamented with now dimmed birds perching amid a darker green vegetation. Curtains, matching the colours of each room, hang in splendid folds at every window — an occasional glance outside will take in the garden's fountains, lawns and flowers. The trust established by the present Duke helps maintain all this beauty; he feels it is important that people should be able to continue gaining so much pleasure from visiting his old family home, which is kept with understandable pride and devotion.

Clumber Chapel

Four and a half miles south-east of Worksop, six and a half miles south-west of East Retford, Nottinghamshire

Chapel open April to end of September, Monday to Friday, 2.00-7.00 p.m.; Saturday, Sunday and Bank Holidays, 12.00-7.00 p.m.; 1 October to 31 March daily, 1.00-4.00 p.m.

Facilities include car, caravan and coach parks, clock tower shop, restaurant, cycle hire, fishing (during the coarse season), ferry, nature walks, orienteering (by arrangement). Facilities for the disabled: wheelchairs available free of charge; tandem and tricycle hire; fishing platform with wheelchair access and rail; toilets.

Clumber Chapel was built in the 1880s for the seventh Duke of Newcastle. It is surrounded by 3,800 acres of parkland, farmland, lake and woodlands.

Denby Dale Pies

Every so often, 'pie fever' hits a village between Huddersfield and Barnsley called Denby Dale. It happened in 1964 when the mad, pie-making light suddenly appeared in the eyes of its inhabitants. They threw caution and everything else to the winds and set about making 'the world's largest pie'; a six-ton affair which raised enough money, when cut up and sold in portions, to buy Denby Dale a village hall.

Eight times in less than two centuries Denby Dale has made a giant pie. Any excuse will do – the victory at Waterloo, the repeal of the Corn Laws or the birth of a royal baby. One pie, probably the first, was made in 1788 to celebrate the recovery of George III from mental illness. Inspired as it was by such loyal and humane sentiments, it deserved to be at least a greater success than the pie made a century later in 1887. That one went bad — and how!

There could be no doubt about its condition; when a pie big enough to need a four-wheeled cart and two horses to move it goes off, everyone knows about it and tries to pretend that he never wanted a pie in the first place. But summat (as they doubtless said in Denby Dale) had to be done so they held their noses, gritted their teeth and (presumably with some difficulty) said, 'Let's give it a funeral'. And since all this happened, not in a fairy tale but in Denby Dale, they did the job thoroughly.

A funeral card was printed 'In affectionate Rememberance of the Denby Dale Pie which died August 27th, 1887, aged three days and was interred in Quick Lime, with much rejoicing, in Toby Wood, Sunday, August 28th, 1887.' The sad occasion was even commemorated in verse:

Strong, strong was the smell
  that compelled us to part,
From a treat to our stomachs to
  a salve to our hearts.

The 'poem' runs for another stanza or two but each line seems worse than the last, giving the impression that it, too, might be succumbing to the fate of the pie itself:

This mystic pie, so large and
  rare,
Smell'd awful as a tomb.

And, if the locals are to be believed, the smell lingers in Toby Wood to this day.

Inevitably, there was an inquest and since such a catastrophe could not possibly be Denby Dale's fault, it was blamed on the fact that foreign cooks from London and such far-flung places had been hired for the occasion!

But you can't suppress pie-mania for long in Denby Dale, hence this footnote on the funeral card:

THE RESURRECTION PIE
Undeterred by previous efforts the people of Denby Dale have attempted another pie, which is to be consumed today, Saturday. This has been made by the ladies of the village and is expected to be a success. It consists of forty-eight stones flour, ninety-six stones potatoes, a heifer, two calves and two sheep.

And so the folk of Denby Dale turned disaster into triumph, doubtless resolving to learn from

their mistakes. But you can never insure against every possible mishap; the 1928 pie, for instance, managed to get stuck in the oven, although it still raised the tidy sum — for those days — of £1,000 for Huddersfield Royal Infirmary.

Traditionally, each Denby Dale pie is bigger than its predecessor. The 1964 pie contained the beef of ten bullocks, a ton and a half of potatoes, half a ton of flour, five hundredweights of lard and fifty gallons of gravy. The pie dish, which weighed a ton and a half, was 18 feet long, 6 feet wide and 18 inches deep — big enough, in fact, for cocktail parties to be held in it as it floated, empty, on the canal. Rather mysteriously it sank, which was very good for publicity. Incidentally, like its predecessor of 1928, this pie got stuck, coming out of the barn in which it had been cooked. To free it, oxy-acetylene cutting tools had to be used.

But all this talk of pies is making me hungry — perhaps it is time they made another . . .

Doddington Hall

Five miles west of Lincoln on the B1190

Opening times: Wednesdays and Sundays during May to September and Easter, May, Spring and Summer Bank Holiday Mondays, 2.00-6.00 p.m. Other times can be arranged for parties of twenty or more people.

Refreshments available; shops; special children's guide to the house; nature and garden trails.

Set in the beauty of a small Lincolnshire village, Doddington Hall rests quietly behind a Dutch gabled gate house, with seventeenth-century brick outbuildings and the church of St Peter close by. Today the gatehouse is the public entrance to the hall and grounds. (It is also a shop, among whose wares locally-made pale, fragrant honey is an attractive delicacy.) From here the visitor walks into the east garden where there are paths, formal lawns and borders, and walls to left and right. At the far end the house's three small domes, mullioned windows, stone quoins and worn, deep red and sand-coloured brick walls dominate the tranquil scene.

The manor of Doddington was bought from Sir John Savile in 1593 by the registrar to the Bishop of Lincoln, Thomas Tailor. Tailor set Robert Smithson, the architect who was responsible for Hardwick Hall in Derbyshire and Wollaton Hall in Nottingham, to work on designing a house. Smithson went against convention and the popular vogue for internal courtyards, and settled instead for an outward-looking building. His uniformity of construction gave Doddington a domestic, yet elegant, charm which has remained over the years.

When Tailor's son died in 1652 the hall passed to his niece, Elizabeth Anton, who was married to Edward Hussey. Portraits of Sir Edward and Lady Hussey hang in the Long Gallery. This must have been one of the brightest rooms in the house when windows were in place along the east, as well as the west, wall. (The east windows were

blocked in during the 1760s so that pictures and porcelain could be put on display.) The Long Gallery has a closet containing a model of the Husseys' son who died in 1643, fighting in the English Civil War. The fatal bullet hole is visible in the top edge of his breast plate.

In 1749 the last surviving member of the Hussey family, Mrs Sarah Apreece, left Doddington to her second grandson, Sir John Hussey Delaval of Seaton Delaval in Northumberland. He had the house completely redecorated during the early 1760s; work included double glazing in several of the bedrooms to combat draughts. At his death the estate was taken over by his younger brother, Edward; in the Drawing Room a letter from Edward to his daughter, Sarah Gunman, is on show in which he discusses a piano for her, one of 'handsome appearance' costing £89 5s. On her death in 1825, because of

George Ralph Payne Jarvis's romantic involvement with Sarah, the hall passed into Jarvis hands. It has been the family's home ever since.

Visitors will find Doddington gently unassuming; it is a house full of very personal touches, — Edward Delaval's letter, for instance, or the refectory table, whose carving was executed by George Jarvis, and the red and white beef bone chess set in the Drawing Room which was made by French Napoleonic prisoners of war at Dover Castle where George was the Castle commandant. He acquired three such chess sets, knowing that it would help the men earn some welcome money.

Doddington has further reminders of life's crueller aspects: the White Hall contains a harshly-wrought bridle that was used to punish scolding housewives, and part of a set of gibbeting irons which were associated with a local man called

East Riddlesden Hall

One mile north-east of Keighley, West Yorkshire, on the south side of the A650

East Riddlesden Hall, following a major programme of restoration work, will be re-opened to the public in 1984. Details about opening hours and arrangements will be available from the Administrators at East Riddlesden Hall or from the Regional Information Office, 32 Goodramgate, York.

This National Trust property is a seventeenth-century manor house with tithe barn, small formal garden and stable.

Ebberston Hall

Eleven miles south-west of Scarborough on the Scarborough to Pickering road (A10)

Open from Good Friday to mid-September, 10.00 a.m.-5.00 p.m. daily.

No wheelchair access.

Ebberston Hall is a Palladian Villa of 1718 and was designed by the architect Colin Campbell.

Tom Otter, who murdered a South Hykeham girl in 1805. (In bizarre fashion, three years later a blue tit made a nest in Otter's iron-gripped skull.) The second half-landing is hung with nautical pictures, details of whose events – battles amid dramatic seas, crashing waves – are recorded in Captain Christopher Gunman's journals, including the blasting away of his left hand.

After the house, it is worth spending some time in the sheltered west garden and the wild garden beyond. The latter is especially picturesque in May when carpets of pink cherry blossom and brilliantly coloured rhododendron blooms catch the eye. The quiet is typical of an estate in total harmony with its surroundings – Mr and Mrs Antony Jarvis maintain Doddington's uniqueness by shunning commercial exploitation.

Elsham Hall Country Park

Elsham, near Brigg, South Humberside

Opening times: daily 11.00 a.m.-8.00 p.m. or dusk from Easter to October (last entry 5.30 p.m. weekdays, 6.30 p.m. Sundays and Bank Holidays); from November to Easter, Sundays and Bank Holidays only, 11.00 a.m.-4.30 p.m. (Closed Good Friday and Christmas Day; may be closed in bad weather.)

The park is ideal for family outings and for large parties; bookings can be made in advance. It has several lakes, an arboretum, an adventure playground, a duck pond and various domestic animals and wildfowl; visitors can feed some of the birds and the giant carp. There are also a tea room, a craftshop — craftsmen can be seen at work most days — and good facilities for the disabled.

THE CALENDAR YEAR

Elton Hall

On the A605, eight miles west of Peterborough, Cambridgeshire

Open Bank Holiday weekends and Wednesdays from May to August, and Thursdays during August only, 2.00-5.00 p.m. Parties on other days throughout the summer by appointment.

No wheelchair access; dogs not allowed; home-made teas available on the terrace overlooking the gardens.

Elton Hall dates from 1475. This family home has collections of books, furniture and paintings on display.

Elvaston Castle

Four miles south-east of Derby on the B5010; signposted off the A6 and the A52

Opening arrangements: estate museum — Easter to October, Wednesday to Saturday 1.00-5.00 p.m., Sundays and Bank Holidays 10.00-6.00 p.m.; information centre, shop and exhibitions — Easter to October, Tuesday to Saturday 12.30-5.00 p.m., Sundays and Bank Holidays 11.00 a.m.-5.00 p.m. The park is open daily until dusk throughout the year.

Free admission to park — small charge for other amenities; toilets for the disabled; parlour tea room in castle (Easter to October, 11.00 a.m.-4.00 p.m.); riding stables (details on application); caravan and camp site (Easter to October).

Elvaston Castle Museum demonstrates the life, work and craft skills from around 1910 of a self-sufficient country house estate, with blacksmith, wheelwright, farrier, restored gardener's cottage, etc. The rest of the castle is closed for renovation. There are also two hundred acres of woodland and landscaped parkland, formal gardens, extensive topiary gardens, a walled old English garden and a nature trail.

Epworth Old Rectory

Sixteen miles from Doncaster, on the A161 between Goole and Gainsborough, Humberside

From March to September the Rectory is open on weekdays 10.00 a.m.-12 noon and 2.00-4.00 p.m. (Sundays 2.00-4.00 p.m.) Visits can be made by prior arrangement at other times of the year.

Wheelchair access limited to the ground floor; dogs not allowed; refreshments and accommodation available by arrangement.

The Old Rectory was built in 1709 and was the boyhood home of John and Charles Wesley.

Felbrigg Hall

Near Felbrigg, three miles south-west of Cromer

House and garden open April to October, Tuesday to Sunday (except Friday) and Bank Holiday Mondays, 2.00-6.0 p.m. (closed Good Friday).

National Trust shop; teas in the old kitchen; facilities for the disabled, including provision of wheelchairs for visitors; woodland walk to Felbrigg woods.

Felbrigg Hall is a seventeenth-century house. Its contents of furniture and pictures are mostly from the eighteenth century. Also of interest are an orangery and a walled garden.

Fulbeck Hall

Lincolnshire, on the A607 Lincoln to Grantham road, one mile south of the junction with the Newark to Sleaford road (A17)

Open Spring Bank Holiday, then daily during August, 2.00-6.00 p.m.

Reduced admission charge for the disabled since wheelchair access limited to ground floor only; dogs allowed in the gardens; cream teas.

Fulbeck Hall is set in eleven acres of garden. Dating mostly from the eighteenth century, it has been the home of the Fane family for 350 years. It has an attractive collection of paintings and furniture.

Fountains Abbey

Four miles south-west of Ripon, North Yorkshire

Opening times for 1984 not yet known owing to the transfer of Fountains Abbey and the Studley Royal Estate to the National Trust.

Fountains Abbey, now ruins set in very beautiful surroundings, used to be a Cistercian monastery.

Georgian Theatre and Theatre Museum

Victoria Road, Richmond, North Yorkshire

The theatre and museum are open daily from 1 May to 30 September, 2.30-5.30 p.m. (last admission 5.00 p.m.) On Saturdays and Bank Holiday Mondays opening time is 10.30 a.m.-1.30 p.m.

The museum houses a collection of original playbills from 1792 to the 1840s, as well as the oldest and largest complete set of painted scenery in Britain (1836).

Every summer, visitors to Richmond have a unique opportunity to return for a while to Georgian days by squeezing themselves into what is surely the tiniest theatre in Yorkshire.

If it were not quite so clearly marked, Richmond's Georgian Theatre (which Ivor Brown said looked like 'a barn that had come to town') might easily be missed — and that would be a pity, for within the grey stone building, entered almost furtively from Friar's Wynd (pronounced *weend*), is a world of magic.

The little paybox is almost unchanged from the time it first took money from the patrons who crowded its narrow forms and small boxes on the opening night, 2 September 1788. And crowded is certainly the appropriate word, for on that auspicious occasion the audience numbered 400; which seems to prove that the Georgians were, on the whole, a smaller breed than we latter-day Elizabethans — today, a capacity house is estimated to total no more than 200.

A narrow flight of stone steps takes you to the boxes, on each of which is emblazoned the name of an eminent dramatist — Shakespeare, Jonson, Dryden, Rowe, Sheridan, Goldsmith . . . Superior folk, segregated here from the common herd, may observe not only the activities on the beautiful little stage, but also the antics of the 'groundlings' packing the forms in the stepped pit below. Above the boxes is the gallery, complete with the barracking-board once kicked by Georgian playgoers who were less inhibited than we in expressing their approval — or otherwise — of those seeking to entertain them.

Richmond, although visited by barnstorming strolling players, had no proper theatre' until one Samuel Butler, who had been running the Theatre Royal in York, proposed to the Mayor and Corporation of the Swaledale town that he should provide just such an amenity to 'accommodate the Town and County in a more commodious manner'. He was offered the site on which the present theatre stands and immediately began building his playhouse. In a mere four months he was ready to open. His first programme consisted of a prologue specially written by himself, two plays called *Inkle and Yarico*, a comic opera by George Colman and Mrs Inchbald's comedy *The Midnight Hour*.

Butler was well supported in the company by his family, some of whom might have served as models for Dickens's Infant Phenomenon in *Nicholas Nickleby*. Butler's own son by his second wife played adult roles in Shakespeare when he was only 14, for a youngster of talent could make his name early in the theatre of those times. Before he was spirited away to London, the great Edmund Kean himself worked for Butler at Richmond as a singer of comic songs and 'gentleman harlequin'. His salary was fifteen shillings a week. When the boy's big chance came, Butler generously paid his fare to London and some years later, when 'the unrivalled' Kean again appeared at Richmond, he is said to have refused his fee out of gratitude to his then deceased benefactor.

In the years that followed the opening of the theatre, many and varied were the delights offered to the theatre-goers of Richmond. Not only Shakespeare, comic opera and farce, but such novelties as a tightrope walker who wheeled a barrow through the air from stage to gallery. Yet for some reason even these excitements were not enough. Samuel Butler's theatre managed to survive him by thirty years but then, despite the efforts of his widow and his son and daughter, it finally had to close.

And now the theatre itself 'played many parts' — it was a corn store, then a furniture store, part of it was used as a wine cellar and eventually, in 1940, it became a wartime salvage store. And that development proved to be one of those quite accidental benefits which surprisingly resulted from the war. For it was during this latest phase of the theatre's life that the discovery of its real character was made.

In 1943 its little stage was trodden again by actors' feet when a brave attempt was made to celebrate, as much as wartime stringency allowed, the 850th anniversary of the enfranchisement of Richmond as a borough.

The 'barn' was now known to have been a theatre, but it was still thought to have had a flat floor level with the stage. Only when three nailed-down trap doors were discovered on what had been the stage was its true Georgian character suspected. Clearly these trap doors had been there to allow the players to appear and disappear in the manner of the Demon King of pantomime. But when one of these traps was opened, some eighteen inches below it was encountered the roof of the brick wine cellar. Even a midget would have had difficulty making his exits and entrances in such a constricted space. What was the explanation? Was it possible that the wine cellar had actually been 'inserted' into the theatre's structure?

The question, it was felt, could not possibly remain unanswered, so the then Town Clerk of Richmond, David Brooks, decided that the only course was to remove the wine cellar and see what happened. The risks were somewhat daunting. What if the theatre collapsed when the cellar was removed? Obviously, steps must be taken to see that it didn't! And so restoration began.

Fortunately there was no disaster. On the contrary, the removal of the wine cellar revealed the presence of former dressing rooms, signs of former steps and doors, and most exciting of all, evidence that before the wine cellar had been introduced there had been a sunken pit. So this had clearly been a genuine, orthodox Georgian theatre. The original, largely green colour scheme was restored, along with paintings on the ceiling and cornice, though some of the painting did not need restoration.

In 1963 there was a gala re-opening of the theatre in which one item was the singing of *Sweet Lass of Richmond Hill*. This song has nothing to do with Richmond in Surrey, as southerners like to

think, but was written in honour of Frances I'Anson by her husband Leonard McNally. (Frances lived at Hill House, which still stands in Richmond.)

Since its re-opening, many theatrical luminaries have trodden the boards at Richmond. And not only actors. Acoustically, said Yehudi Menuhin, it ranks among the best theatres in the world. During the last twenty years it has had no fewer than five royal visits. Behind the theatre, in buildings formerly used as warehouses, is a theatre museum designed by Gregor MacGregor, the theatre manager. Exhibits include a large collection of painted scenery from 1836, playbills and handbills, one of Edmund Kean's snuffboxes, photographs of artists who have appeared at Richmond since the theatre's restoration and the autographs of royal visitors.

Even without its fairy-tale theatre, Richmond would be one of the best loved of Yorkshire towns. According to one investigator, a total of 54 cities, towns and villages all over the world are also called Richmond, though not all of them started life with that name — Richmond in Surrey was originally called Sheen but was renamed in honour of the Yorkshire Richmond by Henry VII (Earl of the Swaledale Richmond)

when he rebuilt the Palace of Sheen.

Richmond Castle, with its keep over a hundred feet high, is said to be the oldest stone-built fortress in England, founded in 1071 by the Norman Alan the Red. Such an ancient pile is bound to have its legends and they are good, satisfying ones in keeping with the rich folklore of the town where they were born. King Arthur, it is said, sleeps beneath the castle in a secret chamber, at a round table accompanied by his knights and his treasures, including the magical sword Excalibur, his great horn and his treasure chest. Anyone who can blow the horn and draw the sword from its scabbard will be rewarded with the chest.

No one has quite managed it yet, but legend tells of one Richmond man who at least had a go. That man was Potter Thompson, and he found the secret chamber after following a tunnel that led him beneath the castle. There he would have drawn the sword and no doubt blown the horn as well, but at the crucial moment a ghostly voice echoed through the chamber:

Potter, Potter Thompson
If thou hadst either drawn the
  sword or blown the horn
Thouds't been the luckiest man
That ever yet was born.

He was much too scared!

Richmond has an enormous cobbled market square in which stands the redundant church of Holy Trinity, now the Regimental Museum of the Green Howards, 'family' regiment of the North Riding. The old twelfth-century church, leased to the regiment by the Church Commissioners for a peppercorn rent, has been adapted to its new role by the Green Howards at a cost of £90,000.

Richmond is alive with history and those old customs which keep history from quite retreating into dusty corners of the library shelf. Once a year the Mayor receives the 'First Fruits' of the new season's wheat. From the Tower of Holy Trinity, the Pancake Bell is still rung on Shrove Tuesday at 11 a.m.

to remind the housewives to stir the fire and get to their cooking! Daily, at 8 a.m., the 'Prentice Bell' is rung, and at 8 p.m. the curfew — though nobody nowadays takes it as a signal to go home and put up the shutters, as they probably did in the time of William the Conqueror.

What was intended as another Richmond church is found not far from the market place — Grey Friars Tower, which was begun, but never finished, by the Grey Friars, who began their building at about the time Henry VIII embarked on the dissolution of the monasteries, so they really didn't have much of a chance! Another tower in Richmond — one that is complete in itself — is the Culloden Tower, built to celebrate the bloody victory over

the Jacobites on a moorland far to the north of those surrounding Richmond.

Gilling Castle

Gilling East, York

Only the Entrance Hall and late Elizabethan Great Chamber are open to the public (10.00 a.m.-12.00 noon and 2.00-4.00 p.m.) since Gilling Castle is a boarding school.

Entry to the house is free; a small charge is made for entry to the gardens; no toilet, wheelchair, etc., facilities; dogs on leads are permitted in the grounds.

Gunby Hall

Two and a half miles north-west of Burgh-le-Marsh, seven miles west of Skegness, Lincolnshire, on the south side of the A158

House and garden open from April to the end of September, Thursdays, 2.00-6.00 p.m.; on Tuesdays, Wednesdays and Fridays by written appointment to J.D. Wrisdale, Gunby Hall, Gunby, Spilsby; also open on a few Sundays for charity events.

Wheelchair access only in garden; no refreshments; dogs should be on leads; access road unsuitable for coaches, which must park in layby at gates half a mile from entrance.

Gunby Hall was built in 1700 in the style of Christopher Wren. It contains portraits by Reynolds as well as an autographed copy of Boswell's *Life of Johnson*.

Haddon Hall

Two miles south-east of Bakewell, Derbyshire, on the Buxton to Matlock road (A6)

Open from Good Friday or 1 April (whichever is earlier) to the end of September: Tuesday to Saturday inclusive, 11.00 a.m.-6.00 p.m.; Sunday, 2.00-6.00 p.m.; Mondays at Easter and the Spring and late Summer Bank Holidays, 11.00 a.m.-6.00 p.m.

Large car park almost opposite the entrance to the grounds; stables tea-room serves lunches and teas; dogs not admitted.

The first sight of this very old and beautiful house, only a short ride from Bakewell in Derbyshire, creates an immediate sense of well-being — as the river Wye gently meanders round the slope on which the Hall is built, Haddon's steeply rising crenellated walls seem to blend softly with the surrounding countryside.
Once inside the courtyard, where large stone flags undulate down a surprising incline, you soon become aware of different architectural features placed side

by side. The mixture derives from the habit of successive Haddon owners of adding improvements here and there — the north-west tower was built in about 1530, whereas the octagonal bell turret was probably constructed around 1450. The tranquil atmosphere is shared by a couple of medieval gargoyles leaning out from the buttery wall to peer down at passers-by.

At the upper end of the courtyard, preceded by several steps, is the porch marking the entrance to the banqueting hall.

The hall is a very lofty room with a large fireplace, minstrels' galleries from which recitals are still given by early music enthusiasts, and, in great medieval tradition, a long table and bench raised on a dais. The table is supported by three legs, and at some time the top has been turned over: so much hacking at the bread and meat must have wreaked havoc with the surface and caused such pits and craters that it became impossible to use. (The bench has suffered similar hurts from Haddon's feasting revellers.)

A major decoration to the room is an impressive heraldic tapestry, probably dating from the 1460s. Haddon is renowned for its tapestries; although some sixty pieces were damaged during a fire in 1925, there are still many left to admire, including the seventeenth-century 'Senses' tapestries. Each of these has a central motif, representing either touch, taste,

sight, smell or hearing, which is surrounded by characters from Aesop's fables.

To the left of the hall, at the end of a slanting passage with well-worn, channelled stones, the dimly-lit kitchen effuses a likeable starkness. Interesting features include dark patches along the vertical wooden beams in the wall adjoining the bakehouse — scorch marks from rush torches — and a U-shaped working bench, on one end of which have been carved out two bowls. During the ninth Duke's restoration work at the beginning of this century he had a hearth taken out in the kitchen and a tunnel made to link the room with Haddon's new kitchens. A further room that should not be missed in the culinary domain is the butcher's, where hanging rack, creviced chopping block, trough for salting meats and wooden bench strike rather chilling chords!

At the other end of the banqueting hall a doorway leads to the dining room; this is often used today for entertaining parties of guests. The ceiling, checkered black and white with interspersed emblematic panels, complements the wall panelling which is rich in heraldic crests. Those of the nobility take a prominent position above the fireplace; the Vernon and Manners families are also well represented — Haddon Hall was owned by the Vernons until 1567 after which it passed to the Manners' family when Dorothy Vernon married John Manners, son of the then Earl of Rutland.

The full history of ownership at Haddon is quite long. In 1087, at the time of the Domesday Survey, the Hall was in the keeping of William the Conqueror's illegitimate son William Peverel. During the next century, in about 1153, William Avenel took over the establishment. A few years later, probably about 1170, Avenel split it between his two sons-in-law, one of whom, Richard Vernon, was to become the first of a four-hundred-year line of Vernons to own Haddon. After the Manners family drifted away from the Hall it was sadly neglected for most of the eighteenth and nineteenth

centuries until the ninth Duke took it upon himself to arrest the decay of this fine building.

The most enchanting room at Haddon must be the long gallery, whose ceiling is decorated with plaster work and walls panelled with elaborately carved rectangular columns. It is narrow and, having numerous mullioned windows, is well illuminated. The panes of glass in these windows are fascinating for they are angled in such a way as to produce an effective bubbled pattern. When the gallery was restored as much of the old glass was incorporated back into them as possible, together with accompanying curious inscriptions. A cursory glance will soon reveal intriguing ditties and signatures, many dating from the early nineteenth century. (Other more famous and recent signatures can be seen in the Earl's Bedroom. A series of royal individuals have penned their names on one of the walls, ranging from George V in 1933 to Princess Alexandra in 1982.)

Before leaving the Hall to walk round the gardens or have tea in the Elizabethan stables, it is worth visiting the chapel, if only to gaze admiringly at the immense size of the fifteenth-century murals. On one side the tall, bearded figure of St Christopher dominates the scene as he strides through swirling, blue-grey waters with a staff in his right hand and the left supporting the Christ child's image. A simpler design, in the form of a repeating floral pattern, surrounds the east window whose stained-glass figures are notably lacking faces.

Much of the pleasure derived from viewing Haddon Hall reflects the hard work of the ninth Duke, who set about the enormous task of having the building completely, and authentically, renovated. A box containing details of all that was undertaken is now secure in one of the beams in the banqueting hall. Such enthusiastic attention to Haddon undoubtedly helped preserve a cherished treasure for many future generations of welcome visitors to enjoy.

THE CALENDAR YEAR

Hardwick Hall

South-west of Chesterfield, Derbyshire, about five miles from junction 29 on the M1

The Hall and gardens are National Trust property and are open from April to the end of October (closed good Friday). Admission to the Hall Wednesdays, Thursdays, Saturdays, Sundays, and Bank Holiday Mondays 1.00-5.00 p.m., and to the garden 12 noon-5.00 p.m.

Hardwick Hall, which is often said to be 'more glass than wall', is a symmetrical, Tudor building with six turrets and huge windows. It contains important collections of tapestries, furniture, portraits and needlework. Rare breeds of cattle (longhorn) and sheep (whitefaced woodland) can be seen in the park. Other facilities here include fishing, boating and canoeing on Millers' pond.

Harewood House

At junction A61/659 on the Leeds to Harrogate road, five miles from the A1 at Wetherby, West Yorkshire

Season runs from 1 April to 31 October, and Sundays, Tuesdays, Wednesdays and Thursdays in February, March and November. The gates open at 10.00 a.m. and the house at 11.00 a.m. Closing times vary according to the time of year.

Dogs must be on leads; most of Harewood's facilities are accessible to the disabled; car and coach parking is free; a self-service café (11.00 a.m. onwards) and restaurant (12 noon-2.00 p.m.) are open daily during the main season.

Attractions include Harewood House (built by John Carr in 1759) and its collections of porcelain, paintings and Chippendale furniture, a bird garden, an adventure playground, a permanent exhibition of Harewood's history, and over thirty acres of outdoor gardens and woodland. Special events are organised throughout the year, such as car rallies and agricultural shows.

Visitors' information: Harewood (0532) 886225, Estate Office, Harewood, Leeds, LS17 9LQ

Harlow Car Gardens

Crag Lane, Beckwithshaw, Harrogate, North Yorkshire

During British Summer Time the gardens are open 9.30 a.m.-7.30 p.m. (or dusk or sunset if earlier); for the rest of the year they are closed at 5.00 p.m.

Only guide dogs allowed; gravelled path suitable for wheelchairs and prams; toilets for the disabled; admission charge for non-members of the Northern Horticultural Society; shop; plant sales area; refreshments available.

The best time to visit Harlow Car is early evening when everything seems to become luminescent and your conversation turns to discussing ultraviolet lobelias and shocking-red verbenas. Colours are always changing here as plants bloom and then fade away again into the background of thick greenery, so each visit is always quite different from the next.

The gardens' history began in 1948 when the Northern Horticultural Society decided to accept the forty or so acres of land offered by Harrogate Corporation as an experimental site to discover which plants could be made to grow in the average garden. One mile from Harrogate, the area is very exposed with a typically northern, heavy and acid soil. It is a challenge to any keen Yorkshire gardener to grow what he sees at Harlow Car.

Now covering some sixty acres, there are sloping lawns, rock, foliage and flower gardens, and a stream and woodland on which to feast the eyes. I came across giant hogweed and thistles eight feet tall and, at the other end of the scale, 'Tom Thumb' (*Pittosporum* to give it its regal name) sitting on some gravel in the Display House among a crowd of foreigners from Japan, Corsica and Sardinia. Cacti, succulents, ferns: all were neatly labelled and obviously thriving in their adopted home. In one of the

trials' areas forty-five varieties of gladioli made a kaleidoscopic mass of colour, while on the way to the rose garden a block of delphiniums exhibited every possible shade of blue. (If you're wanting that extra-special specimen for your own garden it's worth waiting for Harlow Car's biennial plant bring and buy sale, when a large number of rare and unusual plants grown by members are put on sale at reasonable prices. A treat not to be missed!)

For the amateur vegetable grower the allotment is an enviable wealth of first prizers; marrows, cucumbers, leeks, parsnips, carrots, broccoli, tomatoes . . . the list was mouthwateringly endless. If properly managed the garden can supposedly produce a year's supply of vegetables and herbs for a family of four. I would have

thought forty was a more realistic figure! On this occasion the lowly onion also featured in another trial area. There were eleven different types growing side by side in one plot, some the size of small footballs and large enough to make a chef weep for a week.

Animal life cannot be forgotton either; wait quietly in the shade of an oak tree, or, crouch behind one of the subdued lions in the birch wood (six stone pillars and two stone felines were taken from Harrogate, near the Royal Hall, in 1930 after demolition work and made into a 'folly' at Harlow Car), and you can catch glimpses of squirrels tripping the light fantastic along the backs of conveniently situated wooden seats — there are plenty of both about.

One of the Horticultural Society's original aims had been

to provide a library for its members at Harlow Car. This they achieved in 1958 by converting the old bath house into members' room, offices and library. The odd sulphurous fragrance wafts across occasionally from the old closed-up springs. They were first sniffed in 1840 by their discoverer, Harry Wright, who subsequently had the house built in 1846. This then became an integral part of Harrogate's Spa system. Now, although there is no longer sparkling water to take the blues away, just a slow stroll round any part of the gardens will inevitably bring pleasure to the senses and a healthy glow to the cheeks.

Harrington Hall

Five miles east of Horncastle, Lincolnshire (turning off the A158 near Hagworthingham, signposted Harrington two miles)

The house is open each Thursday, from Easter to the end of September, 2.00-5.00 p.m. It is also open on Bank Holiday Sundays. The gardens and garden centre are open every Wednesday and Thursday from Easter to the end of October, 12 noon-8.00 p.m. Also some Sundays for charity occasions.

Entrance and car parking free; dogs allowed on leads; wheelchair access is available if prior notice is given; teas are only provided on Charity Sundays.

Harrington Hall is a Caroline manor house and is the home of Lady Maitland; the gardens are those the poet Alfred Lord Tennyson referred to when he wrote 'Come into the garden Maud'.

Holkham Hall

About ten miles north of Fakenham, Norfolk, off the A149

Opening times: June — Sunday, Monday, Thursday, 1.30-5.00 p.m.; July — Sunday, Monday, Wednesday, Thursday, 1.30-5.00 p.m.; August — Sunday, Monday, Wednesday, Thursday, 1.30-5.00 p.m.; September — Sunday, Monday, Thursday, 1.30-5.00 p.m.; Spring Bank Holiday Monday and Summer Bank Holiday, 11.30 a.m.-5.00 p.m.

Limited access for wheelchairs; toilets for the disabled nearing completion; dogs allowed in park and gardens provided they are on leads; small charge for parking; refreshments available; Bygones Collection; pottery and garden centre.

Holkham Hall has been the family home of the Cokes since the eighteenth century. Its origins lie in the 'Grand Tour' made as a boy by Thomas Coke (1697-1759), Earl of Leicester, in the company of his tutor. During their travels he became acquainted with Lord Burlington's protégé William Kent. Fifteen years later in 1734, with Europe's vistas still in mind and the friendship with Kent firmly established, he was prepared to embark on the building of a mansion in Norfolk. Kent drew up plans, adapted from Palladio's Villa Mocenago, from which Matthew Brettingham, a Norwich architect, made working drawings. The result was a house whose special characteristic seems to be the juxtaposition of classical severity with ornament.

The route by which visitors enter the park from the road takes them to Holkham's north façade, where sharply defined walls rise starkly against the blue of a coastal sky. Thomas Coke preferred the approach to be made from the south, through the triumphal arch to Kent's obelisk (which today attracts throngs of photographers), so it merits walking round to capture the grander view of the hall. But even here, on the south side, there are few architectural embellishments and the topiary bushes and lawns in front of the building highlight its severity.

By contrast with the exterior, much of Holkham Hall's interior is lavishly decorated. The Marble Hall is particularly striking; fluted, brown-veined alabaster columns are an impressive feature, with niched statues behind putting the

room in perspective, and an elaborate ceiling from an idea by Inigo Jones making a spectacular crown. The Saloon, which leads off from this, is also highly ornate — as principal reception room of the state apartments it was naturally intended to be memorable. The burgundy coloured wall covering is the original Genoa velvet and the ceiling is a splendid complex of golden octagonal designs, lozenges and dense floral friezes. Among the paintings here are Rubens's *Return of the Holy Family* and a portrait of Thomas William Coke (1754-1842) by Gainsborough. Other state rooms are dominated by rich tapestries, including a Mortlake and some seventeenth-century pieces; gorgeousness is the theme throughout.

When Thomas Coke was building Holkham he wanted some areas for display purposes; during the eighteenth century

collecting classical sculpture became a popular pastime and Coke was very much part of this convention. His Statue Gallery and tribunes made a perfect setting in which to show his art treasures brought over from southern Europe — one of these is a statue of Diana and is a Roman copy of the fourth century B.C. original. The room is rather bare in its decoration compared with the state rooms, but not unusually so for its intended use and the period. The amount of furniture spaced along the white walls is modest — a piano and Kent's original deep red upholstered armchairs and sofas are the sum total. (Sculpture is not confined to the Gallery — the very classical, and again less flamboyantly ornate, North Dining Room, for instance, contains the busts of Aphrodite, supposedly taken from the Parthenon, and of Emperor Lucius Verus, discovered when clearing the port of Nettuno.)

To imagine life 'below stairs' you can thread your way through underground passages below the state apartments to reach the kitchen. Here you may muse on the feats performed by the domestic staff to keep food hot for

the Earls of Leicester. The room has been restored to be in keeping with a time prior to the Second World War; copper pans and spits now gleam coldly in the sunlight. Not far away is the only private post office in England. This goes back to the mid-eighteenth century when the first Earl of Leicester was Postmaster General. Each of his successors became sub-postmaster at Holkham, and today the duties are carried out by Viscount Edward Coke.

Besides the house and gardens the park is an interesting area to explore. Paths shoot off in all directions, taking the walker to the lake, Kent's obelisk, or perhaps the Great Barn. This yellow brick barn was built in about 1790 to a design by Samuel Wyatt, and is a reminder of the pioneering efforts of the Coke family during the agricultural revolution. For a small charge you can also reach Holkham's beach by a private road. There the charm is in the great expanse of an unspoilt sea-shore, miles of sand fringed by conifers. Thomas Coke's choice of such a bleak landscape in which to create a coastal oasis is to be admired — Holkham Hall and grounds are a credit to his great foresight.

Holme Pierrepont Hall

Three miles from Trent Bridge, Nottingham, off the A52 Nottingham to Grantham road

Open Tuesdays, Thursdays, Fridays and Sundays 2.00-6.00 p.m. during June, July and August, and Sundays 2.00-6.00 p.m. during September. May Day, Spring and Summer Bank Holiday Mondays and Tuesdays 2.00-6.00 p.m. The house is open to parties on any day or evening throughout the year by private appointment.

Car park is free; fresh home-made teas available; rooms can be hired for occasional functions and conferences.

Holme Pierrepont Hall is an early Tudor brick manor house. It was built round a courtyard, though today this is now a formal garden. The house's contents are mainly oak items from the seventeenth and eighteenth centuries, and tend to be regional in character.

Houghton Hall

Ten miles west of Fakenham, thirteen miles east of King's Lynn, Norfolk

Open from Easter Sunday to the last Sunday in September: gates open 11.00 a.m. Thursdays, Sundays and Bank Holidays; house open 11.00 a.m. Thursdays and Bank Holidays, 1.30 p.m Sundays; last admissions 5.00 p.m.

Ample free parking; invalid car park; lift to State Floor; special facilities for wheelchairs; model soldier and militaria museum; shop; tea room; children's playground; stables with heavy horses and Shetland ponies; parkland with white fallow deer.

Houghton Hall, built for Sir Robert Walpole, is an eighteenth-century Palladian mansion.

Hovingham Hall

Hovingham, about fifteen miles north of York

Open by appointment only, from mid-May to the end of September on certain days. Enquiries should be addressed to the Secretary at Hovingham Hall.

No facilities for the disabled; no dogs allowed.

Hovingham has been the home of the Worsley family since it was built by Thomas Worsley around 1760. Thomas was extremely fond of horses and, being his own architect, arranged that the house should have its own riding school.

A visit to Hovingham Hall will also take in the grounds and gardens, the private cricket ground, and the church with its Saxon tower and famous eighth-century Saxon cross and reredos.

Lea Rhododendron Gardens

Five miles south-east of Matlock, Derbyshire, off the A6

Open daily 10.00 a.m.-7.00 p.m. from mid-March until the end of July.

Free admission for those in wheelchairs; no suitable toilets for the disabled; café; plant sales area; evening parties catered for.

The gardens were started in 1935 when John Marsden-Smedley began to collect various hybrid and species rhododendrons. They now cover three and a half acres and include an area of scree rockery and an extensive azalea bed.

Lotherton Hall

One mile east of the A1 at Aberford, West Yorkshire, on the B1217 Towton road

Open daily throughout the year Tuesdays to Sundays, and Bank Holiday Mondays, 10.30 a.m.-6.15 p.m. (or dusk). Late opening until 8.30 p.m. on Thursdays from May to September.

Car park; shop; bird garden; gardens and parkland.

Lotherton Hall, the Edwardian home of the Gascoigne family until 1968 when it was given to the City of Leeds, contains the Gascoigne art collection, nineteenth- and twentieth-century arts and crafts, fashion galleries and an oriental gallery (with Chinese ceramics on display).

Maister House, Hull

160 High Street, Hull

Only staircase and entrance hall open to the public all year, Monday to Friday, 10.00 a.m.-4.00 p.m. (closed Bank Holidays, Good Friday and 1 January).

Unsuitable for parties; no toilet facilities.

Maister House was rebuilt in 1744; its staircase-hall was designed in the Palladian manner.

Mannington Hall and Gardens

Between Aylsham and Holt, eighteen miles north of Norwich, nine miles from the coast

Mannington Hall is open by prior appointment only; the gardens are open from May until September, Thursdays and Fridays, 2.00-5.00 p.m.

Various charity events are held throughout the year.

The moated manor house was built in 1460 of stone, flint and terracotta and was extended during the nineteenth century. It was bought by Horatio Walpole in about 1740 and is still lived in by the family.

Manor House, Ilkley

Behind the parish church in Ilkley, West Yorkshire, through the archway on Church Street

Closed Mondays, except Bank Holidays. Daily opening times: 10.00 a.m.-6.00 p.m. (10.00 a.m.-5.00 p.m. from October to March).

Car park 350 yards away; dogs not allowed inside the museum.

The Manor House is an Elizabethan building, erected on part of the site of the Roman fort of Olicana, near an exposed section of Roman wall. The ground floor gallery has a collection of excavated Roman artefacts and a display of Ilkley's spa resort history. Regional artists are encouraged to exhibit their work in the art gallery.

Marston Hall

Six miles west of Grantham, Lincolnshire, one and a half miles from the A1

Only open a few days a year for charity occasions. Individuals or parties may visit by appointment at other times.

Marston Hall is an old manor house and has been the Thorold family residence since the fourteenth century. The house contains a varied collection of paintings; the garden has an eighteenth-century gazebo and, among its flora, an elm and a laburnum both approximately four hundred years old.

Medieval Merchant's House, King's Lynn

9 King Street, King's Lynn, Norfolk

Opening times: Easter, May Day and Spring Bank Holiday, July and August (Tuesdays, Thursdays and weekends); conducted tours by the owners from 2.00-5.30 p.m.

Dogs must be on leads; wheelchair access limited to ground floor; toilet facilities (though with steps).

This house, in a country town and dating from the early 1300s, is still a family home. Attractions for the visitor include a medieval window, seventeenth-century beams and eighteenth-century panelling.

National Railway Museum

Leeman Road, York, behind the railway station

Open Monday to Saturday 10.00 a.m.-6.00 p.m. and Sunday 2.30-6.00 p.m. Closed 24,25 and 26 December, 1 January, Good Friday and May Day Bank Holiday.

Small car park adjacent to the museum; free admission; wheelchair access; cafeteria.

The museum contains exhibits from all over the world; a Chinese locomotive has recently been put on display.

Newby Hall

On the north-east bank of the river Ure between Ripon and Boroughbridge, North Yorkshire

House open 1.00-5.30 p.m.: April and September, Wednesdays, Thursdays, Saturdays and Sundays; May, June, July and August, every day except Mondays (though open on Bank Holiday Mondays); also open Easter and Bank Holidays. Gardens open 11.00 a.m.-5.30 p.m. 1 April to 30 September, every day except Mondays (open Bank Holiday Mondays).

Shop; information pavilion; licensed garden restaurant; picnic area; adventure gardens; miniature railway; toilet facilities for the disabled; dogs allowed in the picnic area and large woodland car park only.

Newby Hall is well known for Robert Adam's contribution during the eighteenth century to its interior design and decoration. It has a fine collection of sculpture, furniture and tapestries from the Gobelins factory.

Newstead Abbey

About twelve miles north of Nottingham on the A60

The house is open from Good Friday to 30 September (including Sundays and Bank Holidays) 2.00-6.00 p.m. (last admission 5.15 p.m.) Tours out of season by special arrangement. The grounds are open all the year.

Free parking; tea room (in season); prior arrangements can sometimes be made for those in wheelchairs; parkland; rock and rose gardens; sub-tropical garden.

The Byron family converted Newstead Priory into a country mansion during the sixteenth century. It was the home of the poet Lord Bryon for the early part of the nineteenth century and his manuscripts, first editions, letters, furniture and pictures are on display.

Normanby Hall

About four miles north of Scunthorpe on the B1430 to Burton-on-Stather

Opening hours: April to October, Monday, Wednesday, Thursday, Friday and Saturday, 10.00 a.m.-12.30 p.m., 2.00-5.30 p.m.; Tuesday, closed all day; Sunday, 2.00-5.30 p.m. November to March, weekdays, 10.00 a.m.-12.30 p.m., 2.00-5.00 p.m.; Saturday, closed all day; Sunday, 2.00-5.00 p.m. (Hall may be closed any day owing to private functions — check in advance by ringing Scunthorpe 720215.)

350 acres of gardens and parkland surround Normanby Hall; facilities for horse riding under tuition; country crafts; golf course; refreshments; camping and caravanning for organised parties; nature trails; picnic area.

Designed by Sir Robert Smirke and completed in 1830, the Hall has been refurnished and redecorated in period by Scunthorpe Museum and Art Gallery.

North York Moors Railway

An eighteen-mile track runs from Pickering to Grosmont; at Grosmont there is a British Rail connection to Whitby

Passengers are welcome from 1 April to 31 October.

The most impressive aspect of the North York Moors Railway is, alas, missed by the passenger who travels on the Pickering-to-Grosmont section of the twenty-four-mile track to Whitby. I hate to say anything which may diminish that traveller's pleasure, but it's true. The most exciting sight of all is the train itself, whether steam or diesel as it winds, insect-like, through Newtondale Gorge with the 'radomes' of the Fylingdales Ballistic Missile Early Warning Station peering down from the moors like inquisitive visitors from outer space. But that is not to say that the passenger gets anything less than splendid value

for the money he spends on a ticket.

A train ride is pleasant in itself, but a little knowledge of how and why the whole thing is possible can only enhance the enjoyment. Display panels at all the stations tell the exciting story. And yet the original idea wasn't for a railway at all, but for a canal across the moors to link Whitby with Pickering. The idea may seem rather startling today, but in the late eighteenth century canals were in their heyday. Even then, however, railways were beginning to supplant waterways, so it was not surprising that the idea of a railway won the majority of votes.

Many years were to pass before anything was actually done. In 1831 some businessmen of Whitby called in the 'Father of the Railways' himself, George Stephenson, to plan such a line. Stephenson of *Rocket* fame, Stephenson of the 'Stockton and Darlington' . . . there could be no better man, as the engineer surely demonstrated when he chose to include Newtondale on his railway across the North York Moors. Naturally, aesthetic considerations can hardly have weighed a great deal with him; for all its difficulties, the route was probably the only one possible. Yet, whether by accident, design

or necessity, he succeeded in giving North Yorkshire one of the most magnificent little railway journeys in England.

Work on the line began in 1833 and, incredibly, the first seven miles were completed by 1835. By May 1836, the full twenty-four miles of the line had been laid from Whitby to Pickering. To achieve this, rivers and streams had been diverted, a tunnel 120 yards long had been blasted through the rock at Grosmont and many bridges had been built. At Fen Bog, now a nature reserve, Stephenson had to lay his track over a foundation of peat thirty-eight feet deep. To make it firmer,

233

kilns may be seen to the west of the line. They are a reminder of one of the principle purposes envisaged for the line — the transport of limestone (still quarried at New Bridge just a little further along) by rail to kilns at Grosmont.

Between New Bridge and Levisham, a distance of four miles, the track was double from 1845 until 1917, when one set of rails was 'called up' for war service in France. Ironically, the Germans torpedoed the ship that carried them and now, alas, they lie at the bottom of the English Channel, where no trains will ever run — unless or until we get that Channel Tunnel! On to Blansby Park, once a deer park belonging to Pickering Castle and, like the castle, owned by the Crown since Norman times. The park no longer contains the 600 deer it did in medieval days, though deer frequent Newtondale between Levisham and Fen Bog, further along the line. At Farwath trains sometimes stop to collect locally made heather brooms, or besoms.

Soon we stop at Levisham Station. The village of Levisham figures in North Yorkshire's

he sank wooden piles (and even sheep fleeces filled with heather) in the swampy ground. The plan worked well enough at first, but within thirty years the wooden piles had rotted, the rails had buckled during the hot summer and a loco and two carriages were precipitated into the bog.

But none of this was foreseen when the triumphal opening of the line took place in 1836. For the first nine years of its life, the railway was powered only by horses. Then George Hudson of York, the so-called Railway King, came into the picture. Hudson's ruin under the shadow of fraud charges was still years ahead at this time and no doubt his many supporters cheered the 'King' when he bought the line and introduced steam locomotion. Eventually the line between Pickering and Malton was completed. And now Whitby, the old whaling port which had long felt itself too important to live in isolation, was directly linked with the capital.

For almost 130 years the little railway provided a first-rate service. Then in 1965, under the Beeching Plan the Grosmont-Pickering line was closed. Yet this was not the end, for a band of railway enthusiasts — whose drive and determination must have seemed like lunacy to more mundane minds — were working for the re-opening of the line by voluntary labour. They were convinced that it would be viable and their conviction won them practical support in the form of grants from the National Parks Committee and the Tourist Board. On Tuesday, 1 May 1973, the line was re-opened by the Duchess of Kent. In 1982, it was stated to be handling over 350,000 passenger journeys a year and to be the chief tourist attraction on the North York Moors.

From Pickering, with its castle and medieval church frescoes, the traveller sets out on a journey rich in North Yorkshire history. Less than half a mile from Pickering Station the remains of arched lime

industrial history, for iron was worked on the moors here as long ago as 100 B.C. And there was a forge in the parish as early as 1207. Not far past Levisham is the site of the Raindale water-mill which used to grind locally grown wheat into flour until the stream which powered it changed course in 1915. The whole mill was eventually removed to the Castle Museum, York, there to grind flour for the entertainment and instruction of visitors.

There is far more to be seen from the carriage window than can be described here but, for a variety of reasons, Fen Bog deserves mention. To start with, it is a nature reserve rich in bog and fenland plants as well as a multitude of birds. At its southern end is woodland – all that remains of the dense forest of willow, birch and alder which used to cover the moors but which, 5,000 years ago, began to die out to be replaced by the present vegetation.

On then, from the scene of Stephenson's greatest problems,

to the summit, where the line is almost 550 feet above sea level. Soon after this, the line begins to fall to Goathland, with its station opened in 1865.

On its further descent from Goathland to Grosmont the line drops nearly four miles at a gradient of one in forty-nine. That is one of the steepest rail gradients in the country, but by no means as steep as that of the one-in-ten incline up which carriages were hauled by ropes between 1836 and 1865 on the original route, from which the present line diverges for about four miles. Nowadays the track bed of the original Goathland Incline makes a pleasant walk.

After leaving Beck Hole, the line passes Esk Valley, a hamlet which housed workers at the ironstone mines opened in 1860. Less felicitously named was Grosmont itself, which was simply called 'Tunnel' until, presumably, its inhabitants revolted and insisted on its being re-named Grosmont, the name of the mother church in

Normandy whence came the monks who founded a priory here in 1204. At first, 'Tunnel' comprised just cottages and workshops with a warehouse and the inevitable inn. Today the population numbers only a few hundred, but in the 1870s, when three blast furnaces offered employment — as well as stone quarries, lime kilns and brickworks — there were over 1,500 people here. By 1915 both the blast furnaces and the ironworks had been closed.

Nowadays, Grosmont is well known to rail enthusiasts for its loco shed gallery, but the line itself has something for everyone. From each of the stations, signposted walks may be taken, including explorations of the forest from the Newtondale halt deep in the valley. At Grosmont the NYMR line links with British Rail's Esk Valley line from Middlesbrough to Whitby, a route which offers yet another splendid opportunity to enjoy the glorious North Yorkshire scenery — by rail.

Norton Conyers

Three and a half miles north of Ripon, North Yorkshire, on the road to Wath, and one and a half miles from the A1

Opening arrangements: Thursdays in June, Sundays from the beginning of July to the beginning of September, Bank Holiday Sundays and Mondays, 2.00-5.30 p.m.

Wheelchair access to the ground floor of the house; dogs allowed in the garden; parties may be booked in advance; garden centre with unusual hardy plants, alpines and herbs (open all year, Monday to Friday, 9.00 a.m.-5.00 p.m.; Saturday and Sunday, April to October, 2.00-5.00 p.m.); 'pick your own' soft fruit.

Norton Conyers is a Jacobean manor house with a large walled garden.

Nostell Priory

On the A638 Wakefield to Doncaster road, six miles south-east of Wakefield

End of March to end of June, and October: Thursdays, Saturdays and Sundays, 12.00 noon-6.00 p.m.; beginning of July to end of September: daily, except Fridays, 12.00 noon-6.00 p.m.; Bank Holidays: 11.00 a.m.-6.00 p.m. Special party visits and guided tours can be arranged.

Craft centre; picnic park and adventure playground; lake; rose gardens; Wragby Church (sixteenth-century).

Nostell Priory was built on the site of a medieval priory for the fourth baronet, Sir Rowland Winn. It was begun in 1733 by James Paine, and was later completed by Robert Adam. Nostell is renowned for its collection of Chippendale furniture which was specially designed for the house.

Nunnington Hall

Near Helmsley, twenty-three miles north of York

Season runs from April to the end of October: daily (except Mondays and Fridays) 2.00-6.00 p.m.; Bank Holiday Mondays 11.00 a.m.-6.00

p.m.; last admissions 5.30 p.m. Special opening times for school visits: Mondays, Tuesdays and Wednesdays, 10.00 a.m.-2.00 p.m., by prior arrangement with the Administrator.

Large riverside car park; National Trust shop; home-made afternoon teas in panelled dining room or in riverside tea garden. Unsuitable for disabled people; limited wheelchair access; no dogs allowed inside the house.

Nunnington Hall is a sixteenth-century manor house. Various evening concerts are held during the season.

Oakwell Hall

Nova Lane, Birstall, near Batley, West Yorkshire

Open April to October, Tuesday to Saturday 10.00 a.m.-6.00 p.m., Sunday 1.00-5.00 p.m., closed Monday; November to March, Tuesday to Saturday 10.00 a.m.-5.00 p.m., Sunday 1.00-5.00 p.m., closed Monday.

Admission free.

This old manor house is situated just about a mile away from Red House at Gomersal, but it is so different in appearance that the two buildings could be a hundred miles apart. Oakwell's soft, mullioned exterior contrasts with the neighbouring museum's vividly coloured brickwork. There is a certain air of grandeur about the place, perhaps due to its use in former times as a meeting point for manorial assemblies. It overlooks spreading green fields, while immediately in front is a small enclosed garden, and beyond that a sloping lawn graced with the unlikely presence of a stone ram brought over comparatively recently from Dewsbury.

Either side of the main body of the house is a two-storeyed wing; adjoining the one to the south is a stone porch which acts as a front entrance. From here it is but a short step through a passage to the antler-decorated Great Hall. Originally, however, during the fifteenth century, the whole building, minus wings and porch, was a timber construction — evidence of its previous wooden glory is still clearly seen in various places. (Sixteenth- and seventeenth-century stone halls, such as Oakwell, follow the design of earlier, timber-framed buildings very closely — it is quite common for the timber frame of a building to survive inside a later stone casing.) Part of the panelling in the hall can be pulled back to reveal the early wood arrangement, and in the same room joiners' marks, some in the form of three short parallel lines, have been found behind the end wall. Old timber walls were also uncovered upstairs in one of the bedrooms when plaster was stripped away. It is very likely that the major conversion to stone was organised by a man called John Batt, whose initials 'I.B.' are carved over the porch together with the date '1583'. Batt's grandson, another John, was probably responsible for a further change to the house in the 1630s when a massive hall window was installed, with thirty leaded lights reaching from almost ground level right up

to the roof. This window is now a memorable feature of Oakwell.

The Hall has only ever remained within one family for any great length of time — various members of the Batt family were occupants for a period of about 180 years. For much of the nineteenth century it was used as a boarding school; during the 1840s relatives of the Nusseys (Ellen Nussey was very close to Charlotte Brontë) ran the school. Charlotte's friendship with several of the girls there may have encouraged her to give the manor house such a prominent place, as Miss Keeldar's home, in Shirley. Today this link between Charlotte and Oakwell is remembered in the so-called 'Brontë Room' where the ample furnishings reflect the early Victorian era. Items here include a piano, very like the one to be seen in the museum at Haworth; a table set with delicate crockery; a longcase clock made by a local man from Thornton; and, quite suitably, considering the literary bond between Ellen Nussey and Charlotte, an escritoire belonging to the former and a tall, well-filled bookcase.

The word 'oak' in the house's title is extremely apt, since this particular wood abounds throughout the building in many forms. The main bedroom contains an oak chest with a type of linen-fold carving which was apparently popular during the fifteenth and early sixteenth centuries; a small seventeenth-century settle; and a four poster bed covered with elaborate carvings, some, appropriately enough, in the form of acorns. And then there is the seemingly omnipresent, but very beautiful, oak panelling. Charlotte Brontë devoted a paragraph in the chapter entitled 'Fieldhead' from Shirley to the advantages and disadvantages of Oakwell's wood panelling. She described it as 'very handsome' but, as far as cleaning was concerned, 'execrable and inhuman'. In the Brontë room the panelling had been painted 'a delicate pinky white'. This Charlotte again viewed ambivalently; on the one hand she thought it perfectly outrageous to mar such 'handsome...shining,

brown panels', while on the other, she could see that it was a favourable means of reducing the great toil involved in polishing.

Today changes are planned for Oakwell's surroundings rather than its esteemed contents. Encircling parkland is to include picnic areas, a bowling green and facilities for horse riding, while nearby an exhibition hall will provide an additional point of historical interest. It may even be possible to create a trail from the Hall to Red House; the contrast between life in pre-industrial, manorial times and that of hard-working tradesmen from a later period is so well illustrated by these two museums, that visitors will soon discover for themselves why both have been accorded such local importance.

Old House Museum

Bakewell, Derbyshire, above the church

Open from Good Friday to 31 October, 2.30-5.00 p.m.

The Old House Museum is run by Bakewell and District Historical Society. It is an early Tudor house whose contents include costumes, craftsmen's tools and toys.

Opera North

Based at the Grand Theatre,
46 New Briggate, Leeds, West
Yorkshire

Opera North was founded in 1978
to give the North of England its
first full-time opera company.
Today its performances are not
just restricted to twelve operas a
year at Leeds; it has a subscription
series of three seasons (spring,
summer and autumn) in
Manchester at the Palace Theatre
as well as three at Nottingham's
Theatre Royal. It also travels to
venues such as Glasgow,
Newcastle, Hull, Norwich and
Southampton. For those theatres
which are too small to hold
full-scale operas Opera North
presents regular programmes of
'entertainments'. In addition,
various groups and individuals
from the chorus and English
Northern Philharmonia Orchestra
have a number of concert
schedules throughout the year in
and around the region.

Grand Opera
by the Earl of Harewood

When I became a member of the
Arts Council in January 1966, I was
almost immediately recruited to a
committee to discuss the new
Opera House which was mooted
for Manchester. Sir Maurice
Parriser was the moving spirit and
the plan was for a great new
building which would not only
provide opera for the North but
would house a company as well.
We had meetings in London and
Manchester, and enthusiasm was
boundless until the sad news
came of Sir Maurice's death and
support for the project started to
abate. But it did not cease
altogether and other meetings
took place, with which I was also
involved. The idea was always for a
new building and not for an
adaptation of either the Opera
House or the Palace Theatre, each
of which I knew from personal
experience of touring, and in the
end mounting cost proved an
effective deterrent (the eventual
choice of the Palace seemed to me
a fine resolution of the dilemma,

but it came a dozen years later and
effectively lost Manchester the
initiative).

I feared the idea of an Opera
House for the North had died for
lack of generalship and it was
therefore a major pleasure six
years and more ago to discuss
with the Arts Council their
solution to the problem English
National Opera had been
repeatedly putting to them: how
to fit our Coliseum-sized stagings
onto the smaller stages which
were all that were available
outside London, and how to
continue the flow of opera which
was demanded for centres all over
the country. The proposal was that
ENO should start a new branch,
base it in Leeds and tour from
there. Since the Grand Theatre
was then already a splendid
building — much improved six
years later by its redecoration —
the prospect was exciting, but it
could never have come to pass
without a piece of genuinely
imaginative thinking on the part of
the Arts Council (I have always
associated the names of Angus
Stirling and Jack Phipps, the
Deputy Secretary General and
Director of Touring respectively,
with the work behind the scenes
which made the plan a reality).

Even with a rationalisation of
the sums annually spent on
operatic touring, the Arts Council
could not put up enough money to
start a new opera company and
then fund it through the years.
Another source had to be found
and the only one with enough
financial clout seemed to be the
various local authorities. Here
immediately was the dilemma:
even if the local authorities could
eventually be persuaded to put
money into the new venture,
would they fund it from the start?
None of us believed that, though
we all trusted — and our trust has
been abundantly justified — that
once there was something visible
and it was seen to be worthwhile,
local pride would become
involved. In the meanwhile, how
to bridge the shortfall? The answer
we found was simple: start the
company's operations in the
middle of the financial year, but
make the grant available for a full

year! Provided the following year's grant was more or less assured, at least the first full season could be embarked on without serious risk of financial disaster, and by the time it was well under way, some idea about the second season would surely have been formulated.

So it was that English National Opera North gave its first performance in November 1978 with no backing beyond the Arts Council's and the knowledge that, without something extra, that would not in the long run be anything like enough. Leeds came in very soon; other local authorities followed suit and I suspect that it was pure bad luck that West Yorkshire was not amongst them from the start. Now that has all changed and West Yorkshire is a major backer — but we still talk more about finance when we meet than about anything else. And when you come to think of it, that can't really be right. Almost any gathering of operatic professionals degenerates quite

soon, not into shop talk but into a discussion of the gloomy financial prospects ahead. I was at a meeting once in San Francisco and European intendants joined some American colleagues for a public discussion, chaired by the lady responsible for dishing out the bounty Washington annually made available for the Arts. For about forty minutes, talk hovered round the problem of finding enough money to pay for the year's programme. Finally the head of the Brussels Opera, responsible for Maurice Béjart's Ballet of the Twentieth Century, could contain himself no longer. 'I am fed up with all this talk about public money and private money. The money you call "private" in America is really public money since it comes from the tax you don't otherwise pay. In any case, we should not be talking only about money but about the art which brings us together — its present shortcomings, what we can do to remedy them, its future, how to bring back the popularity

which was opera's at the beginning of the century.' And he was right.

All operatic organisations, certainly including Opera North, ought to be mainly involved in sorting out what operatic fare will nourish the people who have already become regulars, and deciding what will attract new people to the medium. We ought to be devising new menus and not just reheating old dishes; we ought to be working to bring television more and more into the picture; and above all, perhaps, we ought to be finding a way of taking opera — Music Theatre — to the many sizeable centres in the North of England which don't at the moment get opera at all, usually because there is no building which conveniently fits the touring pattern all the big companies find it easiest to follow.

Some of the promises the new company made, even before it changed its name from what sounded like an old-style railway to the more accurate Opera North of current practice, were that it would not only provide opera but also permeate the region with orchestral concerts, instrumental teachers, schools programmes, smaller-scale ventures for smaller-scale buildings.

Most of these claims have been substantiated but the last one still remains little more than a promise. We have tended tacitly to forget that for at least a hundred and fifty years after its establishment around 1600 opera was much more flexible than we, reared on the romantic masterpieces of the nineteenth century, have come to feel it. Monteverdi wrote for grand rooms and ducal halls as well as for public theatres, and in the former he got great orchestral possibilities but limited space, while in the latter the orchestra was pared by the impresario to the minimum but the stages were presumably nearer to what we know today. Purcell wrote his one genuine opera for a girls' school; Stravinsky in *The Soldier's Tale* wrote for a tiny ensemble to perform in village halls (but the music was so difficult that the whole thing cost too much for the touring he planned!) Hindemith wrote to whatever level he was asked for and believed that was part of a composer's duty; Benjamin Britten was at home on the largest or smallest scale, and could write for every building and any ensemble ever suggested to him — the tuned bowls of water the children play in *Noye's Fludde* is only an extreme example. If we don't ask ourselves the right questions, we shall never find the right answers, and without the right answers we shall not reach as many of the people in the region we serve as deserve us.

The middle of its fifth season is as good a time as any for Opera North to take stock. Graham Marchant was its administrative and planning head for four seasons, perfectly combining imagination and a hard-headed business approach, and his successor, Nicholas Payne, is as I write only just in the saddle. He started off with a splendidly refurbished theatre as

headquarters, and he will have known of the remarkable chorus and orchestra which the Artistic Director and Chief Conductor, David Lloyd-Jones, built up over the first four years of his regime. Anyone who travels on the Continent will know that, except in major centres such as Milan or Munich or Berlin, there is no hope of finding either chorus or orchestra of such quality. It just won't be like that.

I am reminded of two things which have encouraged me personally over the whole new venture. The first was said at an early press conference we called for representatives of the media and of other interested Yorkshire parties. I outlined the project and the idea was that David Lloyd-Jones would then talk about the programme for the first year. But we had reckoned without our Northern press representatives. I had said that ENO would collaborate and provide a basis for the whole venture — a kind of working capital consisting of

scenery and costumes rather than of cash — immediately somebody asked 'It's all very well having a London collaborator but how do we know ENO South won't cream off the profits?' My wife says I simply looked at him in amazement and said, 'I don't think we have a column for that in our book-keeping', but I maintain that I answered the question quite rationally while trying to maintain the mood of optimism which had hitherto prevailed.

The other remark was at another Northern gathering when the subject was the start of the recession and how it would eventually bite. A hard-headed West Riding businessman said, 'In times like this, you can't afford to buy a new car but you *must* build a new factory if you are not to go broke'. I think that was the spirit which gave Opera North the impetus it needed.

THE CALENDAR YEAR

Peckover House

Wisbech, Cambridgeshire

The house and garden are open every day (except Thursdays and Fridays) 2.00-6.00 p.m. from April to mid-October.

Large free car park to the rear of the property; no dogs allowed except guide dogs for the blind; no toilet facilities for the disabled; wheelchair access limited to the grounds only; home-made teas available in the Old Kitchen.

Peckover House, home of the Peckover family for 150 years, was built in 1722; it was presented to the National Trust in 1948. The garden covers some two acres and contains many rare plants. An original eighteenth-century stable block still stands in the yard.

Red House

Gomersal, three and a half miles south-south-east of Bradford, West Yorkshire

Opening times: April to October, Tuesday to Saturday 10.00 a.m.-6.00 p.m., Sunday 1.00-5.00 p.m.; November to March, Tuesday to Saturday 10.00 a.m.-5.00 p.m.

Admission free.

Red House, as bright and cheery as its name suggests, was built in 1660 by William Taylor in the most unromantic-sounding hamlet of Gomersal (between Cleckheaton and Birstall). He was something of an innovator for it was the first house in the area to be made from red brick rather than stone, as well as being the first to use architectural symmetry on the façade, in the hall and in the parlour. Later, towards the middle of the eighteenth century, the family created a further innovation by building a grand entrance hall.

The Taylors were a middle-class family, hard-working and conscientious. William's trade was cloth, and the various stages in the preparation of wool were carried out in Red House's front yard — a somewhat malodorous task! As time went by and the business developed, they began dyeing red cloth for army uniforms. A water mill was built at Hunsworth (it now lies below the M62 motorway) to help with the process, but the Taylors were never drawn into the world of factory production. Success brought respect in addition to money; one of William's descendants, Joshua (1776-1840), was able to run bank services from an office in his garden, underneath which was an enormous safe, bolted and fitted with an alarm system.

The Taylors were farmers, too. At the time no opportunity for producing food could be ignored. The small piece of land at the back of the house, together with several fields and other land around the village, was cultivated. (The barn, which remains, is a reminder of those days.) Wheat was difficult to grow so oats were the favourite crop — the kitchen, with its motley array of old domestic utensils, contains a rack that must have dried hundreds of large oatcakes.

Joshua Taylor's daughter was at school during the 1830s with Charlotte Brontë, who often came to visit. In Charlotte's novel *Shirley*, set in 1810-15, the house provided a model for 'Briarmains', while the Taylor family were transformed into the 'Yorkes'. Many of the pieces of furniture seen today in Red House, though not the originals, are authentic items from

Taylors' hands. Red House is now run by Kirklees Metropolitan Council, and most of the rooms are open to the public. Plans are being made for the development of several display rooms, and it is also hoped that the success of a recent craft fair will lead to this becoming an annual event for the museum.

Rievaulx Terrace and Temples

Two and a half miles north-west of Helmsley, near Pickering, North Yorkshire, off the B1257

This National Trust property is open from April until the end of October (closed Good Friday),. 10.30 a.m.-6.00 p.m. (last admissions 5.30 p.m.) The Ionic Temple is closed for an hour at lunchtime from 1 o'clock.

Wheelchair access; picnic lunches may be taken onto the Terrace; dogs are allowed (though not in the Ionic Temple).

The half-mile Terrace was laid out and the Temples built in 1758 by Thomas Duncombe. All overlook the ruins of Rievaulx Abbey.

the 1820s — a period more akin with the time of *Shirley* than with Charlotte's social visits.

Besides the Brontë connection, however, this small building with just a handful of major rooms on each of its two floors is of historical interest, both architectural and social, in its own right. Its characteristic symmetry ranges from the special construction of alcoves in the parlour to the faking of a door at the top of the stairs, where a sheet of slate was set into the wall and painted to match the real door on the opposite side of the landing. Red House also boasts a pane of glass bearing John Wesley's signature — be it authentic or not.

At the end of the nineteenth century the family business declined and the last generation of Taylors to be brought up in the area all became doctors — one is said to haunt the house, his two walking sticks making tapping noises round the rooms. It was not until 1920 that the building eventually passed out of the

Ripley Castle

In Ripley, North Yorkshire, three and a half miles north of Harrogate and seven and a half miles south of Ripon

Gardens open daily Good Friday to the end of September, 11.00 a.m.-6.00 p.m. Opening arrangements for the castle: Saturdays and Sundays from Easter to the end of May, 2.00-6.00 p.m.; daily except Mondays and Fridays from June to the end of September, 2.00-6.00 p.m.; Good Friday and Bank Holiday Sundays and Mondays until the end of September, 11.00 a.m.-6.00 p.m.

No access for wheelchairs; shops (e.g. potter's, wine and cheese, saddler's); 'Capability' Brown gardens and deer park; café.

Ripley Castle has been the Ingilby family home ever since 1345. Attractions include a priest's hiding hole, a treasurer's chest, paintings, armour, furniture and panelling.

Sandringham House

Off the B1440 from Dersingham, near King's Lynn, Norfolk

Sandringham House and grounds, the private country home of the Queen, are open daily (except Fridays and Saturdays) from Easter Sunday until the last Thursday in September; House: 11.00 a.m. (12.00 noon on Sundays) - 4.45 p.m., grounds: 10.30 a.m. (11.30 a.m. on Sundays) - 5.00 p.m.

Free admission to the museum; picnics and dogs not permitted inside the grounds; refreshments and gifts on sale; car parking facilities.

Sandringham Flower Show is held annually on the last Wednesday in July.

Sewerby Hall

Two miles north-east of Bridlington, Humberside, off the B1255

Park open all year, daily, 9.00 a.m. to dusk; art gallery open Easter to September, Sunday to Friday 10.00 a.m.-12.30 p.m., Saturday 1.30-6.00 p.m.

Gardens; small zoo and aviary; free car parking.

Sewerby Hall, an eighteenth-century mansion built in 1714-20 by John Greame, is now a museum and art gallery. The gardens are of much botanical interest.

Shandy Hall

Coxwold, North Yorkshire, four miles off the A19 between York and Thirsk

Open Wednesdays from June to September and Sundays July to September, 2.00-5.00 p.m.

Walled garden; shop.

Shandy Hall is famous for being the place where Laurence Sterne, a local parson, wrote *Tristram Shandy* and *A Sentimental Journey* during the 1760s.

Shibden Hall

Halifax, West Yorkshire

April to September: Monday to Saturday, 10.00 a.m.-6.00 p.m., Sunday, 2.00-5.00 p.m.; October, November and March, Monday to Saturday, 10.00 a.m.-5.00 p.m., Sunday, 2.00-5.00 p.m.; February, Sundays only, 2.00-5.00 p.m.; closed December and January. Special evening parties may be booked.

Craft workshops; parkland and boating lake; picnic areas; refreshments; wheelchair access limited to the ground floor of the hall and to some parts of the folk museum; conducted tours available on request.

Shibden Hall is a fifteenth-century half-timbered house with additions dating from the seventeenth and nineteenth centuries. It is furnished throughout with material mainly from the seventeenth and eighteenth centuries displayed in period room settings.

Skipton Castle

Skipton, North Yorkshire

Open throughout the year, except Good Friday and Christmas Day; admission from 10.00 a.m. (Sundays from 2.00 p.m.) until 6.00 p.m., or sunset if earlier.

Skipton Castle is a remarkably complete example of a medieval castle, with dungeon, watch tower, banqueting hall, wine and beer cellars, etc.

Sledmere House

Eight miles north-west of Driffield, North Humberside, at the junction of the B1251 and the B1253

Opening times: Good Friday, Easter Saturday and Sunday, Monday and Tuesday, and all following Sundays until 1 May; daily from May to the end of September, except Mondays and Fridays (open on all Bank Holiday Mondays). 1.30-5.30 p.m. (last admission 5 p.m.) Private parties arranged by appointment only for Wednesday evenings.

Free car and coach parks; café, and restaurant which caters specially for booked parties; a wheelchair is available for use in either the house or grounds; dogs allowed in the grounds.

This Georgian house was built in 1751, but had to be rebuilt from original designs and plasterwork moulds after a fire in 1911. It is now the home of the Sykes family.

Springfields Gardens

Spalding, Lincolnshire

Open daily April to September 10.00 a.m.-6.00 p.m.

Shops; licensed restaurant; free parking and wheelchair hire; no charge is made for accompanied children; dogs not allowed.

Springfields covers twenty-five acres with woodland walks, lawns, a lake, indoor gardens and an alpine house. April and May bring a million spring blooms to the garden, while during the summer there are magnificent displays of bedding plants, dahlias and twelve thousand roses.

Stockeld Park

On the A661 Harrogate road, some two miles north-west of Wetherby, West Yorkshire

Open every day, except Mondays, from mid-July to mid-August, 2.30-5.00 p.m.

Dogs on leads allowed in gardens; tea rooms, shop and gardens easily accessible for disabled persons and help can be provided for access to the house.

Stockeld Park, designed by the celebrated architect James Paine, was built for the Middleton family during 1756-63 on the edge of the Vale of York. A chapel and stable yard were added at a later date.

Sutton Park

On the road between York and Helmsley (B1363), eight miles from York, four miles from Easingwold

House, gardens and grounds, tea room and gift shop open 2.00-6.00 p.m. (last admissions 5.30 p.m.) Good Friday, Easter Sunday and Monday, several Sundays during April, and Sundays, Tuesdays and Thursdays from 1 May to beginning of October. Open all Bank Holiday Mondays; Wednesdays by appointment all the year round; other special openings by arrangement.

Dogs allowed into the grounds but not into the gardens; free car and coach park. Other attractions include a Temple, woodlands and daffodil walks, a nature trail and a Georgian ice house in the grounds.

Sutton Park is an early Georgian house built in 1730. Its contents include Chippendale, Sheraton and French furniture, paintings, porcelain and a display of fans. The park was designed by 'Capability' Brown, and the garden created by Major and Mrs Sheffield.

Tattershall Castle

Three and a half miles south-east of Woodhall Spa, Lincolnshire, south of the A153

Open daily (including Good Friday), 11.00 a.m. (Sunday 1.00 p.m.) -6.30 p.m. or sunset if earlier. Closed 1.00-2.00 p.m. from October to March; also closed Christmas and Boxing Days.

Dogs on leads in grounds only; shop; wheelchair access to ground floor and grounds; car parks (coaches must park in the village).

Tattershall Castle was built around 1440 on the site of a medieval castle by the Treasurer of England, Ralph Cromwell. Today there is a museum in the guard house where a model of the castle as it would originally have looked is on display.

Temple Newsam House

Five miles east of Leeds, West Yorkshire

Open daily, except Mondays (open Bank Holiday Mondays), 10.30 a.m.-6.15 p.m.

Wheelchair access limited to the ground floor; restaurant; shop; dogs allowed in the grounds; ample free parking.

Temple Newsam, a house built on the traditional courtyard plan, is found in beautiful parkland about five miles from the centre of Leeds in West Yorkshire. A large part of the gardens is dominated in spring and autumn by the scent and brilliant colours of massive rhododendron bushes.

Some of Temple Newsam's appeal must lie in the fact that it is a Tudor-Jacobean building; Tudor masons' marks can still be seen on some stone quoins and there is a typical Tudor bay window on the west front. Throughout its history it has also been associated with many intriguing characters, such as Thomas, Lord Darcy. Darcy, who had Temple Newsam built on this particular site probably some time before 1520, met a disastrous end in 1537 — he was beheaded for having sided with a group that opposed the dissolution of the monasteries.

Temple Newsam's origins, however, can be traced further back than the time of Darcy's demise. In the Domesday Book of 1086 it is apparently recorded that William the Conqueror gave 'Newsam' to a retainer called Ilbert de Lacy. Later, in about 1155, *Temple* became incorporated as part of the title when Henry de Lacy granted ownership of the establishment to the religious order of the Knights Templar.

In 1622, Darcy's Temple Newsam was bought by Sir Arthur Ingram for £12,000. Sir Arthur was responsible for the construction of five large houses in Yorkshire — at one time or another he had over forty estates in his possession, most of these being houses he bought and then later sold for profit. At Newsam he erected side wings, created the entrance porch, above which is the family's coat of arms, and put the long inscription 'ALL GLORY AND PRAISE BE GIVEN TO GOD THE FATHER THE SON AND HOLY GHOST ON HIGH PEACE ON EARTH GOOD WILL TOWARDS MEN HONOUR AND TRUE ALLEGIANCE TO OUR GRACIOUS KING LOVING AND AFFECTION AMONGST HIS SUBJECTS HEALTH AND PLENTY BE WITHIN THIS HOUSE' in an impressive position on the roof balustrade. The Ingram crest, a cock standing above a viscount's coronet, is visible on several parts of the building, most notably as the weather vane on top of the single-handed clock fronting the stable court.

The last descendant of Sir Arthur Ingram died in 1871, after which the house remained in his widow's possession. Mrs Maynell Ingram had the majority of the Georgian sash windows taken out and leaded lights and stone mullions put in. In 1904 Temple Newsam was inherited by her nephew Edward Wood, and in 1922 the house was sold to Leeds Corporation.

The building is now run as a country house museum of decorative art. Inside, the fine art collections are displayed against a great variety of architectural features — craftmanship is Temple Newsam's hallmark. The museum's contents are made up of items which belonged to previous owners and others which have been acquired since 1922. They range from a pair of French bellows, dating to about 1780, whose brand marks show that they were owned by Marie Antoinette, to incense burners from K'ang Hsi's reign in the Ching Dynasty. There is much local work, too, including a spinning wheel (1798-1802) made by John Planta of Fulneck, near Leeds, and delicate profile portraits (ink on chalk) from about 1784-5 drawn by John Miers, who was living in Leeds at the time.

As well as being a museum, Temple Newsam is also used regularly as a venue for music recitals. These are held in the Long Gallery — where snails are a fascinating curiosity in the ornamental plasterwork (rather

like the Kilburn 'mouseman''s wooden rodents!) In addition, the house has facilities to cater for school parties, and has its own specialist team to keep up with conservation work. With so much to see, both inside and out, time spent here is always rewarding and immensely enjoyable.

Thorp Perrow Arboretum

Entrance is on the Well to Bedale road, two and a half miles south of Bedale, North Yorkshire

Open daily from 1 April to mid-November, 9.00 a.m. to dusk.

Parking room; toilets; easy access for wheelchairs in reasonably dry weather; dogs on leads allowed.

Sir Leonard Ropner was given sixty-five acres of open parkland by his father in 1927. Throughout his life Sir Leonard collected several thousand different species of trees and shrubs, all of which he planted at Thorp Perrow. The result is an arboretum of immense beauty.

Thrumpton Hall

About seven miles south of Nottingham, off the A684

Thrumpton Hall is open all the year round, during both the day and evening, for arranged parties of twenty or more people.

Refreshment areas; facilities for disabled persons.

Attractions at this Hall, which dates from the sixteenth century, include relics associated with the poet Lord Byron, a fine Carolean carved staircase, a secret passage and a priests' hiding hole.

Treasurer's House, York

Behind York Minster in Minster Yard

Season runs from April to the end of October (closed Good Friday); open every day 10.30 a.m.-6.00 p.m. (last admission 5.30 p.m.)

Wheelchairs can only be taken around part of the ground floor.

The House, which is now National

Trust property, was rebuilt in 1620 on the site of the official residence of the Treasurer of York Minster. It has twenty rooms, with seventeenth- and eighteenth-century furniture, glass and china, and has an attractive small town garden. A series of events is arranged each season, including Coffee by Candlelight evenings.

Walsingham Abbey

Walsingham, Norfolk

Abbey, ruins and gardens open from 2.00-5.00 p.m.: April — Wednesdays, May to July — Wednesdays; Saturdays and Sundays, August — daily except Tuesdays and Thursdays, September — Wednesdays, Saturdays and Sundays. Open all Bank Holidays from Easter to September.

Dogs allowed; wheelchair access.

This Augustinian Priory, with crypt, is often the destination of many modern-day pilgrimages.

White Wells

Accessible only by foot from Wells Road, Ilkley, West Yorkshire

Open 2.00-6.00 p.m. Saturdays, Sundays and Bank Holiday Mondays from the beginning of April to the end of September.

Free admission.

The present house, containing two plunge baths which were originally used as a tonic or cure for various medical ailments, was built by Squire Middleton in about 1760. White Wells is rather an unusual museum and now has a small display on the natural history and geology of Ilkley Moor.

Wilberforce and Georgian Houses

High Street, in the old town quarter of Hull

Open Monday to Saturday, 10.00 a.m.-5.00 p.m., Sundays 2.30-4.30 p.m.

Admission free.

Wilberforce House is the oldest surviving example of prosperous merchant houses which lined the narrow Old High Street. William Wilberforce was born here in 1759, and there are personal relics and displays to see, including a section on the slave trade. The house, together with the adjoining Georgian houses, is used as a local history museum; there are collections of Hull silver, costume and militaria. There is also a Victorian parlour, and the interior of an Edwardian chemist's shop.

Wollaton Hall

About two and a half miles west of Nottingham city centre between the Nottingham to Ilkeston road (A609) and the Nottingham to Derby road (A52)

Museum open daily April to September, 10.00 a.m.-7.00 p.m., Sunday 2.00-5.00 p.m.; October and March, daily 10.00 a.m.-5.30 p.m.; Sunday 1.30-4.30 p.m.; November to February, 10.00 a.m. 4.30 p.m.; closed Christmas Day.

Limited access for wheelchairs at present; toilet facilities for the disabled; dogs on lead allowed in the park; free coach and car parking; refreshments. Fallow and red deer in the park; nature trail round the lake; early nineteenth-century camellia house.

Wollaton Hall, an Elizabethan mansion dating from 1580-88 and built for Sir Francis Willoughby, houses Nottingham's Natural History Museum. Guided tours of parts of the Hall by prior appointment may be arranged.

Worth Valley Railway

The line runs from Oxenhope to Keighley, West Yorkshire, taking in Haworth and Oakworth

The first train usually leaves Oxenhope just after 11.00 a.m. Passengers can get off at any station on the line.

Steam in Brontëland

You can go to the moorland village of Haworth, not far from Bradford, either because you are mad about the Brontës or because you are mad about trains.

The Brontës were there before the trains, of course. Patrick Brontë and his wife arrived at Haworth in February 1820, bringing their six children and all their worldly possessions from the weaving village of Thornton (now part of Bradford) to the bleak parsonage near the top of the precipitous, stone-setted main street. Most of the houses bordering this street were built in the time of the Brontës for occupation by handloom weavers. At one time over a thousand handlooms were being worked in the district: men and women toiled in the upper rooms of these houses, making use of every moment of daylight that came through the long rows of narrow windows, many of which are still to be seen.

Standing at the top of Main Street is the Black Bull Inn, to which the landlord would summon Branwell when a guest from out of town craved more sophisticated entertainment than the regulars could provide. The seeds of Branwell's disaster were

surely nurtured here and across the road at the druggist's (more recently a bookshop) where he bought his laudanum.

The Haworth church we see today is not the one where Patrick preached. That church, all but the tower, was demolished in 1879 and rebuilt. Beneath the present Church of St Michael and All Angels there is still the Brontë family vault which contains the remains of all the family except Anne, whose grave is to be found at Scarborough. It seems that the shadow of tuberculosis stretched far beyond Haworth. Even in the gentler climate of the Vale of York, within easy reach of the sea ('delightful to me at all times and seasons' as she writes in *Agnes Grey*), Anne was not to be spared.

In the Brontë Memorial Chapel is a monument carved by one of poor Branwell's faithful friends, John Brown, the sexton. It was his hand that Branwell seized a few minutes before he died, while John was sitting with him as the rest of the family prepared for Sunday morning church.

Other faithful servants and friends of the Brontës lie buried in the churchyard; here, Tabitha Aykroyd and Martha Brown are sheltered by the Parsonage garden wall, near a vanished gateway once used only for Brontë family funerals.

Haworth was, indeed, a melancholy place, especially for children. But happiness is the business of childhood and the Brontë children had to take their happiness where they found it — in each other and in their joint imaginings. Theirs was an isolated existence, not only because of the surrounding moorland but also because they were 'the parson's bairns' and consequently hardly encouraged to seek the companionship of the other village children, with whom they would, in any case, have had little in common. In fact, Charlotte, Anne, Emily and Branwell clearly felt no need of other children; they were happy in the miniature world they created, which is enshrined today in the tiny books they made, full of near-microscopic writing recording the affairs of their

imaginary kingdoms — Emily and Anne's 'Gondal', and Charlotte and Branwell's 'Angria'. The private kingdoms began when Patrick, their father, came home from Leeds one day with a box of toy soldiers as a present for Branwell. The children immediately 'adopted' the soldiers (whom they christened 'The Young Men'), and set to work to build a world around them which echoed the doings in that greater world outside the village, a world about which the little Brontës were remarkably well informed.

Their lives, though short, were as touching and dramatic as their writings. In September 1821 their mother died from cancer at the age of thirty-eight. Maria, the

eldest girl, died of tuberculosis in May 1825. Within a month, Elizabeth, too, had succumbed fatally to the disease. Branwell, after failing as painter, tutor, railway clerk and suitor, died in 1848 from the effects of drink and drugs. Emily died the same year and Anne the year after. Charlotte, after an unhappy love affair with M. Heger, the Belgian professor she met in Brussels, married Arthur Nicholls, her father's curate, and was in the early stages of pregnancy when she too fell victim to 'consumption' or 'the wasting disease' as earlier generations called T.B., dying in 1855. Despite the sledge-hammer blows which fate had dealt him, Patrick survived to the age of eighty-five and in his old age delighted in talking about the daughters whose achievements had brought him so much pride – though their early deaths must have caused immeasurable anguish.

Today the two-storeyed Georgian parsonage overlooking the churchyard is a museum maintained by the Brontë Society.

The village has changed surprisingly little in essence since the Brontës were here but the amount of tourist development would doubtless bewilder any

visitor from the past. How astonished the Brontës would be today if they knew that 'Brontë Weekends' were being arranged by travel companies, to include visits to Haworth and its surroundings; there are lectures at the Parsonage Museum on the ill-fated brood and lunches at the Black Bull, whose temptations proved too strong a lure for the unfortunate Branwell.

All the countryside around the village has been coloured by the grand if sombre memory of this family. South-west of the parsonage are the Brontë Falls, at whose foot Emily wrote some of her poetry while she sat in a natural stone 'chair' – reputedly, this was one of the sisters' favourite moorland retreats. Not far from here, sited starkly on a crest of the moorland is the ruined farmhouse which in Emily's imagination became Heathcliffe's home, 'Wuthering Heights'. To the north, at the old handloom weaving village of Stanbury is Ponden Hall, which may have provided the model for 'Thrushcross Grange', the home of the Linton family in the same novel. Ponden Hall was beloved by the Brontë girls who had the freedom of its well-stocked library.

Further along the westward road, having passed the Herders, a remote moorland inn, you cross the boundary into Lancashire.

where the brooding village of Wycoller provided a setting for yet another Brontë novel – the hall, now ruined, was included as 'Ferndean Manor' by Charlotte in Jane Eyre.

In the wider surrounding area, too, the sisters are remembered: at Southowram, near Halifax, where Emily worked on Wuthering Heights while earning her bread as a teacher; at Gomersal, where Charlotte was a frequent visitor to the seventeenth-century Red House (now a museum; see p.242), which became the basis for 'Briarmains' in Shirley; and at Birstall, where Oakwell Hall (see p.236) gave her the model for Shirley Keeldar's home in the same story.

There are many other Brontë associations in this corner of Yorkshire, too many indeed to attempt to list, for the gifted sisters wove the history and topography of the area inextricably into the fabric of their writings, recalling not only the 'little and lone green lanes' and 'billowing swell' of the moors, so loved by Emily, but also the harsh struggles of the emergent textile industry with the accompanying Luddite demonstrations and outbreaks of violence.

Only a year or two before the first of the Brontë children was born the manufacturer James Cartwright, with a few workers and soldiers, had fought a pitched battle against the machine-breakers in which two of the Luddites were killed and a number wounded. Rawfolds Mill, the scene of that fight, was close to Hartshead where Patrick Brontë served as curate. Shortly afterwards Patrick saw the Luddites secretly burying their dead in a corner of Hartshead churchyard. He did not report the lawbreakers, but he spoke out against them so vehemently from the pulpit that he considered it wise to keep a pair of pistols handy in case he was attacked.

Patrick and his children lived to see the dawn of the age of steam, which not only brought mechanisation to the woollen industry but eventually criss-crossed England with a

network of steel rails. The Brontë sisters lived at the time of 'Railway Mania', when countless people were ruined by buying railway shares at inflated prices in an attempt to 'get rich quick'.

No doubt some earnest conversation between the sisters took place on this very topic; they wanted to be sure that what little money they had was invested wisely. They were brought into further contact with the railways when Branwell actually became a booking-clerk at Sowerby Bridge railway station during one of the sporadic periods of employment in his short, unhappy life.

Had Patrick lived a few more years he would have seen the birth of the Keighley and Worth Valley Railway which, though it is only five miles long, claims to be 'England's most prestigious steam railway'. It began in 1867, connecting Keighley with the villages of Oakworth, Haworth and Oxenhope. Then in 1962, along with many other lines which had once been indispensable features in the areas they served, it was declared uneconomic and was closed. Six years later a group of volunteers, dedicated to keeping alive the steam locomotive as a part of Britain's heritage, bravely reopened it. That group, the Keighley and Worth Valley Railway Preservation Society, has its headquarters at Haworth, where old locomotives are restored and active ones prepared for their daily work in the engine shed.

From Keighley Station, which the K & WVR shares with British Rail, the trains climb, by way of Ingrow, Damems (once the smallest 'full-size' station in England), Oakworth and Haworth to Oxenhope, where there is a museum of locomotives, carriages and other railway memorabilia. The pride of the line, however, is its own 'film star' station Oakworth (which has been voted the Best Preserved Station in Britain), for it was used in the film *The Railway Children*.

The volunteers take enormous pride, too, in the maintenance and operation of splendid engines which, in the course of their five-mile journey, prove more than

equal to the severe test of climbing 330 feet up an average gradient of 1 in 76 — quite a pull for a steam engine. Every weekend from the beginning of March to the end of October steam trains ply up and down the valley. At holiday time extra services are run, and during July and August steam trains are operated every day between Keighley and Oxenhope. Winter brings the 'Santa Specials' (with presents for the children) and a Carol Service Special on the Saturday evening before Christmas, while a steam service continues to run every Sunday between Haworth and Oxenhope only. In addition to these steam services there are certain diesel services every weekend throughout the year.

Such enthusiasm for an area rich with historical memories will surely continue as long as Brontëland remains intact.

Yorkshire Sculpture Park

Bretton Hall College, West Bretton, Wakefield, West Yorkshire

Open all the year round, 10.00 a.m.-6.00p.m.

Admission free; car parking nearby; lake and nature reserve.

The Park, one of very few in the country, covers about 260 acres. Some exhibits are permanently sited, such as pieces by Henry Moore and Barbara Hepworth. Others are brought in specially for various exhibitions during the year.

Index

General index

Geographical location index

Each named location includes the surrounding area

THE CALENDAR YEAR